"*Finding the Center Within* is a practical manual on the practice of mindfulness which can help many people to embody their Buddha nature and become radiant and peaceful beings. It provides easy steps for practicing mindfulness in day-to-day living."

> —Thich Nhat Hanh, author of *Peace Is Every Step, The Miracle of Mindfulness*, and *Anger: Wisdom for Cooling the Flames*

"I like this book very much. Wise and clear. A further step in the art and science of healing."

> —Stephen Levine, author of *A Year to Live: How to Live This Year as if It Were Your Last*

Finding the Center Within

~o~

The Healing Way of
Mindfulness Meditation

Thomas Bien, Ph.D.
Beverly Bien, M.Ed.

WILEY

John Wiley & Sons, Inc.

Published by John Wiley & Sons, Inc., Hoboken, New Jersey
Published simultaneously in Canada

The authors gratefully acknowledge the following for permission to quote from: *Being Peace* (1987) by Thich Nhat Hanh with permission of Parallax Press, Berkeley, California. (Extract on page 67.) *Chuang Tzu: Basic Writings* translated by Burton Watson. © 1964 Columbia University Press. Reprinted by permission of the publisher. (Extract on page 86.) *The Poems of Emily Dickinson*, Thomas H. Johnson, ed., Cambridge, Mass.: The Belknap Press of Harvard University Press, Copyright © 1951, 1955, 1979 by the President and Fellows of Harvard College. Reprinted by permission of the publishers and the Trustees of Amherst College. (Poem on page 39.)

For general information about our other products and services, please contact our Customer Care Department within the United States at (800) 762-2974, outside the United States at (317) 572-3993 or fax (317) 572-4002.

Wiley also publishes its books in a variety of electronic formats. Some content that appears in print may not be available in electronic books. For more information about Wiley products, visit our web site at www.wiley.com.

Library of Congress Cataloging-in-Publication Data:

Bien, Thomas.
    Finding the center within : the healing way of mindfulness meditation
/ Thomas Bien, Beverly Bien.
        p. cm.
        Includes bibliographical references.
        ISBN 0-471-26394-X (pbk.)
    1. Meditation.   I. Bien, Beverly.   II. Title.
    BL627.B53   2003
    291.4'35—dc21

                                                                        2003003950

Printed in the United States of America

10 9 8 7 6 5 4 3 2 1

To
Thich Nhat Hanh,
who shows the
joy
of the path.

There's a center of quietness within, which has to be known and held. If you lose that center, you are in tension and begin to fall apart.

—Joseph Campbell, *The Power of Myth*

Contents

❦

Preface

∽o∽

Calm in the Storm

The Buddhist meditation teacher Dipa Ma was one of those individuals who exuded a special presence. Just to be around her was an experience of wisdom and love that was almost palpable. It had not always been that way. Married at the age of fourteen, as was the custom in India, she suffered horribly when her husband and two of her three children died suddenly. Her suffering went on for years until, wasting away, she recognized she had to do something or perish. She entered a Buddhist monastery in Burma, where she progressed quickly to deep levels of concentration and spiritual attainment. Later in life, when she had become a teacher with this extraordinary quality of presence, she was asked what was in her mind. She said simply, "Concentration, lovingkindness, and peace. That is all."

Imagine being a person whose whole consciousness consists only of "concentration, lovingkindness, and peace." Most of us would love to be that way. Most of us would love to be happy, loving, and peaceful individuals—people whom it was a blessing just to be around. Most of us wish we knew how to be calm, how to hold our center even in the face of the most extreme storms that life blows onto our path. This desire is the deep reason people come to churches, synagogues, and meditation centers, and it may be the unspoken wish of many who come to a therapist's office as well—simply to find the center within.

The center within is a spatial metaphor for a spiritual reality. It is that which holds us together and keeps us from falling apart. In spatial terms, you can think of it as being at the center of the chest at the heart level. Sometimes this is helpful. But the true center is everywhere. Temporally considered, the center within is a process. It's your ongoing mindfulness as you continue moment by moment to bring calm, accepting awareness to what is going on, without fighting or struggling or judging. To find the center, and hold it, is the capacity to live deeply and fully, with boundless peace and happiness, in any external circumstance.

It is knowing that, since everything passes, peace cannot be found in any thing or circumstance. Peace is the center of awareness itself.

If you are wondering whether that is even truly possible for you, good. You are taking it seriously, and seriously acknowledging your hunger for the center. It may seem unimaginable to dwell in the center continually. It may seem thoroughly beyond your grasp. Yet the Buddha and other great teachers insist that it is possible. You can do it. However hidden or obscured our capacity for peace may be at times, all of us have Buddha nature; all of us share in the divine spark. And therefore it is possible for all of us to learn to be the calm one in the midst of the storm. It is possible because that is our true nature—not something that we are just trying to add artificially to who we are. To realize this true nature, however, we must learn to see things differently, removing the walls that conceal who and what we really are. When we can do that, we discover the calmness and wisdom that are already there, though obscured under layers of misunderstanding and old conditioning. We learn to find and hold the center within.

Integrating the Spiritual and the Psychological

In the pages that follow, we offer ways of breaking down the barriers that prevent us from actualizing our wise inner self. We combine spiritual wisdom—especially the Buddhist practice of mindfulness—with the pragmatic wisdom of Western psychology. When you realize that Buddhism is at heart a form of wise, ancient psychology and a practice for waking up, this combination makes perfect sense. But we also need the psychology of our own day, suited as it is for our time and place and way of life.

For spirituality to be of value in our world, it must connect with the unique problems of our times. It must deal with the problems of rush-hour traffic and complex relationships, of mortgages and telephone bills. The Zen injunction to "chop wood, carry water" must become, as the Zen teacher Charlotte Joko Beck has so aptly said, "make love, drive freeway." Mindfulness is the energy that allows us to do this, while at the same time providing a wonderful point of contact with psychology.

The two disciplines of spirituality and psychology each offer distinctive and helpful insights and ways of change to aid us in our quest. Yet these two areas have remained largely unacquainted with each other—sometimes even hostile.

To understand why, consider Gail, who was depressed. A Protestant minister, she was embarrassed to find herself in a psychologist's office. Even though she referred people in her congregation for therapy, she somehow did not feel that she should be there herself. After all, she was a spiritual leader. She was supposed to be strong, and her faith was supposed to provide all that she needed. She felt like a bit of a failure as a person of faith to find herself in need of the help of a psychologist. But lately there had been too many days that she could barely function. And finally, she had had to admit to herself that she stood in need of the human help that therapy could offer. And so, with deep ambivalence, she found herself in my office.

Gail's feelings are shared by many religious and spiritually minded people, sometimes even taking the form of cynicism and antagonism toward the practice of psychology. They feel they should not have to search beyond the spiritual to find what they need, as though their faith were imperfect if it could in any way be helped along by psychology or other human means. Like many religious people, Gail found that these ideas got in her own way. She could not become the loving person she wanted to be until she could be loving toward herself, until she could begin to be more accepting of the feelings of being less than loving at times. These feelings conflicted with her role as a spiritual leader. She needed the presence of another person to help her learn to accept and be present with these feelings. But once she did—once she could learn to embrace the very feelings that she rejected—she came closer to being the person that she wanted to be.

Religious and spiritual people have no monopoly on distrust of other models. Psychologists and psychiatrists, trained in the model of empirical science, often believe that their approach to learning about the world is the only valid one, and that it should be sufficient on its own. Some behavioral scientists have a hard-nosed, "show-me" attitude. Some of these professionals even chose their field in part as a reaction against religion or a religious background.

Both psychology and spirituality tend to be closed. Both can be mistrustful of other ways of knowing. Yet both also have much to offer.

Spiritual people are prone to what the psychologist John Welwood has called "spiritual bypassing." This is an attempt to use your spirituality to run from the reality of life, to avoid facing your life issues and problems. It is an attempt to get a free pass to avoid difficulties and is-sues. One of the strengths of psychology, on the other hand, is precisely to help us face these things. It can help us acknowledge that our moti-vations are not always as saintly as we would like to think, and starting from there, help us become more whole and behave more effectively.

Sometimes religious and spiritual people lose the connection be-tween their spirituality and their daily life, confining spiritual practice too much to special occasions and rituals, to the meditation cushion or scripture study or a worship service. They may wish to build their lives on a solid spiritual foundation, but to really do so may require that emotional and psychological wounds be acknowledged and healed.

Christ taught that before trying to improve your neighbor, you should take a look at yourself. You should remove the log from your own eye before attempting surgery on the speck in your neighbor's eye. The world would be a much better place if people took this teach-ing seriously. But how does one do this exactly? How can we see our-selves, without distorting our attitudes and intentions in the direction of being better than we really are? How can we avoid the fate of reli-gious people like those we have all met, who, now that they have be-come "spiritual," seem to be more difficult to be around than they were before? Psychology is uniquely positioned to help with these difficul-ties—helping us, through self-acceptance, to know ourselves a little better, so we can see the log in our own eyes. Psychology has also de-veloped useful practices that help us learn to live and deal with others more skillfully. The Buddha would commend the communication skills psychology offers us as a wonderful way to implement what he taught about skillful speech.

On the other hand, while psychology provides us with tools and in-sights, it cannot tell us what to use them for. Answering the "what for" question requires a step outside of pure empiricism into the realm of spirit. The best tools do little good if we don't know what we want to build in the first place, just as our cars and planes can take us faster and faster, but do not provide direction and purpose.

We hold it as a basic truth that we are spiritual beings. That is our essence. There is more to us than we imagine. The scientific view is helpful and important, yet by itself it can too easily flatten out. The world of science limits and truncates, leaving us two-dimensional in a many-dimensional universe. We are more than that. We are not con-fined to the space between our head and our feet, nor to the years between birth and death. And since we are spiritual beings, there are limits to what psychology alone can tell us—valuable though it is.

There are hopeful signs that the boundary between science and religion is not as rigid as it once was. Theoretical physicists sometimes sound like Buddhists. A form of psychology known as *radical behaviorism*—which many think of as a kind of ultimate empirical, scientific approach to the psychology of behavior—ends up sounding surprisingly Buddhist. Many psychologists, psychiatrists, and other counselors these days value both the spiritual and the scientific, and no longer feel the need to separate the two or defend the one against the other.

On the other hand, many religious people have learned to value psychology and therapy. For more than thirty years now, clergy have been receiving basic training in counseling. Religious people may retain some uneasiness about psychology, and therapists may not always quite know what do with people's spirituality, but there is a tendency toward greater acceptance. Scientists, like Edward O. Wilson in his stimulating book *Consilience*, may envision all realms of knowledge as ultimately reducible to science, while spiritual people will claim the reverse. But in the end, we will come to know that all of the different modes of knowing are ultimately one, since all of them are aspects of something larger than what we normally consider either scientific or spiritual. All ways of knowing concern the one reality, and the division between spirituality and science is ultimately as artificial as the division between poetry and prose or between ocean and bay.

Until we can come to see things in a more unified way, we believe it is important to be open both to the spiritual dimension of life—to all that the great spiritual traditions of the world can teach us—and also to psychology, which can help us face ourselves and our lives with greater honesty and give us tools with which to build a well-grounded, decently human life.

Which Spirituality? Which Psychology?

But when we say spirituality, which spirituality shall we consider, and when we say psychology, which psychology?

While there is almost as much conflict among the differing schools of psychology as there is among the differing world spiritual traditions, all of these traditions exist because they offer something valuable and important. Still, neither our treatment of psychology nor our treatment of spirituality can be exhaustive. So we must be somewhat selective in both realms.

Many years ago, I heard Rabbi Zalman Schachter-Shalomi give a talk at a university. As I remember it, he said that the true aim of learning and scholarship ultimately concerns the question, "What is the good life?" The farther we wander from this central, living question, the more abstract, dry, and remote study becomes.

In keeping with this insight, the criterion we have used is a simple one, cutting across different systems and beliefs: We have emphasized those aspects of both psychology and spirituality that are of the most practical relevance, that help us to live the good life and to become who we are meant to be. We emphasize that which most directly answers the question of how to live deeply and well. We emphasize teachings that tell us not only that we should love our neighbor, but also how we can go about doing it. For that reason, prominence is given to Buddhism among the spiritual paths, because it excels at maintaining a focus on practice and has a minimum of the sort of dogmatic beliefs and speculative philosophy that can become an obstacle to those who see things differently. And the heart and soul of Buddhist teachings is the practice of mindfulness. So while we refer to many spiritual traditions, none are as central as mindfulness.

Central to Buddhist teaching are the four noble truths. The Buddha gave this teaching, the record tells us, in his first sermon after his enlightenment, and these teachings set the tone for all of the teachings that followed. The first noble truth is the truth of suffering. This teaching is not so much that everything is suffering, but that suffering is the very thing that points us in the right direction. Suffering is to be learned from rather than ignored if we are to find our way out of it. It is something like the Christian teaching that resurrection must be preceded by crucifixion—that it is in our very struggles that God's presence is to be found.

The second noble truth is that the causes of suffering can be known and understood. The cause of our suffering is not the nature of reality but our own ignorance. Once we see the nature of reality clearly, we know why we suffer. The third noble truth is that once these causes are known and understood, we can stop suffering. We can enter the realm of nirvana, of bliss, what Christians would call the kingdom of God. The fourth noble truth is a description of what a life without suffering would look like. This is the famous eightfold path: right view, right thinking, right speech, right action, right livelihood, right mindfulness, right diligence, and right concentration. It is important to understand that this is not so much a moralism as it is a practical teaching. The eightfold path describes the way to live that is "right" (meaning effective) in eliminating suffering, in helping us cross to the shore of nonsuffering.

The Buddha maintained at the end of his life that he had taught nothing except the nature of suffering and how to end it. To some, this seems a little negative. And just as Christians can get too focused on the overwhelming sufferings of Christ on the cross, or Jews too focused on the vast atrocity of the Holocaust, there is a risk for Buddhists to get too caught up in the negative here. But doing so is a distortion. Since we are already spiritual beings with a divine nature, with Buddha nature, we do not have to do anything in particular to become those things. We are them already. All we need to do is know how to remove that which gets in the way. All we need to do is know how to work with that which causes us to suffer, so the shining joy underneath can be revealed. In this way, all of this talk of suffering is nothing negative at all.

Every word in this book is also about suffering and how to transform it so as to cross to the other shore. It does not matter so much whether the method is something labeled spiritual or something labeled psychological.

The psychology we draw on in this book is similarly aimed at transforming our suffering. Among psychological approaches, the practical focus of cognitive-behavioral psychology earns it some prominence for the same reason—having a minimum of speculative assumption and a maximum of practical validity, though once again, we draw freely from other psychological schools as well.

Our Journeys

Beverly and I came to appreciate the value of both spirituality and psychology from opposite directions. Both of us were struck by the similarity between the practice of mindfulness and the basic principles of psychotherapy. Mindfulness teaches that wherever we shine the light of awareness, transformation and healing take place. A basic tenet of psychotherapy is that difficult and painful problems gradually yield to an accepting attention. Mindfulness uses breathing and meditation to calm our thoughts and feelings sufficiently to look deeply and find healing. Therapy uses the presence of another person who is accepting and nonjudgmental to accomplish the same goal. The similarity is not accidental, but reveals a primary and potent healing force viewed from different angles.

I (Tom) began my professional life as a minister, deeply drawn from an early age to the spiritual dimension of life. From there, I became interested in pastoral counseling, and was gradually drawn to psychology. Eventually, this became a career change. Beverly, on the other hand, began her career in mental health and human services. As her need to stay centered in a difficult field became increasingly important, she slowly gravitated toward spirituality. From different starting places, we both met in the middle and arrived at the same place, with a deep conviction that both the psychological and the spiritual are of value and importance. Through the holy truth of our sufferings and struggles, we both felt psychology helped us to understand ourselves and other people and taught us how to cope with many kinds of difficulties. And at the same time, we both also clearly saw that we needed to connect with the spiritual center of life in a way that went beyond psychology.

The combination of the spiritual and the psychological can be a powerful help in finding greater peace, joy, love, and well-being in your life. For those who would like to work at this in a systematic way, we offer a step-by-step program for inviting and deepening your capacity for psychological and spiritual well-being. It is a kind of retreat that you can give yourself, but one that you can take without traveling to some far-off place. In a way, it is even better than a retreat, for on a retreat there is always the difficulty of integrating the mountaintop retreat experience with the valleys of everyday life. Here, however, your retreat and daily life are one.

A Retreat in Daily Life

Week one: During this week, we explain the difficulties in modern life and how mindfulness helps heal them. Introductory exercises initiate you gently into the program.

Week two: During the second week, you become acquainted with mindfulness as the essential ingredient for becoming more centered.

Weeks three and four: In the third and fourth weeks, you learn how to begin a meditation practice.

Week five: In the fifth week, you learn how to bring the meditative attitude into daily life.

Week six: During the sixth week, we invite you to look deeply at your life and explore an alternative vision of what life is about.

Week seven: In this week, you learn to use dreams to become acquainted with all of who you are and achieve maximum wholeness and self-acceptance.

Week eight: In this week, we teach you how to work with and transform negative emotions.

Week nine: This week focuses on practices to bring mindfulness to your relationships to make them healthy and healing.

Week ten: In week ten, you learn to meditate on paper, using journaling as a tool of mindfulness.

We of course know that your spiritual growth is unlikely to be complete after ten weeks. These ten weeks are unlikely to remove all of your psychological issues or make you a saint or an enlightened person. But if you follow the program faithfully, you will have a good foundation for new habits and practices that can provide a solid basis for continuing spiritual growth and wholeness.

How This Book Is Organized

This book is organized into four parts. In Part I, "The Key," we describe the problems of modern life and how meditation and mindfulness help. This is the background information you need in preparation for the journey.

Part II is called "The Door," since it leads us out into a new life. In these chapters, we teach you how to meditate and how to use a meditative approach to daily living. This section is primarily spiritual in orientation, but includes supplemental information from psychology.

In Part III, "The Path," we show you how to deal more effectively with negative emotions and relationships, and how to work with dreams and use a journal. This is the most directly psychological part of the book, though as usual, spiritual themes are incorporated throughout.

In Part IV, "Arriving Home," we offer thoughts about what your continuing practice might be like beyond the formal weeks of the program, and about what a mindfulness-based spirituality might look like in our own cultural context.

A unique feature of this book is the sections in first person entitled "The Experience." In these sections we try to convey to the reader something of what it may be like to put the ideas in the book into practice based on our own experience. The gulf between understanding the concepts of this book and putting them into practice can seem wide at first. By sharing some of our experience, we hope readers will know that their experience is normal, and that their struggles with practice are normal ones. We hope these sections provide encouragement to continue the practice. For the essential thing is always just to continue.

At the end of each chapter, you will find a section with an outline of the practices for that one- or two-week period.

How to Use This Book

How you can best use this book will depend on what kind of person you are. Some people will want to read straight through first and become familiar with the entire book before trying the exercises. If you want to do this, that is fine. But to get the most out of this book, we hope you will then come back and read it more slowly, following the suggestions for practice either according to the program, or at your own pace and in your own way. This is a book to work with. Allow time for the content to be absorbed and practiced.

If you tend to be a little compulsive about following rules and programs, it might be best if you take a leisurely pace through the material without worrying too much about following the practices for each week exactly as they are outlined. Spend as much time on each section as feels right for you. Relax and enjoy the process.

On the other hand, if your good intentions about spiritual practice tend to evaporate—if you don't follow through—it might be best to follow our suggestions programmatically, step-by-step and week by week. At the end of the ten weeks, you can always return to any areas that appeal to you or that you would like to strengthen.

There is a lot of information in this book. We hope that you will make this book a kind of companion, a spiritual friend that you keep coming back to again and again, dipping into it frequently for inspiration and guidance. Just reading will do little for you. But using it as a spiritual friend to whom you keep returning, taking your time with the exercises and suggested practices, will be far more powerful and helpful, whether you follow the weekly program, or work through the book in your own way.

Finding the Time

When I was so distressed I nearly dropped out of graduate school, my friend and classmate David Greenway asked me: "How much do you want to be a psychologist?" I didn't like the question at first. But later on, I realized how apt it was. If I wanted to be a psychologist, I had to face the difficulties I was experiencing.

A similar question to ask yourself is: How much do you want to find the center within? How much do you want to find release from suffering and be the calm one in the storm? Would it be worth, say, the time you would give to a college course? Would it be worth a tithe of your time, just 10 percent? If you want this a lot, the time requirements of the program in this book are not onerous.

However, this is only one way to think about it. More important, we realize that the means must match the ends. You cannot achieve peace and joy by pushing yourself too hard into practices that are not themselves full of peace and joy. The key is to practice in a way that is delightful all along, so that the path and the ultimate destination are the same. If you do this, it will not be difficult to find the time.

Language and Anonymity

Except for sections titled "The Experience," the first person is used to refer to the first author (Tom Bien). The second author is referred to by name (Beverly Bien). We generally rotate use of "he" and "she" to refer to a nonspecific individual person. Sometimes we may use masculine pronouns in a religious context where this is traditional usage. There is no intention in this to ascribe male gender to the deity.

Most of the case examples in this book, while based on our experiences in life and in therapy, are composites rather than being drawn from specific individuals. When a specific person is used, identifying characteristics are changed to preserve anonymity.

PART I

~o~

The Key

If you want peace, peace is already there. If you want joy, love, harmony, understanding, wisdom, and happiness—these, too, are already present, right in the nature of things. You do not need to travel to Tibet or India. You do not need to find the perfect teacher or the perfect retreat. You do not have to do anything special whatsoever. All you need to do is open yourself gently to receive what already is, as the earth receives the rain, as a flower opens to the sun.

Perhaps the most painful and damaging illusion of all is the notion that peace and happiness are to be found in the future. When we finish that degree or find the right job or the right relationship, then, we believe, we will be happy. And these may in fact be good things. But peace and happiness can only be now. If we can touch peace and happiness in this moment, future moments will also contain peace and happiness. If we cannot touch peace and happiness now, when will we?

Practically speaking, however, we are prone to lose our way. Both spiritual and psychological practice are a kind of medicine to help us find the means to recontact peace when we no longer seem to know how.

In Part I, we describe the nature of the problems we face in the modern world, and how mindfulness or holding to the center can help. Today many of us see life as a problem to be solved rather than an experience to be lived, looking everywhere but within, everywhere but at our own experiencing. We suffer from fragmentation, disconnection, negative emotions, and low self-esteem. We burden our primary relationships with impossible expectations, and live for the never-arriving future.

Mindfulness, on the other hand, centers us in our own lives, empowering us to find our own internal authority. Mindfulness is deeply connected also to the practice of no self, which we introduce in this section.

Part I provides you with the essential background and understanding of mindfulness. It eases you in to the more formal practices beginning in Part II.

Week One

KNOW WHERE YOU ARE

If you are trying to know God, you must imagine that death is already gripping you by the hair. If you are trying to win power and fame, you must imagine that you will live forever.
—Swami Vivekananda (1863–1902)

Pushing the Stone Uphill

Judy flew home from the peaceful retreat center on the northern California coast. The day was cold and gray. Newark airport was busy as ever. Though she half expected it, the indifference and suspiciousness of the travelers and the airport workers shocked her. Reflexively, she smiled at one person as she had been doing all week on her retreat. He looked away quickly, as if to say, "What do you want? Leave me alone." Men touched their pockets to check for their wallets; women guarded their purses.

The airport atmosphere contrasted dramatically with the smiling, happy people at the retreat with the famous author. She felt well, whole, and calm just being there with him and all those friendly people.

3

As she stepped into the dark emptiness of her house, everything she'd left behind engulfed her: the loneliness, the half-completed plans and projects, all the unfulfilled good intentions. Even her cat's gaze induced guilt for leaving him. As cats sometimes do, he punished her for her absence by pointedly ignoring her. Six messages from work nagged at her, and her heart sank when she heard them. They were like a strong undertow pulling her down with great force. She reminded herself quickly that her next retreat was only two months away. For although this had been her fourth retreat this year, she always had the next one planned. Her friend Mark said it was *the* workshop, and though she did not recognize the name of the famous leader, she nodded knowingly when he mentioned it. Yes, of course she'd heard of her from the *Oprah* show.

Seekers like Judy deserve credit. They have taken a crucial step. They have paid attention to their sense that something is missing and are trying to do something about it. At least they are looking in places that actually contain help, instead of the more indulgent, destructive paths some follow. The difficulty is in connecting these insights to their lives.

Judy tried to bridge the gap between the mountaintop experience of her retreats and workshops with the valley experience of everyday life by staying one step ahead of herself—always having the next retreat or workshop planned before returning from the present one. Her real life was overwhelmingly complicated. It was easier to live with vague fantasies of self-improvement than to face the complexities. Someday she would get it all together. Someday she would have the right job, the right relationship, enough money, live in the right place, and have all the right thoughts and feelings. Someday she would know peace and wholeness. It all seemed to depend on finding the right workshop, getting the right prepackaged answers.

Judy had been a retreat and workshop junkie for years. Her strategy of always having the next workshop planned succeeded just enough at staving off anxiety that she never saw its futility. She kept pushing that stone up the hill and ignoring that it always rolled back down. The retreats and the workshops that she attended were wonderful, and she found wisdom and supportive people at them. The problem was not with the retreats. The problem lay with something deeper, with the way Judy kept the focus off of herself and her own life, the way she kept looking outside herself for the answers. Judy could not resist the urge to tinker with herself. The more she did this, the more the peace she sought eluded her grasp.

Connect Where You Are

The essential thing people want to know from teachers and therapists comes down to this: How can I be happy? How can I find peace?

The essential answer is always the same: Begin where you are.

If the 1970s were the "Me Decade," and the 1980s were the decade of greed, today we look back on a century of growing self-preoccupation. Freud published his first major work, *The Interpretation of Dreams*, right at the birth of the twentieth century. And from that point on, we have been increasingly fascinated with ourselves. Yet at the same time, our anxiety and uncertainty have only increased. For all this fascination and preoccupation, we are more estranged than ever from ourselves and our world.

The reasons we have failed to find peace through all this astonishing effort are doubtless complex. But part of the answer is that we are looking in the wrong place. Part of the answer is that all of our searching leads nowhere if it is rooted in a fundamental distrust of ourselves and our nature. Psychology can help and spirituality can help. But as long as our searching is rooted in self-distrust, we will always be trying on someone else's answer. Workshops and retreats and other tools can only be helpful if you use them to help you connect with *where you are*.

There are many different complications, roles, and roadblocks in our lives that contribute to pushing the stone uphill. There are also many attitudes and beliefs that contribute to our incessant motion that leads us nowhere and in fact keeps us stuck in the same place. But before trying to understand the way out, we need to take a look at how we got into this mess in the first place.

Look at Life's Curveballs

Sometimes life throws a major curveball at us. Times of major change, for good or ill, are obvious challenges to our capacity to remain centered. At such times, even the most spiritually advanced and psychologically whole among us will be thrown off.

Among the negative changes, there are the obvious traumatic events, such as the death of a spouse, parent, child, or other loved one; the unexpected and undesired divorce; the major health problem. These are difficult passages, requiring time, patience, and a lot of support from others. We are thrown out of rhythm and balance. And indeed it would be strange and unnatural if death or major loss did not affect us deeply. For a time, life is empty and pointless. But as time passes, we resume our lives and go on. As we move through our grief, we begin to heal and gradually we are able to return to center. Eventually we integrate the loss and function again, though we remain changed by the experience.

Less generally acknowledged is that positive changes, such as promotions, marriage, career changes, graduations, significant success, and the birth of children, are also difficult curveballs. While we may feel incredibly happy, the earth is shifting beneath our feet, and it can be difficult to stay centered and peaceful. And so even in the face of good fortune, we may lose our center.

Life's curveballs, while difficult, are nonetheless opportunities for learning and growth to take place. Life is a school and the universe is constantly sending us lessons. But we need a way to come back to the center so that we can look at the havoc that these events can wreak on our psychospiritual well-being, understand them, and continue on our path.

But perhaps even more important are the background tensions, the chronic conditions of modern life that make it difficult to stay centered during times of major change.

Open to Abundance

So why do we lose our way even when there are no major losses or changes? What knocks us off course and prevents us from holding onto that balanced, peaceful place: the center within?

In Buddhist cosmology there is a strange and peculiar realm called the land of hungry ghosts. The land of hungry ghosts overflows, as the Bible would put it, with milk and honey. It is a land of abundance. The beings that dwell there, however, are a little strange. They have huge, empty, distended bellies and tiny, pin-size openings for mouths. This is a picture, in other words, of a huge appetite, but an inability to satisfy it no matter how abundant the surrounding world. In fact, the hellish aspect of this realm is not that anything is lacking, but rather, that everything is there, right in front of you, readily and easily available. Only you cannot avail yourself of it because you can never get enough of it through your tiny mouth. *It is not lack, but the inability to open to the surrounding abundance that is the source of the torture.*

In some ways the developed nations of the West are just such a realm. We live in a land overflowing and abundant, but we are plagued by anxiety, depression, and dissatisfaction. Instead of enjoying the abundance, we focus on what is lacking. Like hungry ghosts, we never get enough. The abundance only convinces us that we are not getting our share, increasing our already swollen appetites. No matter how much we have, the focus remains on having more.

The point is not so much that desire is wrong per se. You are not a materialist for wanting abundance or a careerist for desiring success. The universe is generous and longs to bless you with your heart's desire. But these things can become problematic when we put them at the center. Desire can lead to an endless cycle. While we imagine a particular level of wealth will suffice, once achieved, this level is no longer quite enough. We then need still a little more. The attempt to find peace by such means is an attempt to quench our thirst with saltwater: the very nature of our efforts only makes it worse.

Escape from the Future

Another reason we lose our center is that we postpone life rather than live it. Planning is unavoidable to some degree, and planning is no more the enemy than desire is. But when planning for the future takes over the present to such an extent that the present becomes unreal, insubstantial, and ghostlike, we have lost our center. Planning mindfully means knowing we are just planning. We do not confuse it with the present reality. When done in the right spirit, there's a lightness about planning. You know reality is endlessly complex and endlessly evolving beyond our capacity to foresee. And since our plans therefore need continual refining and adjustment—if not total revision—there is no sense to get too caught up in them.

Can you enjoy future food? Can you drink tomorrow's water? Most of us try to do just that, yet you can only nurture yourself with the food and water that are here and now.

Judy avoids living today by focusing on the next retreat or workshop. The student postpones life till he gets his degree, the businessperson till she achieves some imagined height of financial success. Is that person out running around the track truly happy? Perhaps not. His head may be filled with visions of what he will be like six months from now, when he can run farther and faster, when his body-fat percentage is even lower. And in the meanwhile, all of us are missing it. We are missing our lives. The irony is, a life full of so-called purpose and planning and goals is ultimately without point. For while we are preoccupied with our plans, life is happening. Life is not waiting until we are done planning. And while we are defining our goals, we are missing the whole thing. For life consists only of this present moment—the very one we are so busy running away from.

∼ PRACTICE ∼

Where Are You?

Right now: *Where are you?* Come back from your worries and plans, to where you are now as you read. How are you breathing? How are you sitting? How does your body feel? What is the quality of your thinking, your self-talk? Don't criticize or try to change any of this. Just spend a few minutes being quietly aware, as much as possible without judgment.

This is it. This is your life.

∼∼∼

THE EXPERIENCE (TOM)

As I write this, my fingers feel cold. I feel the precise resistance of the computer keys, feel the pressure of my wrists where they rest on the edge of the desk. My stomach anticipates lunch. I hear birds outside my window trying to sing spring a little closer while the cold, March New Mexican winds try just as hard to keep it winter. There's a slight tightness in my abdomen as I focus intently on writing. There is both a sense of curiosity about how this chapter will turn out, and the effort to get the sentence and the paragraph to come out right.〰

Become Aware of Fragmentation

A special problem of present-day life that detracts from our well-being is the fragmentation we experience as we are pressed between conflicting roles and tasks. The many masks we wear and the roles we play can lead us away from the center.

Our work can be fragmenting, and it doesn't matter how complicated the job is. Sometimes other people's work looks enviably easier than our own. But when you're in that apparently simple job, it still has many aspects and demands. Being a homemaker, for example, is not the simple task others romantically imagine: "What is most important for me to do now? Should I do the grocery shopping or go to the cleaner's? Do the banking or vacuum the carpet? Have I done enough now to be able to take a break and do something I enjoy, like watching my favorite program, reading my book, listening to my favorite symphony, or just calling a friend and talking for a while? Or do I need to do more first? And, oh, I forgot to defrost something for dinner tonight." And just when you think you've got it figured out, the kids come home from school and demand your attention; the phone rings and that aggressive long distance carrier tries yet again to sell you its services (how did you ever get on its list, anyway?); the doorbell rings; you suddenly remember you need to pay the mortgage.

There is nothing easy or simple about running a home. Even within this one role, there are many competing demands. And of course it is more complicated than this for many of us. Most of us must deal not only with the complexity of one role, but with balancing the complexity of many roles.

Is it any wonder that we sometimes find ourselves yearning for some other, simpler time; some past or future Eden; some time when we know what is expected of us; some time when things are easier; some time when we can *just* earn a living, or *just* be a homemaker, or *just* be a parent or a friend or a spouse; or some time when we do not have to do any of that at all and can just sit on the beach and sip margaritas? Beverly says, let's move to the islands and sell T-shirts. Yet she knows *this* is the time we have, the life we have.

～ PRACTICE ～

Acknowledge Your Many Roles

Get out pen and paper. Sit quietly for a few minutes, breathing gently. Start to think of the many roles and aspects of your life. List all the roles that you play.

Of course, you may think first of your role at work—the first thing we're asked at parties and social gatherings. But that one role has many subroles. For example, if you're an attorney, you may be part counselor, part litigator, part actor, part researcher, part businessperson, and so on. Also include the roles that you play as husband or wife, parent, son or daughter, and so forth. Make your list as long as possible, coming up with at least twenty-five roles or so, considering even aspects that are quite small such as salon customer or mail recipient.

When you have listed as many roles as you can, read your list over meditatively. Now ask yourself gently and repeatedly: *Who am I?* without trying to answer the question, just holding it in your awareness for a few minutes.

～～～

The Experience (Tom)

As I wake up this morning, I am grateful that I didn't schedule appointments today. There's a feeling of freedom in this, and I'm glad to be able to start my day without having to be at a certain place at a certain time. But this feeling is short-lived. I start running through the list of things I need to do. I try to remind myself that my plan is to write, but just as I do, I remember that I also have to go to the bank. I should get some laundry done, too. Outside, the fruit trees demand pruning and fertilizing. I tell myself: First, I will read for a little while over coffee. But as I'm reading, the ideas in the book spark associations, and I think: I've got to remember to add that insight to the talk I'm giving next week. And when will I get in that application to teach at the university? And don't forget to check the phone messages at work. I meditate for a while, and accepting these crosscurrents, returning again and again to the breath, I emerge from my meditation with a clear focus: to write. I turn on the computer and begin. Just then, my cell phone startles me. Will it be a crisis, or a wrong number? A million tasks, great and small, pull at me, each one a pretender to the throne in the moment it occupies my consciousness, each one claiming to be the most important thing.

And I could add more, just describing the demands experienced within the space of an hour or so on one particular morning, balancing responsibilities for domestic tasks, teaching and speaking, running a psychotherapy practice, and writing. The catalog of activities does not include some major pieces of my life that did not happen to figure prominently that morning, such as being a parent and being a spouse. And I'm not complaining. I'm pretty lucky. Many people are juggling more and enjoying it less.

Breathing in and out, in and out, feeling each breath all the way in, feeling each breath all the way out, not only breathing, but knowing that I am breathing, deeply aware, I let each demand come and go. No resistance. No struggle. This is my life. Just as it is. Its many pulls and demands. Breathing in and out, I know I am worrying about what to do. Gradually, without trying to do so, I grow calmer. I trust my sense of what is important to do now, what is important to do next. I am aware again of the coldness in my fingers, the wind, and the birds. I know that I am alive, as fully as I can be at this time. ∽

Recognize Disconnection

Though my father's father came from Europe, the next generation lacked all wanderlust. Most remained in the same city. When my father moved an hour south to the suburbs, it was as if we had moved to the moon. If we were to see his family, we were the ones who traveled. They could scarcely imagine leaving the city and going so far. Later some cousins moved all the way from New Jersey to Florida, venturing far beyond my father's journey. But for the most part, that generation stayed put, as if honoring some cross-generational need for balance and stability after the emigration of their parents.

Disconnection and separation from our families of origin and friends, coupled with periodic change in geographic locations, all add up to a loss of center. There are many side effects to disconnection from family and friends. And sometimes these side effects distract us from our sense of balance and peace and cause us to lose our way.

For most of human history, people didn't venture beyond a radius of a few miles. Our bodies and nervous systems are no different from our ancestors who lived their quiet, local lives. Most human beings intimately knew the place where they were born, and knew the same set of family members and neighbors their whole lives. For us, it is unimaginably different. We scarcely know the place where we live. Our cars whisk us past them too quickly. We don't have a village, not even a neighborhood. And then every few years or so, we move and start again. Lifelong friends are rare. What we have are friends from different chapters in our lives. And the majority of these fade into the past as we move to new places and occupations. Whether we like living this way or not, our Stone Age bodies and brains are ill equipped for it. There is a constant background stress to lives so disconnected from the roots of place and community. Then when life throws us a major curveball, it is no wonder we lack the resources to cope with it.

But this is only the familiar piece. This is the piece we all talk about. There is much more. Disconnection runs deeper.

Recognize Disconnection in Time

In contrast with our own culture, consider the importance of ancestors in Confucianist Asia. Traditional Vietnamese homes, for example, usually contain an ancestral altar. Every important event in the family's history—every death, every birth, every marriage—involves ritual offerings and pronouncements before this altar, keeping the ancestors informed of all these events, and seeking their guidance and support. This is not a practice most Western people could imagine undertaking. Here, parents and adult children often have troubled relationships. Sometimes they have no relationship at all. Some ancient argument severed the connection. And if we cannot connect back even one generation, how could we possibly entertain the notion of making a place for ancestors in our awareness?

Ancestor worship may not fit our Western context. But it does demonstrate another dimension of our disconnection. We are disconnected not only in space, but in time as well. We lack continuity with the past. Nor do we feel connected with our offspring and with the future. In the past, people were like oak trees, changing slowly, having the strength of deep roots—roots that sank not only into a particular place, but also into the stream of life flowing back into the past and forward into the future. Now we are like the tumbleweeds that roll incongruously across our southwestern interstates, rootless and blown by every wind.

It is impossible for most Western people to think like Confucians. But we do need to find our own ways of maintaining a sense of connection with the past and the future, with the people we came from, the traditions we were born into, and with future generations. Maintaining connection does not mean whole and uncritical acceptance of all people and traditions. Perhaps some of the actions of our parents and ancestors were misguided; perhaps some of the traditions no longer compel in our fast-paced, pluralistic society. We do not need to ignore shortcomings and errors. But if we are radically disconnected, we pay a tremendous price.

Sometimes We Need Separation: Jerry's Story

Jerry had not talked to his parents in ten years. He could no longer even say exactly what that last argument had been about. But he vowed at that time never to talk to them again. He kept his word and took pride in it.

Jerry had his reasons. His parents were alcoholics. Their disciplining would be considered abusive by today's standards. They terrorized him as a child. Coming home from school, he never knew whether his mother would be passed out on the couch or greet him with an angry tirade. Passed out was often preferable. At least then she would leave him alone. And likewise, when his father came home from work, Jerry never knew what mood he would be in. Jerry tried to be outside when his father came home. He would listen at the door for a minute to test the water before going inside. Sometimes he didn't go inside at all, but stayed overnight at a friend's house.

In rejecting his parents, Jerry rejected their religion, too. It was so hypocritical of them, he felt, to spout their Christian platitudes and sit in church on Easter and Christmas with smiling faces, dressed in their best clothes. But Jerry went further. He didn't just reject Christianity. He rejected God. He rejected religion. He rejected spirituality. He rejected any sense of meaning and purpose in life. He saw it all as childish and hypocritical.

Jerry adapted the best he knew how. He tried to make a family out of his closest friends. This was not altogether satisfactory, however, for his friends had their own families. On major holidays and for birthdays, weddings, and funerals, Jerry's friends were with their blood families, and unavailable to him. Sometimes Jerry felt subordinate to his friends' families, and it bothered him. But he was doing the best he could.

Find Your Roots

The point is not that Jerry was wrong. His reaction was understandable. In some situations, it may be the best a person can manage. While none of us are born to perfect parents, some of us are born to parents who are so wounded it may be impossible to reconcile. So perhaps Jerry needed to take the stand he took. Perhaps he needed to avoid speaking to his parents and to see their faith skeptically. But even so, can he look more deeply? Can he, at least in memory, acknowledge that they were people, not monsters? Can he allow himself to remember those admittedly rare moments of positive connection? Though they gave him little and hurt him much, someone clothed him, fed him, changed his diapers—enough for him to have survived early childhood's dependency. And even if he rejects his parents' religion for himself, can he acknowledge the positive yearnings religion represents for others? Does he have to close himself off in bitterness and cynicism? Continuing in such a disconnected way creates grave risks to Jerry's well-being.

Over months of therapy and meditation practice, Jerry slowly began to heal. He learned to relate differently to his thoughts and feelings, experiencing them more fully and clearly while identifying with them less. He eased his grip on his anger and resentment, and eventually recontacted his parents. He did not want to become close to them and at least to this point cannot envision ever doing so. But neither does he have to completely ignore them.

Someone else might make a different choice than Jerry. Someone else might in fact feel that any contact is impossible. Still others may try to reestablish true familial closeness. But Jerry felt this was the healing choice for him. And he made that choice out of his freedom and mindfulness.

Not all of us are as disconnected from our roots as Jerry. But most of us probably have some disconnections to contend with: friends who were once close that we have lost touch with, a sibling we have nothing in common with, parts of our heritage that we have rejected. The world being what it is, this is to some extent unavoidable. But the fewer gaps of this nature we have, the stronger, the more resilient we can be.

It is hard to grow tall without deep roots.

∼ PRACTICE ∼

Reconnect with Your Roots

Spend some time considering the people who have been important to you. Be sure to think about all the different times and places of your life. Now write down the names of the significant people you have lost touch with. For each one on your list, consider the circumstances under which you lost contact. Was it just drifting apart as one of you moved away? Or was your disconnection the result of some conscious choice, based on disagreement? Or was it perhaps unclear how you drifted apart? Notice any patterns. Try to see beyond blaming either them or yourself.

Then for each person on the list, consider whether you might want to reestablish contact in some way. Form a plan to recontact anyone you might like to. There will be some people you may not be able to contact because you no longer know how to find them, and others who, for one reason or another, you judge it best not to be in contact with at all. That's okay. Such choices must be made in freedom and not forced. For those you do not want to contact or cannot contact, spend a few moments visualizing them. See them as happy, smiling, and fulfilled. If you have bad feelings about them, release them by reminding yourself that, whatever they did to hurt you, they were just trying to be happy and avoid suffering in accord with their best understanding at that time. Don't just say the words, but do your best to let this be a deep intention.

THE EXPERIENCE (BEVERLY)

I just returned from a hike in the Sandia Mountains. As always, I feel refreshed. My hikes in the New Mexico landscape always help me to recenter when I find myself getting a bit off track.

But I had that feeling today: that Where am I? feeling that I sometimes experience since moving to New Mexico. It happens less often now, but still washes over me occasionally. It's a moment of feeling strangely disconnected from my New Mexico environment, which is so drastically different from where I grew up in the Boston area.

The moment passes and the landscape once again feels comforting and familiar. I stop for a few minutes and sit on a rock overlooking an expanse full of cactus and piñon trees. Breathing in and out, feeling the hard rock beneath me, I meditate on being at home right here.

Negative Emotions and Low Self-Esteem

When the Dalai Lama started coming to the West, he encountered the problem of low self-esteem for the first time. When first asked about it, he did not know what the term meant. And this was not just a problem of translation: The very concept was unknown to him. From a Buddhist point of view, there is never any reason to feel bad about oneself. No matter what mistakes you have made, you are a future Buddha. Nor is this just a philosophical attitude. Tibet had not been infected with the vicious microbe of low self-esteem.

Of course people everywhere experience negative emotions, and Tibetans are no exception. But negative emotions *with* low self-esteem and negative emotions *without* it are quite a different matter. If you feel positive about yourself overall, it is not terribly difficult to pass through negative moods, learn their lessons, and come out the other side, perhaps stronger and wiser. But if you do not feel good about yourself at the root level, negative emotions grab you more deeply. They pierce you to the core and are more difficult to heal.

In the West, negative emotions present a special problem due to the background of low self-esteem. Our combined fragmentation, disconnection, and low self-esteem make us less resilient to negative emotions and mood states. They also present some special difficulties in learning to be more mindful and tapping into the healing and wisdom this brings. We will suggest ways to negotiate these difficulties in chapter 7, drawing upon both psychological and spiritual wisdom to help you in your work toward psychospiritual well-being.

∾ PRACTICE ∾

Be Aware of Self-Punishing Thoughts

Spend a day practicing awareness of your tendency to engage in self-critical, negative thinking. Label each instance you notice and number them consecutively: "Self-abuse number 1, self-abuse number 2, . . . self-abuse number 37," and so on. If you lose count, just start at one again. Do this in a lighthearted way. Laugh.

If you do this deeply, you will notice that many thoughts may contain an implicit self-critical element rather than a direct criticism of yourself. Count these also.

If you have a lot of these thoughts, you might like to continue this practice for several days. See if, by the process of awareness and without trying to correct the thoughts, they automatically begin to decrease. Awareness itself is healing.

Relationships: Great Expectations

Nothing affects us as deeply, makes us as happy, or causes us to lose our balance as much as romantic relationships. Love is said to make the world go round, but it often sends us spinning as well. Relationships, particularly romantic ones, often get in the way of our holding to center.

The modern view of romantic love seems so fixed and absolute and is so much a part of the psychological landscape of our time, it is difficult to see it in its historical and cultural context. But romantic ideals of love are not universal, they are a phenomenon of the Western world. The creation of what we consider love in this sense can be attributed to one very powerful medieval woman, Eleanor of Aquitaine. Eleanor (1122–1204) was married successively to two different kings—Louis VII of France and Henry II of England. She used her attractiveness to spur Louis on to dangerous endeavors. As a patron of the arts, she encouraged the romantic poetry of the troubadours, which instilled an almost divinized view of woman as the unobtainable, ideal lady, thereby increasing female power and influence. It is hard for us to imagine a world without love, in this sense of the word, yet it is absolutely an invention of culture, scarcely existing before Eleanor's time.

In contrast with romantic idealism in the West, in traditional societies parents arrange their children's marriages. Our culturally conditioned reaction to this is generally one of horror. Imagine having to marry someone you had perhaps never even met. Where's the romance? Where's the love?

While romantic love can be wonderful, older ways contain their own wisdom, and people who do things differently than we do are not necessarily less intelligent or wise. Of course, marriages were arranged among royalty in former times to cement political alliances and strengthen family fortunes—reasons that from our perspective are horribly crass. But consider the consequences of our ideal of romantic love, of soul mates living happily ever after. For one thing, falling under the spell of this myth, we often fail to see the reality of the other person clearly. And for another, this ethos creates tremendous overexpectation. Somehow by just meeting that special someone, as the songs all say, all our dreams should come true. That's it. No more strain and struggle and striving. Instant happiness.

This sets up inflated hopes, and subsequently, painful disappointments. What we experience is inevitably at least somewhat different from the happily ever after of fancy. For one thing, all the other problems of life continue. We still worry about earning a living and what career to pursue, where to live and how. We still confront health problems and emotional problems. While it is often easier to face these things with someone we love than to face them alone, the problems themselves do not disappear. Moreover, the relationship creates problems of its own: How to get along with her when she's grouchy. How to get along with her when you're feeling grouchy. Whether to have children and how to share these responsibilities if you do. Working out differing financial priorities. Whose family to spend holidays with. How to share housework. How to deal with it when one person wants more sex than the other. Whether to rent *The English Patient* or *Terminator II*. These are problems internal to the relationship, but factors outside the relationship also affect it.

Disconnection also affects our relationships. In the village of old, even in the neighborhoods of a few generations ago, people enjoyed considerably more closeness. For this reason, people did not expect their primary relationship to meet all their emotional needs. What you didn't get from your partner, you got in part from Uncle George or Aunt Sophie, from the friend next door or across the street. Even the neighborhood grocer might supply a piece of what you needed, just by noticing that you looked a little tired. For many people, all of this burden of caring is placed squarely on the shoulders of the primary relationship. And the heavier the burden, the more likely the eventual collapse. This lack of broader social support can strain even the best relationships.

Other external factors affect relationships. If your partner is not happy at work, guess what? You are going to be less happy also. If your partner has an argument with a friend, undergoes a change in health status or earning capacity, has a fight with his or her parents—all of these things and more will have a direct effect on you and on your relationship.

The hidden factor in many divorces is overexpectation, so that when these predictable crises hit the relationship, we feel something is terribly wrong. For it certainly does not resemble the fairy-tale fantasy, no matter how sound the relationship may be at its core. Because of these expectations, it is all the more important to take especially good care of our relationships. But in practice just the opposite is the case. Somehow the relationship is just supposed to be there for us, no matter how many years of neglect and indifference it has suffered. Often we lack the basic skills for relationship care. And if we have them, we may still feel something is wrong if we have to work at it. For this reason, to be mindful in the West involves special attention to relationship skills, which we address in chapter 8 with both spiritual and psychological practices.

Living in the future, becoming fragmented and disconnected, expecting all of life's problems to be solved by our partners—these are all common sources of suffering. These problems point us all the more urgently in the direction of mindfulness. In the next chapter, you will learn more about mindfulness—what it is, and how it can help you meet these challenges and difficulties. We then move on to the specifics of mindfulness practice and relate it to the special problems of negative emotions, relationships, and other needs. You do not have to be superhuman. You do not have to be a saint to practice mindfulness. Every step taken in mindfulness helps reduce our very human, very common, but very painful suffering.

∼ PRACTICE ∼

Become the Beloved

With paper and pen in front of you, think of the person you feel closest to—perhaps your partner if you have one, perhaps a friend or relation if not. With eyes closed, imagine yourself becoming that person. Be him physically. Think his thoughts. Feel his feelings.

Now open your eyes. Let this person express his deepest feelings, his hopes and fears, his strengths and self-doubt, everything. Also record this person's feelings about you. Write this all down.

Do not worry whether this is accurate or not. In fact, do not assume that it is. It is not the particular things that are of importance, but making the effort to see it from the other's point of view. By doing so, you may begin to notice whether your guesses are correct, because you begin to observe more closely. Perhaps you even ask. It is all about paying attention.

∼∼∼

See Yourself as a Flower

In *Psychotherapy East and West*, the author Alan Watts described a similarity between the activities of the Zen master and those of the psychotherapist. In Rinzai Zen, the master gives the student a koan, a kind of unsolvable riddle such as "What is the sound of one hand clapping?" He instructs the student to meditate continually on this intellectual jawbreaker until he attains insight. The student approaches the teacher many times attempting to answer with the required insight, which the teacher just as many times rejects, until something of a different quality emerges in the student's answer. It is not any particular words that the teacher is looking for. He is looking for an answer that demonstrates spontaneity and trust of one's own being. But this understanding only emerges out of finally *giving up* the effort and relaxing into a knowingness. Zen masters are tricky fellows and have a knack for knowing the difference between a true, spontaneous emergence and a fake one.

Watts wrote that Western psychotherapy accomplishes something similar. The psychotherapy patient in essence approaches the expert therapist and says, "Fix me." Now every master therapist knows at some level that this is an absurd proposition. One human being cannot fix another human being any more than, in the Zen context, the teacher can make the student into a Buddha. So the therapist dispenses her own unsolvable riddles. If the therapist is a classical Freudian, the riddles will be about mother, toilet training, penis envy, and castration anxiety. If the therapist uses a modern cognitive approach, she will tell you to identify your irrational thoughts and counter them with more rational thinking. The patient keeps coming back, thinking he just does not get it, and the therapist keeps giving out more riddles, until eventually, the patient *gives up* and allows himself to just be as he is. The problem, you might say, is our perception that we are a problem that we have to fix. And once we stop thinking of ourselves as a problem, we discover that we are (and always have been) okay. In Buddhist terms we uncover our Buddha nature.

Of course, this is an oversimplification of both Zen and psychotherapy. It is like saying that bread is just water, yeast, and flour. So why bother with all that baking? Just eat the separate ingredients, then jump up and down for a while to mix them, and let them bake in the heat of your body. Isn't that the same thing? But this oversimplification has a point. Who told you that you were a problem to fix? *You are not a problem to fix any more than a flower is.* A flower is there to appreciate. You are much more like a flower than like a Rubik's Cube. Be wary of anything that teaches you that you are a problem to fix, that sets you at war with yourself, diminishes you, and reduces your capacity for peace.

Practice for Week One

1. Do the practices contained in the chapter:
   - "Where Are You?" (p. 8)
   - "Acknowledge Your Many Roles" (p. 10)

- "Reconnect with Your Roots" (p. 15)
- "Be Aware of Self-Punishing Thoughts" (p. 17)
- "Become the Beloved" (p. 20)

2. Try this special daily practice: "Take Up Your Robe, Sandals, and Begging Bowl" below.

∽ PRACTICE ∽

Take Up Your Robe, Sandals, and Begging Bowl

Wearing special clothes contains power. I knew a minister who wore a clerical collar every day. At one point he considered leaving the church, but in the end he decided to stay. What held him was a simple thought: He couldn't imagine not putting on his collar in the morning.

When a traditional Buddhist monk or nun wakes in the morning, there are no choices to be made about what to wear. Every morning, he puts on his robe. Every morning, she puts on her sandals. Every morning, he takes his bowl to beg food for the day.

Every time you put on your clothes in the morning this week, or change them during the day, or take them off at night, say to yourself, "This is my robe, these are my sandals." Whenever you take out your wallet to pay for something, say to yourself, "This is my begging bowl that the universe has filled." Use this as a way to remind yourself that, whatever role that you may be playing at the moment, your central calling is the same as that of anyone under religious orders: to be a person of peace, of calm, of mindfulness, of lovingkindness and compassion, of joy, and of equanimity. This is your true career.

2

Week Two

FIND A PATH TO THE CENTER

In the immediate experience of the Presence, the Now is no
mere nodal point between the past and the future. It is the seat
and region of the Divine Presence itself. No longer is the ribbon
[of time] spread out with equal vividness before one, for the past
matters less and the future matters less, for the Now contains
all that is needed for the absolute satisfaction of our deepest
cravings.
                    —Thomas R. Kelly, *A Testament of Devotion* (1941)

P eace can be elusive. If you seek it but fail to find it, the problem is
not always lack of effort. Sometimes you are looking in the
wrong place. If the problem is something lacking in you that
needs to be filled from the outside, then whatever experiences you seek
will only disappoint you. You are left in the realm of overexpectation,
fragmentation, and disconnection. You find yourself in the land of the
hungry ghosts, where you remain empty and unsatisfied despite the
abundance all around you.

Of course, if you lack the necessities of food, shelter, and clothing, it
is difficult to find peace. Moreover, if you need more success and appreciation, if you need a partner, or if lack of money prevents you from
enjoying many of the good things in life, these are important, too. It is

a mistake to be so spiritual that you do not honor such needs. But if peace means having all our needs met in a totally satisfactory way, we will never find it.

For most of us, our dissatisfaction is not about fulfilling basic needs. It is about endlessly searching outside of ourselves and our own experience for what was never missing in the first place. *We do not need to fill ourselves with new things—we need to experience more fully what is already there.*

So how do we learn to soften and open to what is already present? How do we come to live fully and deeply *this* life and not some imagined life that we hope someday to have?

In this chapter we describe the main principle for finding the center within, the Buddhist practice of mindfulness, and show how it meets the dilemmas of modern life.

Mindfulness

Mindfulness is a quality of gentle presence. Mindfulness is the capacity to be present with what is going on here and now, without judgment or resistance, without evasion or analysis. It is a willingness to experience without reservation what is happening in our lives in the present. It is the practice of *radical acceptance*.

This is easier to understand as a concept than it is to experience or practice. But the practice is what matters. Often we dislike what is happening in the present. This is why we keep so busy, trying to push ourselves ahead to some future time when things will be lined up more the way we like, engaging in all manner of fantasy about how it will be in that illusory future. It's a good thing that life does not come equipped with a fast-forward button. We would all be dead already. For instead of experiencing what is going on, we are busy trying to avoid it. Even when we try to come into the present moment in a mindful way, most of us experience the wild, intractable nature of the mind. This "monkey mind" is a total restlessness and jumping about from limb to limb and tree to tree, never stopping anywhere for very long, not finishing this bite of our banana before we are already stuffing the next one in.

Fortunately, there is help. There are time-tested ways to develop greater presence or mindfulness in your life. There are ways to learn to keep your appointment with life in the only place it can be kept:

the present moment. That is the good news. And we will introduce you to some of these ways, both Eastern and Western, both ancient and modern.

Work with Three Kinds of Experiences

Though mindfulness is a single thing, it is helpful to distinguish three types of objects: things that are difficult and painful; things that are delightful, healing, and restoring; and things that are somewhere in between or neutral. The practice of mindfulness involves all of these.

If you are doing walking meditation along a forest path and suddenly remember that there isn't enough money in your bank account to cover a check you wrote earlier that day, you should be aware that you are walking down the forest path. Come back to the present. Feel the earth beneath your feet. Smell the pine trees. Feel the wind caress your hair. Notice the little wildflowers along the side of the path. Be where you are. This is the practice of being in touch with what is healing and restoring. This does not mean that you should try to repress your financial fear. You have to respect these feelings and work with them. But don't forget to experience walking in the forest when you are walking in the forest. Some fear or worry or concern is always lying in wait for us. What is the point of being alive at all, if we let these things dominate our attention? This is cultivating mindfulness of what is delightful.

The second type of practice is to work with the negative feeling itself—in this case, the financial fear. However, even then, you need to be in touch with the present moment. To practice in this way is in effect to tell yourself: "Here I am walking in the forest, and also worrying about my checking account. I hold these feelings of fear tenderly, and smile at them. I am completely willing to be here, walking in the forest, and also having these thoughts and fears about money." With gentle persistence, you learn what your fear is trying to teach you and integrate it, but are no longer captive to it. You may even be able to come back to just walking in the forest. This in itself is a miracle.

Evolution has provided us with a gastrointestinal system that is skillful at digesting the food and nutrients we need to maintain a healthy body. It is not always perfect. Some people have allergies to certain foods. These types of food will not be digested well and may cause problems. All of us lose digestive enzymes as we age. Food that we once could digest easily now no longer agrees with us. Many people, for example, lose the ability to digest dairy products.

Similarly, the human mind is the gift of evolution as well. It has become skillful at anticipating problems and solving them. It has become good at digesting unpalatable experiences. Troubling experiences may be metabolized in dreams, or by thinking and talking about them until we are through thinking and talking about them. Sometimes, however, this system of mental digestion breaks down. Sometimes the mind gets stuck in its processing. We may have recurrent dreams, or even relive traumatic experiences as if they are happening all over again. Someone with post-traumatic stress disorder (PTSD) may relive wartime experiences again and again, caught in an endless and frightening loop.

When we get caught in such a loop, when our minds are not digesting difficult feelings and experiences, we need help. At this point we need some way to bring calmness to our experience. Just as we do not digest properly if we eat while we are agitated, so we cannot process feelings if we are not calm. If we cannot do this on our own, psychotherapy aims to restore our ability to digest difficult experiences, so we can learn from them without being dominated by them. Key in this process is the ability to recognize that what you are experiencing is a memory and not a present reality. The presence of a therapist helps clients realize that they are not *reliving* this old experience, but they are safe with a caring person at their side, *remembering* it. When this happens, the mind's capacity to digest the difficult experience is restored.

We get stuck when fears, worries, or old traumas put us into a trance of pain that takes us out of the present moment. So with the person walking in the forest and worrying about money, it is important that he knows he is walking in the forest. If he gets so caught up in his fear that he is overpowered by it, with the same thoughts and feelings looping endlessly, he will get stuck there. It is already helpful when he realizes that he is in a lovely forest, walking in peace, even while at the same time he has this fear and worry. That way, he is not completely engulfed in the negative material.

Neutral experiences can become positive if we receive them with calmness and clarity. The bluebird that flew right across our path this morning as Beverly and I took our morning walk was very beautiful.

But if our minds were agitated, we might have experienced it as neutral or not even have noticed it at all. Wouldn't that have been a shame? Similarly, drinking a glass of water may be neutral, but if you experience it fully, it can be a pleasure.

The breath is often experienced as neutral, but it can be quite enjoyable if we give attention to it. Breath also can help us calm down and digest negative experiences, transform neutral events into positive ones, and reduce our suffering from negative experiences.

∼ PRACTICE ∼

Count the Breath

Sit comfortably. Loosen any tight clothing. Let your mind turn toward your breathing. With the first in-breath, count one. With the first out-breath, count one. With the second in-breath, count two, and with the second out-breath, count two, continuing up to ten. When your mind wanders, come back to the breathing, and begin again with one. When you reach ten, go back to one. Continue for five to ten minutes. Practice in an easygoing, relaxing way. When you are ready to stop, pause for another minute, and feel the effect of having done this on your body and mind.

∼∼∼

THE EXPERIENCE (BEVERLY)

It's about 5 A.M. on Thursday morning and I'm sitting in meditation. I felt so peaceful sitting down in my usual meditation chair. But as soon as I close my eyes, my work projects and worries are bouncing in my head, ricocheting in and out of my meditation. I decide to focus on one current personnel issue and hold that person in my attention for several minutes. I invite the universe to present possible solutions and then just hold her in my attention. No miraculous answers are evoked, but as I continue to focus on holding her in my attention, my mind calms down a bit. Breathing in and out, I feel more peaceful. My bouncing mind quiets and my focus shifts to my breathing. ∼

Killing the Buddha

There is always a risk of getting so caught up in your technique that you miss the point. The goal of spiritual practice is to come into your life more fully, to be more aware of the life you actually have. The second-century church father Saint Irenaeus said that the glory of God is a human being fully alive. The true goal is to be just that. As you become more fully alive, what initially felt unsatisfactory, boring, or even painful, becomes full and satisfying. But in the meantime, you can get caught up in the means and forget the point.

Meditation, for example, is about learning to be more mindful, about coming into your actual life and experience, about enjoying the present moment. But many people turn meditation into a project. As a project, meditation can become rigid and goal oriented. You fantasize about a time when you can meditate so well—when you are so enlightened—that life will always flow smoothly and everything will fall easily into place. Or worse still, you start to think of yourself as "spiritual." This becomes yet another role you play, an image to live up to. And in living up to that image, you become selectively open to certain experiences and closed to others that you would prefer not to notice. You may allow yourself to experience peaceful feelings. But you may resist noticing that you feel bored, because boredom does not fit your idea of yourself as a spiritual person. And it is even harder to admit that you are angry.

Any teaching, any approach or method, becomes an obstacle if we let it. The Buddha described his teaching as being like a snake. It must be taken up very carefully, or you will get bitten, and be worse off than you were before. You can take any teaching, no matter how useful, and make an idol of it, constantly checking your experience against it. And if your experience doesn't fit, you force it into the mold of what you think you should experience.

This is not the way. The way is to be with whatever you are experiencing, and to acknowledge it not only as legitimate, but even as primary.

There is a Zen saying that if you meet the Buddha on the road, kill him. This is a shocking notion. But the shock impresses the point. As with religious language in general, this is not to be taken rigidly or literally. What is implied is that even the Buddha—a fully enlightened being—can be a danger to you. If the Buddha becomes an idol, if you try to conform to your image of what a Buddha is like, this becomes destructive. In fact, conforming to any image whatsoever is the opposite of mindfulness. Whether the image you are conforming to is positive or negative, mindfulness is absent whenever we try to make our experience be what we think it should be instead of allowing it to be what it is. This struggle within ourselves to have only certain kinds of experiences is the main reason we lack peace.

Accept Your True Face: John's Story

John was in psychotherapy for the first time. He thought he knew what to expect. But his ideas about therapy were drawn from indirect and questionable sources, such as movies and television, newspaper and magazine articles. His therapist wanted to help him face his anger, and he gave John an assignment to record his anger-related fantasies. John immediately translated this assignment to fit his preconceptions about therapy. His task, as he took it, was to really get into his anger. He felt that his anger was some awful thing that needed to be exorcised. Instead of looking deeply into the anger that was there, he went way beyond his actual feelings, trying to record what he thought he should feel. He described in great detail the horrible tortures he imagined doing to the person he was angry at, in this way trying to be a good therapy client and do what he should do. After writing this exaggerated version of his anger, John only felt angrier. Worse still, he felt bad that all this hostility and violence was in him.

When he read this material to his therapist at their next meeting, the therapist said, "Wow, you really were angry!" Since John was constantly scanning for cues about whether he was being a good client and having the kind of experience in therapy he was supposed to have, John took this comment to mean he had done it wrong and had gone too far. John was no closer to getting acquainted with his own anger, so anxious was he to conform to what he thought he should be feeling.

A Zen koan asks: What was your original face before your parents were born? This question points toward the real you and your true experience, before you were trying to be anything other than who you are. This is the point of mindfulness, and not trying to make your experience conform to anything. If your philosophy is that matter is the only stuff in the universe, but you have an experience you can only call spiritual, let it be. If you consider yourself a spiritual being, but continue to only experience the body and the material world, let it be. If you think of yourself as gentle but experience anger, or think of yourself as calm but experience anxiety, let it be. Be willing to experience whatever comes. See what happens as you become more accepting of your true experience, of your true face.

Acknowledge All Your Experience: Joe's Story

Joe had a very stressful job. He was a middle manager for a technology firm, which was not doing well. Management blamed the workers, and the workers blamed management. Joe constantly got caught in between. Joe believed in being optimistic and strong. He boasted that he had never had a bad day. He would tell you this, if you asked him, even last Tuesday when half of the workers under him took a sick-out and his boss scolded him mercilessly right in front of the people Joe managed. That evening, Joe had what his doctor called a "cardiac event."

Joe's philosophy has merit. Optimism helps us through some tight situations. But taken to extremes, it causes as many problems as it solves. In one way there are no "bad days," if what you mean by "bad" is a day with no positive elements whatsoever. There are always some positives, no matter how extreme the situation. But if this means that there's nothing going on that is less than wonderful or that causes pain, then this is not only absurd, it's destructive. If Joe had allowed himself to realize earlier how uncomfortable his job had become for him, he would have felt his pain. By acknowledging it, he might have foreseen his need for a change. He might have combed the Sunday paper for jobs or done something to manage the stress he was feeling. Quite possibly, that "cardiac event" would not have happened.

Joe was, in a sense, the opposite of John. John's image of emotional health emphasized expressing negative feelings. John believed this so strongly that he actually cultivated his anger. Joe had adopted a life philosophy that seemed optimistic, adaptive, and useful, but he misused it to deny his own experience. That's getting it backward. He was trying to impose his philosophy on his experience, rather than taking his life as it really is and working with that. And because Joe used his philosophy to deny negative aspects of his experience, he failed to heed the warning that the negative feelings were trying to give him.

Reclaim Your Authority

One day, sitting in theology class, I realized: Everything I was learning was simply an appeal to authority. How does one decide to believe this or that? You choose an authority, and go with what the authority says about it. The authority might be the Bible, or church tradition, or to some extent even the professor. What this ruled out was one's own direct experiences.

I liked psychology because the scientific method seemed different from such blatant appeals to authority. It took a few years to realize that psychology only substituted one authority for another. The authority was not the Bible, but data, research, and experimental design. It was not church tradition, but Sigmund Freud or Abraham Maslow or Aaron Beck. There is a lot that is good about research, just as there is a lot that is good about scripture and tradition. But the real authority still resides in yourself, since only you can decide what you will accept as authoritative. All external authorities are an attempt to bypass the authority of your own experience.

The humanistic psychologist Carl Rogers said it this way: "Neither the Bible nor the prophets—neither Freud nor research—neither the revelations of God nor man—can take precedence over my own direct experience." This is actually a good description of mindfulness. Rogers was talking about the refusal to allow for any mediator, the insistence on what he himself thought, felt, and experienced. If some external authority told him he should think or feel one way, but his own experience did not fit this, he trusted his own experience. Nor does this mean that you have to then fight the authority or try to convince someone with a different experience that yours is more valid. All that is needed is to abide with good-natured inflexibility by your own experiencing. You do not have to lock horns with anyone.

When you begin to do this simple thing—to just be mindful of your own experience in a gentle, nonjudgmental way—you find a path through the wilderness where you thought none existed. The knots of long-standing, difficult life problems are gradually loosened. And this happens—not by trying to force a solution, not by trying to feel peaceful and calm when you are anxious and afraid, not by trying to feel happy when you feel sad, and not by trying to force anything in particular—but just by being more present to all of it, softening to accept what is really happening. If you could force your way through whatever problems you have, if there were some simple solution, you would already have done it and already have found it. Mindfulness is the art of deep presence, without struggle, without trying to fix anything. The best solutions occur when you are not trying to find a solution, but when you are just allowing yourself and everything else to be.

This is not pacifism. This is not fatalism or just giving up. In fact, the opposite is the case. When you are deeply mindful and no longer trying to impose anything on your experience or trying to force a solution, you suddenly find yourself acting with surprising clarity and strength, with action that is both efficient and effective, because your action is in touch with what is really going on.

The Trappist monk and noted author Thomas Merton wrote about this quality of action in his book *Mystics and Zen Masters*. In the passage below he describes the actions of the sage, the one who follows the *Tao* or principle of harmony in all things. Note the blend of activity and passivity, without violence or force:

> The sage . . . accomplishes very much indeed because it is the *Tao* that acts in him and through him. He does not act of and by himself, still less for himself alone. His action is not a violent manipulation of exterior reality, an "attack" on the outside world, bending it to his conquering will: on the contrary, he respects external reality by yielding to it, and his yielding is at once an act of worship, a recognition of sacredness, and a perfect accomplishment of what is demanded by the precise situation.

The problem in other words has something to do with trying too hard, with attempting to perform acts of force and violence on ourselves and the world around us. Such action may have good short-term results. But the long-term results are never good. When we stop forcing, and allow ourselves to experience what is happening clearly, effective action flows naturally and easily. The whole force of human evolution, indeed the whole force of the human spirit, cannot be harnessed and pushed. It can only be impeded or allowed to flow.

When I began as a therapist, I focused on evaluating what was going on: Was I doing a good job? Did this person like me? Was he responding well to me? Or even worse: What is this person's problem? What diagnosis fits? What kind of flaw in his early experience created this problem? What does the literature say I should do about it? More and more, I find that my job is both easier and harder than that. Harder, because I no longer have these judgments and evaluations as a buffer between me and this person. Easier, because I know that what is most important is to attend to this person deeply. The question, What am I noticing? replaces the evaluating, judging, and diagnosing. When I am present in this way, I say and do things spontaneously that often have a rightness about them that I can't explain, even when they contradict my pet theories about therapy. And when I respect the other person's experiencing, he begins to respect his experiencing, too. He finds his way through the problems without struggling so much with himself. I think many therapists come to discover this.

By simply being willing to be present to what is going on, we find our way.

Release the Illusion of Control

Because of past conditioning, we inevitably import attitudes into the practice of mindfulness that do not belong there. If you were in the military, you might hear the call to mindfulness as the voice of the drill sergeant: "Straighten up, soldier! Pay attention!" Or, since almost all of us have been to school, you might hear the voice of old Mrs. So-and-So, the mean schoolteacher who filled your life with terror the year you were in her class: "Now listen up! I do not want to have to say this twice!"

Mrs. Reston loved to lay traps for her students. A year or two from retirement, she had been teaching since 1929 when I had her for a teacher. To us twelve-year-olds back then, the year 1929 sounded prehistoric. Mrs. Reston seemed like the dinosaurs we saw on our field trip to the Museum of Natural History. Sometimes she would tell us to remain at work quietly while she went to the office. This was a ruse, fabricated solely to entrap us. She would then wait in the hall outside the door until we gradually began to loosen up and talk. When the noise and activity reached a crescendo, she would pop in, walking stiffly erect, the sternest of looks on her face. She would scold us at length for not following her orders and not paying attention to her instruction to work quietly. This was her way of teaching us a lesson. And lessons were learned, though not necessarily the ones she intended.

Mindfulness is not like this at all. It is gentle and forgiving. When we are mindful, we lose our illusion of being in control. Then we can settle back and experience fully and deeply. And of course, if we are not in control, how can we blame ourselves or be ashamed? Mindfulness doesn't tell us that we are bad when our mindfulness slips, but that mindfulness is always a miracle. And whenever we come back to the present moment and to what is actually going on, the spirit of mindfulness smiles on us. It does not matter whether we come back five times or five hundred times in the space of an hour. What matters is that we come back.

Don't Worry about Doing It Right

Some of us sabotage ourselves by the very intensity of our efforts. Our desire to be right and correct interferes with coming into the present moment. If you are even a little bit more present to your life, even a little less distracted by thoughts and worries and plans, then you are doing it right. You are moving in the right direction.

THE EXPERIENCE (TOM)

Today I am giving a talk to some colleagues. I am more nervous than usual before a talk. There is something intimidating about all those Ph.D.'s in the room. I hear the voices of my graduate school instructors in my head making their most damning comments—as if I were revisiting my oral comprehensive exams. I find myself imagining one criticism after another, then struggling to rebuff them. As if coming out of a fog, I somehow fight my way back to the cup of coffee I'm drinking. I smell it deeply, then take a sip. I know I am having a difficult time being mindful this morning. But I remind myself it is a miracle to come back to the present at all.⌒

See That the Island Is Beautiful

Sometimes we can coax our feelings along a little bit, especially if we are gentle and patient about it. We can cultivate happiness, joy, and peace. But feelings can never be forced. Peace and happiness emerge out of the practice of mindfulness. They are a by-product. The whole point is to experience whatever you are experiencing. You force nothing.

There is a Korean Buddhist story about a man who hears that a beautiful island is inhabited and goes to find the one who lives there. He searches the island up and down to find its inhabitant, but fails to do so. Finally, at some point, the searcher gives up and stops all his searching. He suddenly realizes the island is beautiful.

Beginning to practice mindfulness is like that. At first, we are looking for something that we expect should be there. We search and search. But when we finally give up a little, and relax into where we are with no special effort, we experience an epiphany; the beauty of the place reveals itself.

While we employ methods and techniques of practice in order to find peace, peace is not a method. When peace unfolds on its own, we can ease our grasp of the method. At that point, there is no method, there is only peace.

Practice Radical Acceptance

The practice of mindfulness is a kind of radical acceptance. It is not so much that we seek to be peaceful, no matter what is happening, as it is that even when we are not peaceful, we accept *that* experience, just as it is. If in this way we tune in to *what is*, even if *what is* is something we do not particularly want, peace emerges. To put it somewhat differently, much of what interferes with our enjoyment of life is the continual struggle to impose a different kind of order on experience than what is already there. Peace is found when we cease this struggle. And the doorway to the cessation of struggle is first to accept that right now, struggle is what is going on.

Some object at this point that radical acceptance is dangerous, that our own experience is not to be trusted. But once again, you have no choice. If you do not accept your own experience, what else can you do? Even if you place your faith in some external authority, it is still you who must decide which authority you will accept. So how do you know you can trust your decision?

The German philosopher Friedrich Nietzsche spoke of human

development in his famous parable of the camel, the lion, and the child. At first, we are the camel. We need to take on the load of tradition, of rules and guidelines for our behavior. If we do not do this in early life, we are not civilized beings at all. Instead, we live in the world of fangs and claws and ruthless aggression. But then we must make the transition to the lion. At this point we come into our power. We still follow the rules, but we use them to achieve and succeed. We become something in the world. But finally, we become the child, and as the child, we throw off the rules we took on as the camel and return to innocence and freedom. This is like Saint Augustine's dictum, "Love God, and do what you will." If you do what you will while having the love of God in your heart, there's no danger of your doing wrong. The person who reaches the child stage is still a civilized being, but the rules and traditions no longer restrict her freedom.

THE EXPERIENCE (TOM)

Sitting outside this morning, I am glad to live in a climate where I can do this even in March. I delight in everything: the blossoming of the fruit trees in the yard, the greening of the grass, the feel of the warm sun on my skin. Before I am fully aware, however, my delight begins to shift. I start to notice the many things I need to do out here. Some trash has blown into the yard. The vegetable garden needs planting. The peeling skin of my house portends paint buckets and brushes and ladders in my future. And so in a short time, my peaceful sitting has become a review of things to do. Whereas before I could feel the trees as something real, as living presences, now they exist in a kind of abstract way: They are a task that needs doing, an item on the list. I have worked with mindfulness long enough to know I cannot force myself to feel peaceful when I am like this. So I just gently breathe in and out, watching these thoughts come and go, letting them jump around as they will. All on their own, held lovingly by the energy of mindfulness, they calm down a little. And there are some moments when the trees are trees once again. ∾

Discover No Self

The practice of mindfulness is embedded in the Buddhist teaching of no self. And while it is not our intention to make Buddhists of our readers, it can be helpful to understand a little about what this means.

Student: How can I make myself enlightened?
Teacher: What would you do with a self?

In the West, we are preoccupied with self. We want to be ourselves, free ourselves, make ourselves be the best we can be, grow ourselves to the fullest extent possible, fix ourselves, and accept ourselves. While Buddhists are not allergic to using the word *self*, this talk of *self* can sound a little strange from the perspective of Buddhist teachings.

The self is made entirely of nonself material. You may feel that you are quite solid—a real, separate person—until you look a little more deeply into this. Where do the molecules of this solid body come from? There is not one molecule of your body that does not originate elsewhere. Every molecule, including the 70 percent of you that is water, comes from outside. The calcium that makes up your bones is not your own but comes from the earth. And do you think that your genes are you? They, of course, came from your parents and your ancestors.

Although we have a sense of being a solid and separate self, this feeling does not stand up to examination. We are used to thinking as if there were a solid boundary at the skin. Everything within that boundary is self, everything outside of it is nonself. But look more deeply. Skin is porous. Material is constantly coming out of these openings, constantly coming in through them. Every moment, we inhale or exhale—again, exchanging material with the world around us. How much sense does it make to say that the molecules of air that have just filled my lungs are now me, whereas a few seconds ago they were not me? Likewise, we eat and drink and eliminate waste. What wasn't self a moment ago is now self, and what was self a moment ago is no longer self. And whereas we are used to thinking of ourselves as separate and solid, as if we are a solid self moving through the emptiness of space, we know this is not the case. At the boundary of the skin, the slower-moving molecules of our body meet the faster-moving molecules of the surrounding air.

And we can go further. If we go beyond the molecular level to the subatomic level, we know that we are mostly space. Our hand may appear quite solid to us, but looking at it at the quantum level, we know that it is really more like a cloud or a field of energy. When our hands appear to pick up an object, the reality is more like one field of energy interacting with another. There is nothing solid there at all. So where is the self?

In *Star Trek: Voyager*, there is a character known as the EMH, or Emergency Medical Hologram. This doctor is actually a computer program. His outer form is actually light, photons emitted from a holo-projector. He appears to have a personality, full of little quirks, oddities, and idiosyncrasies, but these, too, are just his programming. He seems to learn from experience because, of course, he is programmed to do so.

Now here is the point: How are you or I different from the doctor?

We want to protest immediately that we are more than computer subroutines and photons. But are we? How much difference does it make that we are made of water and carbon rather than photons, or that our programs are the result of the interaction of neurons rather than microcircuits? Where in any of this is a self—either in the doctor or in us?

If I am not a separate self, then what am I? At the deepest level, at the level where the word *I* no longer has clear meaning and reference, I am life itself. I am the universe. I am one with all of it. And I see that your needs and my needs only appear to be in conflict, but cannot ultimately be so, since you and I are not separate. We are in fact so deeply connected, you might say we "inter-are."

∼ PRACTICE ∼

Find Your Self

Try this experiment to have an experience of no self. Sit for a few moments and watch as thoughts and feelings come into your mind. Where do they come from? Where do they go? We believe we think, but if we look more closely, the experience of what we call thinking is more like thoughts just coming and going on their own. They appear, elaborate on themselves, then go again. We are no more in charge of this process than we are of clouds passing through the sky.

Now ask yourself: Where is something which I can call "I"?

All there is is just this stream of thought and feeling and experience. You can say you are the experiencer, but that is just another thought.

≈≈≈

The Purpose Is to Be Fully Alive

At a talk I gave, someone objected to the idea of no self, saying that the self is what is doing the observing. This is an insightful comment, and shows that the person took the idea seriously. However, what happens when this self stops observing? Where is it then? If the self exists only intermittently, then it is something quite different from what we usually mean when we talk about self. It is considerably less solid and substantial. The reality, according to Buddhist teachings, is that self is just another thought in the stream of our thoughts.

This may sound a little esoteric. But this principle is actually quite practical. The key to understanding Buddhism is to see it as always about practice, about suffering and the end of suffering. The Buddha was always practical. Sometimes he refused to answer speculative metaphysical questions posed by curious disciples—not because he could not, but because he did not feel it was helpful to get distracted by such things.

It may seem frightening to question such a basic idea as the existence of a self. It can give you that feeling of being on no solid ground, as if there's an earthquake going on. But once you get past the initial shock, it is liberating. This is well stated in a poem by Emily Dickinson:

I'm nobody! Who are you?
Are you-Nobody-Too?
Then there's a pair of us!
Don't tell! they'd advertise-you know!
How dreary-to be-Somebody!
How public-like a Frog-
To tell one's name-the livelong June-
To an admiring Bog!

It is freeing to lay down the burden of having to be a somebody, and come out onto the broad, easy plane of just being.

Consider driving. When you drive from the perspective of self, it becomes important who is in front of whom and who gets there first. Driving becomes a competition and a race. Sometimes, as with road rage, it even becomes a war. But what is the purpose of driving? Even within relative, goal-oriented thinking, the purpose of driving is to get safely from here to there, and only secondarily to get there quickly. It makes much more sense to think of driving as a situation that we are all in together, with a goal of getting from one place to another safely and efficiently. In fact, it actually works better that way. When we approach it in a no-self way, there are fewer accidents. We all get where we are going in one piece, and are far less distressed and worn out. It costs us a great deal when we cling to the idea of a separate self.

We can go even further here. When you really examine it, all we have is our experiencing. It is not so clear that there is anything solid that does the experiencing, even though the convention of our language insists there must be a subject and a predicate for every sentence. But when we realize there is no solid, unchanging thing that experiences, we can see that the purpose of driving is not to get there but to drive, and the purpose of living is to live—to be fully alive.

Abandon the Chase

There's a bumper sticker that reads: "Life is a game. The one with the most toys in the end wins." Funny, yes. But also sad. Wins what? Wins the heart attack? Wins the prize of dying early from one of the many other stress-related diseases? Wins the prize of missing the whole thing because you are never quite where you are, doing what you're doing, but are always racing ahead to the next thing, as if life itself were a race or a competition? We pay an awful price when we think we are in a self situation but are actually in a no-self situation. And we are actually always in a no-self situation.

Take another example—a job interview. You have researched this position, and you feel that you want it very much. Because you are thinking of it as a self situation, which is to say a win-lose situation, you get competitive. Your heart races and your sweat glands become overactive. This in turn makes you self-conscious. You second-guess yourself constantly: "Was that the right answer? Boy, that was stupid!" Because of this attitude, you are tight and anxious, and you don't make the impression you could make if you were more relaxed.

Even a job interview is a no-self situation. What good is it to win the position, if you then hate it, if next month you find yourself combing the classifieds again? If you see this as a no-self situation, then you know that there is no winning for you alone unless everyone in this situation also wins. Both you and the employer must be happy, or the results will not be good for anyone. If you get the job because you have made an overly positive false impression, what have you really succeeded in doing? You have created a situation that can only cause bad feelings and disappointment for everyone concerned, including yourself. Ironically, if you see the truth of this, you are more likely to create a good impression, because you are more relaxed and more yourself.

The idea of no self is to experience reality in a different way, to see our interconnectedness with all things. It is a way of removing the veil from our eyes, so we can see that we, like everything in the universe, are constantly changing, not some solid unchanging entity. Don't get caught by this as an idea to argue about. It is not something to defend, nor something to debate against. It is an experience. It is a way of seeing.

So no self is not esoteric. It is pragmatic and effective. It works. The practice of mindfulness is exactly this simple, moment-by-moment attention. It is peaceful and refreshing to be in that place: Now this is happening, now this is happening, now this, and so on. It becomes a struggle as soon as ideas of self creep in: "Am I doing it right? Am I being mindful enough? Boy, I'm not very good at this!" Noticing the difference between these two kinds of awareness is itself the way out. But more about that later.

∾ PRACTICE ∾

Tea Meditation

Take a break. Perhaps give yourself a cup of tea or a piece of fruit to enjoy, or whatever your body would like right now. Prepare your tea or snack in a relaxed way, aware of each movement. Let it be like opening a Christmas present: Instead of doing it in a hurried and uncivilized way, take your time with it, enjoying the whole process. Preparing your tea is as valid as drinking it. Stay in the present moment. When your thoughts get ahead of you, gently return to the present and to what you are doing.

Before you begin to eat or to drink your tea, pause. Appreciate the prospect of your tea or food. Then slowly begin to eat or drink. While sipping or eating, savor each taste, smell, and sensation. Notice what it is like to chew, taste, and swallow. When other concerns arise, acknowledge them, and remind yourself you can deal with them later. Right now, only this cup of tea, this piece of fruit, exists. Give yourself the gift of being in the present moment.

Practice for Week Two

1. Perform the practices for this week:
    - "Count the Breath" (p. 27)
    - "Find Your Self" (p. 38)
    - "Tea Meditation" (p. 41)
2. Try this special daily practice: "Moments of Mindfulness" below.

～ PRACTICE ～

Moments of Mindfulness

There are many opportunities during the day when we are engaged in a relatively simple task that we usually do on automatic. For example: doing the dishes, taking a shower, vacuuming, going to the bathroom, drinking a glass of water, walking from your car to the office or the store, getting dressed, waiting at a red light, and so on. Choose one of these activities, and in the coming week, resolve to do it with total mindfulness, breathing in and out, aware of what you are doing, not getting lost in your plans and worries. When your mind wanders, bring it back to the present without wasting any energy in self-recrimination.

PART II

~o~

The Door

How then are we to open the door of mindfulness, and use it in our daily life? If meditation is the answer, it has been presented in ways that make it seem daunting and difficult to most Westerners—a practice for the spiritual Olympians among us. But when the essence of meditation is understood, this need not be the case. And when we can take meditation out of our meditation room and into daily life, a quiet power emerges that, while at first almost too subtle to notice, gradually transforms every moment and every experience.

Part II is drawn primarily from traditional spiritual practices. In this section, we teach you the formal practice of meditation (weeks three and four). We tell you what meditation is and how to do it, and we answer questions regarding common difficulties. Psychological sources help us understand the effects of meditation and teach us how to give ourselves encouraging messages. In the chapters for weeks five and six we show you how to begin to integrate the meditative attitude into daily life. Spiritual sources are again supplemented with psychological input, such as comparing mindful living with the psychology of "flow," and keeping a balanced lifestyle.

3

(Weeks Three and Four)

A GENTLE APPROACH TO MEDITATION

> We already are what we want to become. We don't have to become someone else. All we have to do is be ourselves, fully and authentically. We don't have to run after anything. We already contain the whole cosmos. We simply return to ourselves through mindfulness and touch the peace and joy that are already present within us and all around us. I have arrived. I am home. There is nothing to do.
>
> —Thich Nhat Hanh, *Transformation at the Base* (2001)

Befriend Your Inner Life: Kate's Story

Kate was a trial lawyer. She was bright, dedicated, and hard-working. And though she was reasonably successful, something seemed to block her from living up to her full potential. In therapy, Kate came to see how thinking oriented and intellectualized she was. The moment she started to feel an emotion, she immediately converted it into thinking and reasoning, as though it were altogether intolerable to feel emotion. This was by no means all bad. It helped her stay in a problem-solving mode when others were losing their calm. But it also limited her effectiveness. To convince judges and juries, she needed emotion. She needed passion, and not just reason.

In meditation, she learned that she could let emotions come up without being afraid they would sweep her away. Over time her emotional energy became more available to her, and she learned that she could draw on this when she needed to. She became more powerful in giving closing arguments, and her success rate—already good—improved still more.

The Meditative Attitude

There is no better method for deep transformation and finding inner peace than meditation. Psychological research such as that conducted by the Harvard psychiatrist Herbert Benson has detailed the profound physiological effects of meditation. When we meditate, our pulse slows down and our blood pressure drops. Our brain activity shifts toward alpha waves—reflecting a state of calm awareness. These changes inoculate us against many stress-related illnesses, and they occur in even novice meditators. Yet these physiological changes barely touch upon the change of consciousness that advanced meditators report. For meditation is not just for fine-tuning the body and the mind (which it does), it is a path of enlightenment, a way to come into that place of unshakable peace called nirvana, moksha, satori—the kingdom of heaven.

However, the practice of meditation is riddled with paradox. Trying to find peace, we first experience anxiety. Trying to just be, we experience the wild busyness of our minds, endlessly worrying, anticipating, planning, or regretting. This initial experience makes some of us recoil from meditation, glad to return to the distraction of our busy lives.

Is it possible for ordinary human beings—who are neither saints nor ascetics, not monks, nuns, or gurus—to become meditators and to use this method of peace and transformation for themselves? Absolutely. The only catch is that although you start to meditate for a reason—whether it's to reach enlightenment or just to inoculate yourself against stress—you must give up this very goal, allowing your meditation practice to unfold as if you were not seeking to accomplish anything at all.

Meditation Is a Natural State

Meditation is natural. Just as you do not have to work to see the color blue or hear the sound of traffic going by, you do not need to try to force yourself to accomplish anything special in order to meditate. Encouraging meditative awareness is a little like encouraging sleep. You can do things to facilitate sleep: waiting to go to bed until you feel sleepy; turning off bright lights and putting yourself in a comfortable, safe, and quiet place; avoiding caffeine or stimulating activities before you go to bed; and so on. But you cannot force sleep. You cannot make sleep happen. Going to sleep is not something accomplished with willpower and flexed muscles and knitted brow. In fact, the art of falling asleep is the art of getting out of your own way enough to allow sleep to occur. As everyone who has been up in the middle of the night knows, the more you worry about how tired you will be the next day, the more you think that you've got to get to sleep right now, the more sleep eludes you.

Meditation is a state of calm, alert attention rather than sleep. But as with sleep, it can only be encouraged and not forced. If you sit with an attitude of accomplishing or forcing, you quickly come to recognize that you cannot control this process. The more you try to force yourself to feel peaceful and not feel sad or anxious, the less peaceful you become. Meditation is the art of getting out of your own way and of letting the process unfold at its own pace and rhythm. It is the simplest thing of all. But we are so used to doing—to being occupied and entertained—that it takes a while to reeducate this capacity for being. What makes it possible in the first place is that we are already Buddha. We are not trying to force ourselves to be something inimical to our nature: We are just uncovering what we already are, allowing something vast and unfathomable but normally in the background to come into the foreground of awareness.

Meditation is a little bit like what happens when you sit before a campfire in a quiet, beautiful place. It is more focused, but like your campfire reverie, you are not trying to accomplish anything. You are not looking at the fire because it is good for you, or to create peaceful feelings. You are just looking at the fire. And as you look at the fire, your mind settles down on its own. As your mind gradually quiets down, you get closer, layer by layer, to your underlying Buddha nature.

And these are not empty words. Your Buddha nature is there. In the film *Phenomenon*, John Travolta plays a character named George who has suddenly developed super intelligence. In one scene, he studies the trees as they gently sway back and forth in the wind, allowing himself to sway gently in their rhythm. Wisely, the meaning of this behavior is never expressed in words; but what it shows is a person in harmony with nature, in contact with instinctive wisdom. When the woman he loves complains of anxiety about how to live and handle her life and its problems, George tells her, of course she knows what to do. He asks her, for example, how she held her children when they cried as infants. She pantomimes holding her baby and rocking back and forth, just as George had rocked in harmony with the trees. In this way, he puts her in touch with her own wordless knowing, her own instinctive wisdom. He puts her in touch with her Buddha nature, which is not always about knowing deep mysteries, but is sometimes just knowing how to comfort a child, or for that matter, how to comfort ourselves. Meditation is getting in touch with that.

Remember Who You Are

If you have been doing the exercises to this point, you are coming to know just how busy your mind is. The mind is always doing something. If it is not focused on drinking your tea or coffee, or on your breathing, it will be focused on your worries and plans and regrets and heartaches, gibbering and jabbering away with its incessant noise and chatter. In order to touch Buddha mind or big mind, it helps to give little mind something to do. Whenever we are fully engaged with something, there is an opportunity to become aware of big mind. When we touch big mind, there is a sense of coming to ourselves.

In an interview John Lennon gave shortly before his death, he discussed a time in his life when he was having great difficulty. He was using drugs and experiencing a deep alienation. One day he took a warm bath, which he called a great female trick. Suddenly he came to himself, saying he knew who he was. What he described was a moment when he got back in touch with his true self, and not just the role he played as a former Beatle and rock star. The simplest things can help bring us to this space. Meditation is just the simplest.

Cow Taming

The Zen teacher Shunryu Suzuki wrote: "To give your sheep or cow a large, spacious meadow is the way to control him." In other words, the more we try to clamp down on our awareness and force it in a particular direction, the more resistance we get. But if we give our thoughts and feelings plenty of space to romp around in, they begin to tire themselves out and settle down, all on their own.

In practical terms, when you sit down to meditate, say something to yourself like, "I welcome all that I am into this sacred space." Sometimes this is not easy.

THE EXPERIENCE (TOM)

It's my first day back to work after vacation. My mind is racing. I'm thinking about the pile of mail, about how many phone calls I will have to return, about the clients who will cancel after my being away, and about a million other things. I know I cannot force these feelings to settle down, so I just breathe in and out, and let myself be present to the roller coaster ride of my thoughts. I just sit, breathing in and out, watching all these thoughts come and go. After a while, they begin to calm down. And when the meditation bell sounds, my mind is clear, energized, ready for the day. I am no longer resisting either my worries or my return to work. I have stopped struggling with myself.~

Peace Is the River

The flow of thoughts and feelings is like the flow of a river. Each thought and feeling as it passes is just one drop in the river. Sometimes if there is rain or melting snow from the mountains, the river flows with a lot of energy and noise. The current is strong and dangerous, and we know we need to be careful if we are to avoid drowning in it. At other times, the river flows along more peacefully and gently. And watching the river is more pleasant.

Some of the water drops in the river are peaceful thoughts and feelings. Some are drops of worry, fear, anger, hatred, and other emotions we would rather not experience. But all of them are drops in the same river. Beginning meditators often try to make more and more peaceful drops in the river and less of the more painful ones. When we try to do this, we end up frustrated. We wonder whether we are meditating correctly, or whether meditation is really for us. But the frustration is itself a teaching, telling us that we are attempting to do something that we cannot do. We cannot force the river to be calmer. It is what it is. Peaceful feelings, like all other feelings, will come and go. The deeper peace is found, not in these temporary thoughts and feelings, but in the river itself. As we learn to accept *all* the thoughts and feelings passing by, we come to see that peace does not reside in any particular mood, but in the whole flow. As you look more deeply, you see that no matter what is happening on the surface of the river, deep down it is always the same: cool and calm and serene.

The true, solid foundation of peace does not lie in forcing feelings of calmness, but in a radical willingness to experience whatever comes up.

Coffee-Break Attitude

If in your meditation, you try to restrict yourself, or struggle with yourself, your meditation imprisons you. Then it will be no wonder if you give up on it. *The purpose of meditation is to enjoy it.* The proper attitude to take toward it is a little like your attitude toward a coffee break. You know that a coffee break is good for you. You know it increases your productivity and helps you feel better. But that is not why you take a coffee break. You take a coffee break to enjoy it. You do not have to push yourself to do it. You don't end up arguing with yourself: "I know I should take a break. It's very good for me. It lowers my blood pressure and helps me work more efficiently." More likely, you look at the clock, anticipating break time. "Twenty more minutes and I can take my coffee break! Hooray!" Then you use the coffee as something to do to get your mind out of your work and into a different space.

It is the same with meditation. Meditation is not like taking castor oil or forcing yourself to jog if you hate jogging. It's a little like the coffee break. It is something to look forward to, something you will miss if for some reason you are unable to meditate on a particular day. The Zen master Thich Nhat Hanh says, "We practice sitting meditation to have liberation, peace, and joy, not to become a hero who is capable of enduring a lot of pain."

It is important for people from the Western world to approach meditation in this spirit. We inevitably want to turn meditation into more doing and accomplishing. So forget about meditation being good for you. Just sit for a few minutes, and enjoy your breathing in and out. If you become too goal oriented, you will miss how wonderful it is to simply have this time set aside from your busy life and many worries and enjoy your breath.

Finding the Discipline

When we teach, we are often asked, "How do you find the discipline?" In a way, the question itself is misleading. The ancient Chinese sage Ma-tsu expressed the paradox of discipline this way: "The *Tao* [the way of harmony and balance] has nothing to do with discipline. If you say that it is attained by discipline, when the discipline is perfected, it can be lost . . . If you say [on the other hand] there is no discipline, this is to be the same as ordinary people." (Bracketed material added.)

If you observe a meditation master in traditional meditation posture, what you see is a careful balance—upright, but not rigid, alert, but relaxed. This posture demonstrates meditation as a balance between discipline and effort on the one side and a peaceful, relaxed state of being on the other. It is easy to err on one extreme or the other.

Some teachers focus on strict posture, allow no movement, and require even beginning meditators to undertake long periods of sitting. They teach you to be present with the pain in your legs or back, and to use it rather than give in to it. If these stricter approaches appeal to you, by all means follow them. But there are dangers. You might view your meditation as a personal achievement and develop spiritual arrogance. You might lose the freshness of your "beginner's mind." Too much discipline results in a cold, frozen, abstract kind of awareness, which is quite different from the living, warm, flowing water of true meditative awareness. When that kind of awareness results, there is a great risk that you will stop meditating altogether, and become one of the many who say they "tried meditation for a while." We have met far too many people in this category—people who may have done better with a gentler, more patient approach.

Let the path you choose be based on an honest self-knowledge. If you are a highly disciplined person and can follow a strict approach without losing your zest for meditation, wonderful. If that is not you, however, proceed more gently and slowly—as we teach in this book.

Practice Meditation as Self-Love

We cannot stress enough the importance of not forcing anything to happen. If you feel anxious and you try to force yourself to feel peaceful, you have declared war on yourself. You have divided your original wholeness into warring factions: the part that wants to feel peaceful and the part that feels anxious. At this point, you trade one problem for two, because now you are not only feeling anxious, but you are also struggling with yourself not to feel that way. You are both anxious, and anxious about being anxious, and you are worse off than you were to begin with.

Obviously, it is not good to wallow in negative feelings. But at the same time, when you feel anxiety (or some other emotion you would rather not have), that feeling is you. You cannot force it to change. To destroy the anxiety is to destroy yourself as well, since you and it are the same. When you learn to be present with it in an accepting way, breathing in and out, the energy behind the anxiety can be gently transformed, without any special effort to do so. You just meet the energy of this anxiety and observe it lovingly. If you try to disown it or push it away from you, you are damming up psychological energy. You are becoming a person whose energy no longer flows freely. When this happens, you will only feel more anxious.

Do not declare war on yourself. You need all that you are and all of your energy. If right now, some of your energy is coming to you in a form that you would rather not have, the practice is to let it be so for the time being. As you bring a gentle, accepting awareness or mindfulness to this feeling, it changes and shifts.

When we declare war on ourselves by trying to disown some of what we think and feel, we are a house divided. And when we are divided, this gets reflected back to us externally. We find ourselves in conflict with many people and at odds with our life situation. As *within*, so *without*.

The things about ourselves that we want to disown get projected onto others, and cause havoc in our lives.

So meditation is an exercise in self-love, not by trying to force anything, but by accepting whatever is happening just as it is, by being willing to experience our thoughts, feelings, and emotions, just as they are. When we do this, we create a harmony within that has a way of being reflected back to us in the outer world as well. When we do not struggle with ourselves inside, we see this reflected back to us as lack of struggle on the outside.

Refuse to Compare: Betty and George

As Betty sat in meditation, her thoughts ran off like this: "Well, here I am again, sitting at the meditation hall. I don't know why. (Oh yeah, remember, breathing, in, out . . .) Look at these other people around me. They are sitting so straight and tall. They look so peaceful. And here I must sit in a chair instead of a meditation cushion because of my weak back. None of these other people seem to struggle with wandering thoughts the way I do. They all look like they know just what they're doing. Like George there across from me. He always seems so happy and peaceful. I don't want to admit it, but I don't think I know what I'm doing at all. (Oh yes, the breath, in and out, in and out . . .)"

In the meantime, George was thinking: "Here I am again, meditating with these same people, in this same place. I know this is helpful to me. As busy as my mind still is, I have felt different these past months now that I have been meditating regularly. (Breathing in, breathing out, watching these thoughts, in and out.) But I wonder: Am I really doing it right? All the other people here seem so peaceful. That woman Betty looks radiant. And she's only been coming here a couple of weeks. She can't even sit on a cushion but has to use a chair, and yet she seems more advanced than I am."

Stop. Meditation is not a competitive sport. Sometimes it can indeed seem like everyone is better at it than you are. But that is because you lack direct access to their wandering thoughts, while you are acutely aware of your own. Remember that you are not trying to get anywhere, and not trying to accomplish anything. So what does "better" mean? It has no relevance. If you are able to sit and smile and enjoy this time for meditation, you are doing just fine.

Buddhism teaches that there are three kinds of problems you can have with self-esteem: thinking that you are worse than others, thinking that you are better, or thinking that you are as good as others. Why include thinking that you are as good as others? Because you are still comparing.

If comparing yourself is a problem, give yourself some encouragement: "I am doing just fine," or, "All that matters is to enjoy my sitting," or, "I am just as I should be."

Make a Start

All you need is a relatively quiet place, a comfortable way to sit, a bit of time, and something to focus on besides your usual planning and worrying. You don't need to feel that the place has to be a perfection of silence. In fact, any sounds or distractions can actually be used as part of your meditation. But especially in the beginning, it helps to find some quiet. If you know your phone may ring, for example, turn the ringer off. Let the answering machine do its job. Just taking the action to set the stage is an expression of your commitment and already a help.

Find a Comfortable Position

If you don't know what the full-lotus or half-lotus positions are, wonderful. That's one less obstacle in your path. If you do know, you may need to let go of some images of how you should look when you meditate, unless you are one of the few Americans who can sit comfortably in this posture.

Recently we saw a show on public television concerning a Third World country. One thing stood out for both of us at the same time: *They were all sitting on the ground.* It is no wonder that meditation teachers who come from these cultures teach that you have to sit cross-legged on the ground to meditate. For them, the lotus position is just a variation on normal sitting. For many of us, however, backs, legs, and knees, unaccustomed to such positions, protest at such abuse. And for us, that's just what it is—abuse. Remember, meditation is the art of enjoying your moment-to-moment awareness. It is a way of being more deeply and fully alive—something to look forward to and treasure. How can you enjoy it if you are in pain?

You can meditate lying down, walking, sitting, kneeling, or standing. The reason you hear so much about the sitting posture is that it is relatively comfortable and stable. Many traditions emphasize the importance of sitting upright. There are many esoteric reasons for this, concerning opening up the spiritual channel to the chakras, or energy centers in the body. But if you sit comfortably but upright (not wooden or stiff), you can be relatively relaxed and alert, and less likely to fall asleep than if you are lying down. So for sitting meditation, just find a way to sit that is relatively comfortable and upright.

We love those statues of the Buddha sitting in that wonderful lotus posture. But killing the Buddha here means letting go of images that don't fit our own circumstance. Once when I had injured my back, I could not sit in my usual meditation posture. Though I was glad to get back to my regular position, I found that I could even meditate quite nicely with my feet up on my recliner. Don't get caught by preconceived ideas.

Set the Stage

It is helpful to use props to set the stage for meditation. Whatever invokes a sense of peace, wholeness, or holiness may help. This may involve incense, a statue of a holy person, a bell to sound at the beginning and end of your meditation, a flower, and so on. Choose these items with care. If you have a statue of the Buddha, for example, make sure it is one that expresses peace and is very beautiful.

Though meditation purists may object, sometimes you may wish to use some gentle music in the background. If you are a musician, you may want to meditate on the music itself. Otherwise, it is best to choose something quiet and repetitive, something that does not call attention to itself. If there is a lot of activity, sound, and commotion around you when you meditate, it may be helpful to mask this with some peaceful music. After working with music, sometimes you begin to hear all sound a little differently, as though it, too, were music coming from your stereo. This gives you a deeper perception of sound in general. For meditation, choose music that helps you to feel peaceful, calm, and happy.

Remember to Smile

From early on in my meditation practice, I meditated with a little Buddha smile on my face. I had not heard or read anything that instructed me to do this; it just felt right instinctively. Many years later, I read about the importance of smiling while meditating. This confirmed my original instinct.

Smiling calms the muscles in our body, and helps put us in the right mental attitude. In fact, I would go further: When you meditate, pretend you are the Buddha and are already an enlightened person, full of joy and peace and wisdom. If you smile like a Buddha, you tap a little more deeply into your Buddha nature, your true self. And your meditation will be much better.

It is so important to touch joy and happiness when you meditate. When you touch joy in your meditation, your meditation becomes easy. When you cannot touch joy, meditation can be very difficult.

So go ahead. Smile!

Use a Timer

Some people have a kind of romantic notion that they can just meditate for whatever feels comfortable at the moment. But for formal practice, it is good to set a specific time. This is a way of honoring your intention to keep coming back to your mindfulness, whether meditation on a given day is easy and peaceful, or whether you are very distracted. With a timer, you do not have to worry that you might be late for work or whatever you should be doing next. You can let the timer take over that worry for you.

When doctors prescribe antidepressant medication, they follow the principle "Start low and go slow." You begin with a low dose to see how it is tolerated, monitoring for troublesome side effects. Then you gradually increase the dose. Similarly, in our program, we have you gradually increase the length of your meditation time.

There are two considerations to keep in mind. First, if you overwhelm yourself by trying too hard and lengthening your meditation too quickly, you may give up altogether. Second, however, if you stay stuck in only brief meditation periods, you do not reach the fruit of your meditation practice. The first fifteen or twenty minutes of meditation is often the period when you are most scattered, and is therefore the least rewarding part. If you never get past this, you don't know what you are missing.

Of the two dangers, we think the first outweighs the second. Above all, don't overwhelm yourself. For if you stop meditating, the whole venture is lost right there. So above all, keep your meditation enjoyable. Maintain a positive spirit about it. And increase your sitting time slowly and gently.

Move Mindfully During Meditation

Some meditation teachers strictly forbid movement during meditation. While there is a lot to be gained from cultivating stillness, we feel that if you prohibit yourself from moving, you may get caught up in a struggle between your desire to move and your intention not to. This is a frustrating way to spend your meditation time, and actually *prevents* the stillness you are seeking. So go ahead and move if you need to. When you move, however, do so *mindfully*. Resist the temptation to move as a kind of reflex. Slow the process down a little, so it is less automatic. Be aware of what is making you want to move, be aware of your decision to move, and be fully aware of each movement. Then notice the result: How do you feel after moving in that way? For example, if you are sitting in a position and suddenly become aware that your back is hurting, you might respond something like this (putting a nonverbal experience into words): "Hmm, pain in my back. Let me just take a minute to breathe in and out and be aware of this pain. Do I need to shift position or stretch? I think that would be good. Let me do this slowly and with full awareness, breathing in and out. There, that's better."

If you do this mindfully, you learn when moving is helpful and when it is not. For example, if you use a timer for your meditation period and are tempted to peek at it from time to time, try to do this mindfully. Notice for yourself what effect this has and whether it is helpful or not. Does peeking at the time make you more or less anxious, or more or less rooted in the present moment? Or are there times when it is helpful and times when it is not? In this way, you are not just imposing an arbitrary rule on yourself, but you are learning by experience what helps. Since meditation is about awareness and experience, no one's experience is more important in your practice than your own.

I'm Sitting: Now What?

Some meditation traditions answer this question very simply: What you must do when you are sitting, is *just sit!*

In practice, however, most find it helpful to give the mind a focal point. The mind will be doing something, after all, and if we don't give it some job to do, chances are good it will run off in its familiar patterns of worry, fear, planning, scheming, reviewing the past, and so on. And if that happens, your meditation will probably not be enjoyable or healing.

The degree to which your mind is busy is a matter of individual personality. Some people have minds like a cat curled up by the fire. They settle comfortably, sensually, easily, into whatever circumstances they find themselves in. Many more people have minds like a sheepdog. Sheepdogs are most comfortable when they have a job to do. They become uneasy without a task. The more you are like comfortable tabby, the more you can "just sit." The more you are like the sheepdog—the more you need something to do—the more you need a focal point for your meditation.

There are many focal points that you can choose. You can meditate on a flower, on Buddha, or on Christ. You can meditate on a mantra— a kind of prayer or chant that you say to yourself, such as *om mane padme hum* or the famous Hare Krishna mantra *(hare Krishna, hare Krishna, Krishna Krishna, hare hare, hare Rama, hare Rama, Rama Rama, hare hare)*. Mantras are usually chosen because of their harmonious, healing sounds, and not so much because of their meaning. So from this perspective, it does not matter whether the mantra is in Sanskrit, Japanese, or English. Sometimes the simplest are the best, such as "om" or "ah," drawing the sound out long and resonantly. However, if you want to use English and employ your own spiritual background, that is also a wonderful practice. In the Judeo-Christian tradition, you can choose a line from the Psalms ("The Lord is my shepherd") or the Jesus prayer ("Lord Jesus Christ have mercy on me"). The Christian mystic Julian of Norwich's triple refrain, ". . . all will be well, and all will be well, and every kind of thing will be well," is a wonderfully positive focal point for meditation. Jews may choose the Shema, a meditation on unity and the oneness of God: "Shema Yisrael, Adonai Elohenu, Adonai echad" ("Hear O Israel, the Lord is our God, the Lord is One"). These are all great mantras.

The hands-down winner of all time in Eastern meditation traditions for a meditation focus is the breath. There are so many wonderful reasons for this. Breathing is the fundamental act of life. Focus on the breath therefore puts you directly in touch with the miracle of being alive. The breath is closely connected with our feeling states. When we are anxious or worried, we catch our breath and breathe shallowly. This creates a vicious cycle. Feeling anxious, we start to breathe in an anxious way. This causes us to feel even more anxious, which causes us to breathe even less freely and easily, and so on. Fortunately, since the breath is at the meeting point between voluntary and involuntary action, it functions both ways. Anxiety makes us breathe anxiously, but when we calm the breath, breathing in a normal, relaxed way, we also feel more calm.

There are many other discoveries about the breath that you can make as you work with it, but it is best to leave that for your own developing insight. You will see, if you use this means of practice, that the breath is a very good thing to work with. Conscious, aware breathing is very healing and calming. More than that, in the Buddhist sutra (discourse) on the full awareness of breathing (*Anapanasati sutra*), the Buddha shows how awareness of the breath is a very deep practice, one that can in fact take you all the way to enlightenment.

Let go of fixed ideas about how you should practice, and find the ways that work for you. Your practice may change from week to week or month to month. The important thing is to not be trying to live up to any idea or image of how a "spiritual" person should do this. Adopt a joyful, pragmatic attitude. If you feel light and happy when you practice, you are doing it right.

So Here's What to Do

Once you are sitting, take a moment to just let your body relax. Let your mind ease its grasp a bit on whatever you've been thinking about. If you like, spend a few moments visualizing divine light all around you—a light that is completely loving, that seeks your total happiness and fulfillment, that wants to give you all that you seek.

Then gently turn your attention to your breathing. Feel each breath all the way in, and feel it all the way out. This is called "following the breath." Can you see that breathing is enjoyable? One meditation student complained that following the breath was boring. So one day her teacher grabbed her, covering her mouth and nose so she couldn't breathe for a short time, then asked her if the next breath she took was boring or not! The student realized how wonderful it is to breathe.

THE EXPERIENCE (TOM)

Okay, I'm sitting. So what am I supposed to do? Oh yes, become aware of my breathing. In, out. In, out. But actually, I notice I'm not feeling my breath; I'm *thinking* about feeling my breath. How can I come back to the experience, the sensation of the in-breath, of the out-breath? There, there it is. Ahh! It is good to be sitting, just breathing. It is a pleasure. I notice there is a profound difference between thinking about the breath, and being in deep contact with the breath. And there are shades between these extremes, with more or less thinking about and more or less actual experiencing. I see, too, that each breath is different. This time, my body seems to need a deep breath. Now it needs a shallower one. The pause between breaths can be short or long. I don't interfere with any of this, but just let my body determine how it wants to breathe. I can feel my breathing gradually calm down, and with it, my body and my mind.~

Common Problems in Getting Started

Become Aware of Your Active Mind

Once you have started to meditate, you may immediately become overwhelmed at the busyness of your mind. You may feel that you simply cannot do this, that you have no aptitude for it whatsoever.

But don't give in to this feeling. If you have reached this point, congratulations on how well you are practicing! All that has happened is that you have become more aware of the activity of the mind. And that's great. Becoming aware is very important. In fact, becoming aware is the main thing. This mental overdrive is going on all the time. Only now, you are aware of it. That's all. This may feel a little humiliating if you have a vision of yourself as already a calm and spiritual person. But inner peace is not about having a constant, unchanging mood of peace and happiness. As you have already seen, thoughts and moods and feelings are constantly changing. *True peace is not about an unchanging mood but about the capacity to accept and experience whatever mood you find yourself in. The real peace is that something deeper from which you observe all of this.*

When I work with clients who are addicted, one of the things we inevitably discuss at some point is how to handle urges. Clients often believe that if they are experiencing no urges, they are doing well, and if they are having urges, they are doing poorly. They can be so convinced of this that they even try to deny that urges are occurring, believing that this means they are a failure or at least on the way to failure. Sometimes they are shocked when I tell them that whether they are having urges or not is unimportant. People cannot control whether or not an urge occurs; urges are involuntary. To make yourself responsible for what you cannot control is the essence of self-defeating neuroticism.

What you do have control over is how you *respond* to the urge. And this is what really counts. Of course, the client may feel a lot more comfortable when urges are not occurring, but what really counts in being successful in changing an addiction is what you do about it when they occur. That is something that is within your control.

Similarly, you cannot control whether your mind will be restless or restful. You are no more a success as a meditator if your mind is calm than if it is restless or agitated. What matters is what you do. If you give up, then, of course, you are not being successful. But if you continue despite the fact that the mind is restless, letting it be and not struggling, willing to experience whatever is there, that is already success. By doing this, you are honoring your deep intention to hold calmly to the center even in the midst of the storm. What is more, sessions in which you gently persist despite mental agitation can be far more important and healing than sessions that are easy and peaceful.

So if your mind is agitated or restless, just come back to your intention to persist and accept. You're doing just fine.

And if your mind is peaceful, don't worry: It will pass.

Practice Mere Recognition

Though you are not ultimately in control, there are ways to work with a restless mind. The first thing to do, is come back to your breath, and just watch these changing thoughts and feelings. This is called mere recognition. It is as if you are walking down the street, and you see a number of people that you know. "There's Harry. There's Sally. There's Mitch." You nod and greet each one, smile, perhaps say hello. Then you move on. Or in the case of your feelings, it's: "Hello, sad feeling. Hello, happy feeling. Hello, my anger. Hello, planning and thinking," and so on.

The most important thing is not to get into a struggle with all of this. Though not cold or analytical, you are a little like a scientist of your own psyche, just watching, observing. If you get angry because Sally comes along and you don't want to deal with her, then you are in a fight—a fight with yourself. At this point you get all entangled. That is why it is important that you take the attitude of welcoming all that you are into the sacred space of meditation—so you don't get into a fight with yourself. However, even if you do get into a fight with yourself, just breathe in and out, and watch. "Now I am struggling with myself. I want to feel peaceful, but instead, I am feeling anxious. And I am struggling to try not to feel anxious."

Many people, many moods, and many thoughts pass you on the sidewalk. You don't have to get stuck in a full conversation with each one. Often it is enough just to smile and say hello. However, just as some people insist on getting your attention, so do some thoughts. When that happens, it may be something you need to pay attention to. Remember, *anything* can be the object of your meditation. If you are trying to focus on your breath, but you keep thinking about your relationship, then meditate on your relationship. Do not struggle. Just breathe in and out in such a way as to gently calm the feelings, and observe all that comes up about it. Do not try to fix anything, just shine the light of simple awareness on your relationship. You thought you needed to meditate on your breathing, but that day, you really needed to meditate on your relationship. Meditation on your relationship or any other concern is no less holy than meditation on the Buddha or Krishna or other overtly religious topics. If you are mindful, the Buddha is there in your mindfulness.

The breath gives you the power to hold the center. The breath is an anchor. All thoughts and feelings stream by in the river. Sometimes this current is very strong. Sometimes these thoughts and emotions are so strong, they threaten to sweep us away. With the breath as anchor, however, we are not swept away. We are able to stay in place as we watch these strong currents flow past. This allows us to be less agitated. If we overidentify with these strong currents, they can destroy us. If we put our inner experience into words, it might sound like this: "I feel so sad! This is terrible! I can't stand it! This has to stop!" When our inner dialogue gets like that, we are in danger. We may do something that makes things even worse for us and not better.

But the inner dialogue of someone who is using conscious breathing is different. There may be the same emotions, but without the agitation, helplessness, and despair. The inner experience of such a person may be more like this: "There is sadness happening in me. I am sitting here, breathing in and out, and feeling the sadness. There is a strong feeling, as I continue to breathe, of wanting this sadness to go away. But I know I can be with this sadness, and breathe with it. I know it will not stay forever."

Cope with Sleepiness

If you feel sleepy, there are three things you can try. If you want to continue meditating without falling asleep, you can take several deep, slow breaths, or get up and practice walking meditation for a few minutes. You can also try a third solution: Go to sleep.

In some ways, the best answer is to go to sleep, if circumstances permit. This is most in keeping with the premise of honoring all that you are into the sacred space of meditation. It is also in keeping with the spirit of Zen: When I'm hungry, I eat; when I'm tired, I sleep.

As a rule of thumb, if your mind is overactive, focus on the abdomen as you breathe in and out. If the mind is dull or sleepy, focus on the point where the breath enters the nostrils.

Be Patient with Anxiety

As we discussed in chapter 1, our fragmentation and disconnection have made ours a culture of anxiety. So for some people, the moment they slow down and tune into themselves, the first thing they become aware of is their anxiety and worry.

Congratulations! This is a sign of initial success, because what has happened is that you have slowed down enough to begin to hear more clearly what is happening with you. What you need at this point is some way to touch this anxiety, to be present with it, without being swept away by it. You do not try to fix the anxiety. You do not try to make it go away. In fact, you adopt a willingness to be present with it, to let it hang around as long as it needs to. This takes a little courage and persistence, but it is the best way. It is cow-taming meditation, allowing it to be just what it is and to run freely in the large pasture of big mind. When you become perfectly willing to experience the anxiety just as it is, without trying to change it, it has a way of calming down, all by itself.

Sound difficult? It does take persistence and patience. But you really can do it. What makes it difficult is that we have been taught that we are slaves to our emotions. It is as though we somehow think we must always express and act out our emotions, or we are in denial. The truth is somewhere in between. We cannot "control" our emotions, but we can learn to work with them. Between acting them out in destructive fashion and denial lie a wide range of alternatives.

When difficult emotions like anxiety come up in meditation, imagine your mind becoming as open and spacious as the sky. The sky can embrace many clouds. It is vast and untroubled, whether many clouds appear or none at all.

Practice Returning

Over time, your meditation will deepen. So will your ability to concentrate on the breath or whatever focus you are working on. However, if you become too goal oriented—if you are continually tracking and evaluating your progress—you are interfering with that which you are seeking. The best results come from not seeking results.

When we use language to describe meditation, inevitably some misunderstandings are created. To talk about getting better at or improving your meditation or achieving enlightenment sets one up for struggle. If we are improving or achieving, then we are not being. We are struggling. And almost inevitably, one can start to worry about whether one is meditating correctly.

The antidote for this is to realize that your meditation practice is not about getting better or achieving. It is not about concentrating. It is really a matter of returning. Our thoughts go galloping away in the wide pasture of our Buddha mind. We realize this, notice the process, and bring the mind back to the breath. Again, and again, and again. "Return," says the ancient Chinese sage Lao-tzu, "is the movement of the *Tao*" (the way of harmony).

Meditation strength is the strength of water, not stone or steel. It is the strength of returning again and again, of gradually wearing down the harder elements. From time to time, you may notice that the hardness in you has been softened. You are like a shard of glass found on the beach, worn smooth by the waves.

Until we fully realize our Buddha nature, the task is really about practicing this gentle return. It does not matter whether your mind wanders a thousand times during a half hour of meditation, or just one time. It doesn't matter whether you wandered away for a second or for many minutes. *What matters is returning*.

Encourage Yourself

Cognitive psychology teaches the importance of giving ourselves realistic encouragement. Use positive messages to encourage persistence in meditation. Notice that these examples are realistic; it is not a matter of telling yourself, "Everything is always wonderful."

- I can worry about this now, but I can also worry about this later if I choose to.
- All I have to do right now is be with my breath.
- My mind wandered, but I found my way back to my breath.
- All of these thoughts and feelings are okay just as they are.
- I know that my mind will race for as long as it needs to, and calm down when it is ready.
- The best meditation sessions are not always the easy ones.
- It does not matter how many times I return (to my breath). It only matters that I do so.
- I am giving myself a wonderful gift by meditating.
- I accept all of my thoughts and feelings just as they are.
- Breathing in and out, help is already here.
- Even one minute of mindfulness is a miracle.

A Word about Words

Words are powerful. In the Bible, God created heaven and earth and everything in it by speaking. Adam was allowed to name all the animals, thus giving him power over them. Jesus is called "the Word of God." Magicians and sorcerers have always known the power of words as incantations and magic formulas.

Words can be powerful for good or for evil. Politicians know the importance of putting the proper spin on things. As a profound example on the dark side, the Nazis knew the power of words when they referred to the murder of millions as "the final solution of the Jewish question."

Cognitive psychologists also know the power of words. In research that examines how memories are interconnected in light of different moods, researchers in this field have developed word lists that induce a mild, transient depression or euphoria. Just having someone read a positive or negative list of words temporarily changes his mood. The thought patterns of depressed people involve a lot more of the words linked with depressed mood than the thought patterns of nondepressed people.

It is no surprise, then, that spiritual teachers past and present have taught helpful ways of using words.

Use Gathas

Gathas are short poems that you can use to help achieve more focus in meditation. Gathas are a lot like mantras, but instead of being words chosen for their sound properties to evoke certain moods and energies, gathas are used more to focus attention. Since it is the nature of the mind to think about something, you can respect the nature of the mind by giving it something to do. One of the best gathas was taught by the Buddha:

Breathing *in*, I know I am breathing in.
Breathing *out*, I know I am breathing out.

After the first time or two, you just use "in" on the in-breath and "out" on the out-breath. It is also helpful to return to the full form and use all of the words once or twice when your contact with the breath gets a little fuzzy. Another gatha from Thich Nhat Hanh is one we come back to again and again. It is deceptively simple, but summarizes a lot of Buddhist teaching, and has many layers of depth to it.

Breathing in, I *calm* my body.
Breathing out, I *smile*.
Dwelling in the *present moment*,
I know this is a *wonderful moment*.

Again, after the first time or two, just use the words in italics, and come back to the full version when your concentration wanes. This is not about saying the words mechanically, but about using the words to keep focusing your attention. After you have tried working with some of these gathas for a while, try making your own. Often our own gathas are ultimately the most useful.

Dwell with a Word or a Phrase

A Christian tradition of contemplative prayer is to simply dwell with a word or a phrase. Unlike gathas, the words are not coordinated with the breath. In the traditional usage, these were often words or phrases drawn from Scripture, such as from the Psalms. For example, "The Lord is my light and my salvation." Alternatively, you can use any words that appeal to you, such as "peace" or "light"—simply repeating the word or phrase whenever you wish to or when it begins to fade or lose substance.

If you can draw from your own heritage, that is wonderful. Don't be caught by concept and paradox and terminology. Don't be confused, for example, by the fact that what Eastern religion calls meditation, Western religion calls contemplation, and vice versa. Look to the practice.

Breath, Body, Thoughts, and Feelings

The *Anapanasati sutra* outlines a natural progression to follow in meditation. It starts with the breath, then moves to awareness of the body, then to thoughts and feelings, and so on. You may enjoy following this progression. Begin your meditation with a focus on the breath. Become one with your breathing.

After you have used the breath to become centered, then focus on the body. You can begin by visualizing your breath being transported to every cell of your body. Notice the sensations in your body. If you wish, conduct a body scan, focusing on each part of the body for a few breaths, giving thanks for that body part. Create a short gatha to help with this, such as

Breathing in, I am aware of my left hand (or eyes, ears, heart, etc.).
Breathing out, I am thankful for my left hand.

Be sure to *sense* your body, rather than just *think* about it. Once feelings of calm begin to emerge, you may wish to use the *calming/smiling* gatha on page 67. Good body awareness is very important. How can you ever hope to calm your thoughts and feelings, if your body is not calm, and if you are not grounded as a physical being?

It is perfectly fine to let just this breathing/body awareness be the subject of a meditation period. It can even be helpful to stay with this theme for a period of days or weeks. However, you can also move on, if you wish. You can let yourself become aware of your thoughts and feelings. The idea is to experience your thoughts and feelings without getting caught up in them. If you find yourself worrying about paying the rent, the attitude is: *I am sitting here, breathing in and out, and worrying about the rent.* In this way, you are awake and aware of your worry. You are recognizing it without trying to push it away or make it change. You are learning that you are larger than your worries, plans, thoughts, and emotions.

When you get caught up in your thoughts and emotions, you may wish to refocus on your breathing for a moment, and come back to the attitude above: *Here I am, breathing in and out, and feeling sadness/embarrassment/ happiness/pride, etc.* If you tend to berate yourself for losing concentration, see if you can take a lighthearted attitude as you return to the object of your meditation. Laugh at the playfulness of the mind. Employ a coping thought, such as "Good going! I found my way back to my breath!" Be encouraging and positive with yourself, as you would with a small child taking her first steps.

Practice the Four Immeasurable Minds (Brahma-viharas)

The brahma-viharas, or four immeasurable minds, are another helpful way to practice. The word *brahma-vihara* is composed of the word *vihara*, meaning abode, and *Brahma*, a Hindu term for God. Thus the brahma-viharas are the abodes of God or divine dwelling places. The four brahma-viharas are *love, compassion, joy, and equanimity*. The Buddha promised that those who practice these "will feel secure, strong, and joyful, without afflictions of body or mind."

Love, in the sense intended here, sometimes translated as lovingkindness, means the intention to offer joy and happiness to other beings. Compassion means the intention to offer skillful help to relieve suffering. The *brahma-vihara* of joy is filled with peace and contentment. Some traditions emphasize joy in the good fortune of others rather than of oneself, but in the light of interbeing, it does not matter whether joy is for ourselves or for another. Equanimity is the capacity to see things clearly and without attachment or reactivity. It is a kind of peace that comes from not insisting that things always go as we would prefer them to. It is letting go and letting be.

To meditate on *love*, use this gatha: "Breathing in, I radiate love to all beings. Breathing out, I smile to all beings." After saying it to yourself this way once or twice, then just use the words *loving, smiling*. As you do so, stay in touch with your breathing. Imagine yourself as radiating light outward toward all beings, with an intention to offer them joy and healing. To make this concrete, it helps sometimes to think of specific people. These can be people you feel close to and love, or, as a more advanced practice, people with whom you have difficulty. You yourself can also be the object of this intention. For in love, there is no discrimination between self and others. So offer yourself the same loving intention. Then do the same with *compassion*—remembering that compassion means the intention to relieve suffering.

To work with *joy*, use the following gatha from Thich Nhat Hanh: "Breathing in, I feel joyful. Breathing out, I smile to my joy." After the first time, just say "Joyful, smiling." Joy is always there. No matter what is happening in your life, it is possible for you to contact the joy that is within you and nourish it. There are always joyful elements available.

You can work with *equanimity* in the following way: "Breathing in, I feel *peaceful*. Breathing out, I feel *centered*." Cultivate an open, nonreactive attitude.

Alternatively, dwell with each of these words quietly, as in the contemplative prayer tradition described earlier in this chapter ("Dwell with a Word or a Phrase").

If you have trouble touching the reality of the brahma-viharas and experiencing them vividly, there are two things to do: work more imaginatively, and examine the resistance. If you have trouble feeling joy, for example, focus on the good things in your life right now. For example, "Breathing in, I am aware I have a healthy body. Breathing out, I smile to my body." Or, "Breathing in, I am grateful for the love of my partner. Breathing out, I smile to this love." Or, "Breathing in, I am glad I have good food to eat. Breathing out, I smile to my food." In this way, some quiet feelings of joy may begin to emerge. If you have trouble experiencing compassion or lovingkindness, summon whatever memories you can of when you were the recipient of these—even in small ways. Or to vivify your experience of equanimity, remember a time when you felt something like that—perhaps looking at the ocean, or camping in the mountains, or noticing a beautiful tree in the park that gave you a feeling of calm.

When you encounter resistance to the cultivation of these attitudes, simply note the nature of it, breathe with the resistance, and then let it go. Remember that resistance is natural. Its surfacing shows that your practice is beginning to have an effect and to loosen some of your conditioned patterns. Neither deny it nor struggle against it.

This practice is like cultivating a garden. If you have a vegetable or flower garden, you want to encourage your flowers and vegetables to grow. You want them to be well fed and watered, and not strangled by weeds. So you weed, fertilize, and water to help your flowers and vegetables thrive. Meditating with the brahma-viharas is watering and fertilizing the love, joy, and peace that is in you. For while there will always be weeds—as any gardener knows—that is not so bad as long as you have taken good care of your plants so that they can survive. Cultivating love, compassion, joy, and equanimity will help you survive many difficulties. When you bring this into your daily life, the power of this practice is very great.

Go from Sound to Silence

Sometimes you might enjoy moving from sound to silence within a period of meditation. Begin with full phrases and sentences, such as in the gathas and mantras noted above. For example, "All shall be well, and all shall be well, and all manner of thing shall be well," or, "The Lord is my light." Then as you begin to calm down, just dwell on a word, such as *well* or *light*. At first, as you move into the single-word phase of your meditation, you can time it with the breath by saying the word to yourself on the out-breath. Then, as you go a little deeper, just let the single word sit on the edge of your mind without connecting it to the breath, saying it to yourself whenever your focus gets fuzzy. Then finally, if you reach a deep enough level, let go of words completely, and open yourself to silence.

Go from Motion to Stillness

A Jewish style of prayer called *davening* involves rocking slightly back and forth as you pray. This can be very calming and soothing, like being rocked by your mother when you were an infant. If you are agitated, try rocking back and forth for a while, and then gradually bring the rocking to a halt. The movement from motion to stillness can help you feel still inside.

Inner Light Meditation

In the Quaker tradition, one meditates on the inner light. Similarly, some Buddhist traditions talk about a "clear light." You can picture this as a white radiance at the center of your chest. This area is known as the heart chakra—a powerful center of spiritual energy.

Inner light meditation can seem quite different at first from mindfulness meditation that focuses on direct experiences, such as the breath or a flower. But it will appeal to people who resonate with religious symbols and imagery. If this appeals to you, you might enjoy this form of meditation. Any practice that calms the mind can prepare you to be more awake and enlightened.

Take a Break

It is okay to take very short breaks when you sit, especially if you are working on extending your meditation period. Simply allow your mind to blank out for a moment or two. You might stretch your legs out a bit, or just allow yourself to look out the window and let your mind go into neutral for a few moments. Try to do this mindfully and intentionally, rather than just being pulled out of your meditation. That is, decide to take a short break instead of being pulled out of your practice by thoughts or distractions. Then decide to return. Notice where your mind goes as you gently come back to your breathing or other focus.

Practice Walking Meditation

Many Zen teachers consider this an essential meditation practice. Learning to meditate while walking is also a good bridge to sitting meditation for active people. In most Zen centers, walking meditation is interspersed between periods of sitting. This is in part to stretch the legs, wake up, and promote circulation. But it is more than that. Walking meditation connects sitting meditation with the rest of your life.

The basic instruction for walking meditation is to become deeply aware of the act of walking. If you are in a private setting, you can walk very slowly. As you take the first step, breathe in and say the word *in* to yourself. Then you take another step, saying the word *out* to yourself. The words are not there to be mechanical, but to encourage you to focus on your breath and on the sensations of walking. The words give your active mind something to do with itself besides run in the well-worn channels of your worries, fears, and regrets. Let them gently pull you into the present. Feel your feet as they touch the ground. Get in touch with how wonderful it is to simply move on the earth in this way, making peaceful steps.

In some forms of walking meditation, you focus on the process of walking by saying the word *lift* to yourself as you lift your foot, *move* as you swing it forward, and then *place* as you set it down. You might like to experiment with this, as long as it doesn't become mechanical and interfere with a sense of enjoyment of walking.

If you are walking in public view, you probably want to walk at a more normal pace. In this case, you might take three steps on an in-breath, and three on an out-breath, telling yourself, "In, in, in, out, out, out." Vary the relationship between the number of strides per breath in accord with your body's needs. You may even have a different number of steps for the out-breath than for the in-breath.

Use other words besides *in* and *out*. Thich Nhat Hanh recommends *arrived/home* and *here/now*. You can also create mantras that are meaningful to you—anything that has the effect of helping you stay in the present. "Walking in the Buddha land" or "Walking in the kingdom of heaven" are examples. Make up words spontaneously that help keep you focused. If you are in a more devotional mood, imagine that Jesus or Buddha is walking beside you and taking your hand, helping you be present in the here and now. Then imagine that the person merges into you and you continue as one.

Take Refuge

Buddhists take refuge daily in the three jewels of Buddha, the dharma, and the sangha. There are powerful lessons in this for non-Buddhists as well.

To take refuge in the Buddha is to take refuge in the wise person within yourself. For a Christian, this might be to take refuge in the mystical Christ, the Christ within; for the Hindu, to take refuge in Krishna or other enlightened person. But you do not need to be religious to understand that what you are doing is affirming the wisdom that is already within you and that it is possible for you to come into a more intimate relationship with that wisdom.

Dharma, in this context, means teaching. Again, the important thing to realize is that in taking refuge in some teaching, you are ultimately taking refuge in the teaching that is within you. When you are in touch with this inner teaching, then every experience that you have teaches.

The *sangha* is the community. It can be very helpful to have some kind of community of practice to provide support and encouragement. However, this is not always possible in a literal sense. You may be better off on your own than part of a practice group that is unhealthy or just not right for you—especially early in your practice. Even then, you do not have to be without a sangha. Your sangha might be, in part, a small set of books that you read and reread in the morning. Your sangha might be the bird outside your window as you meditate. It might be one friend or your partner or spouse if he or she meditates with you.

Walk the Path of Devotion

In Hinduism, there is a way of practice called *bhakti yoga*. This is the way of devotion to a realized person or enlightened being. While yoga practices might prescribe meditation on "the lotus of the heart" or on the realization that "atman is Brahman" (God immanent is God transcendent, or the God within is the God without), many people find it difficult to simply sit and meditate on something so abstract. It is much easier to devote yourself to some enlightened person— to imagine what it would be like to be with such a person or to even be that person.

Most of us need human examples to follow, so this practice is a natural one for many people. Perhaps that is why it is found in many religious traditions all around the world. The oldest teachings of Buddhism do not involve any form of bhakti, but emphasize one's own direct experience (such as the breath). But later Buddhism also developed this kind of practice. One might focus on some sage or bodhisattva (one who is dedicated to saving others) or the pure land where Buddha dwells. Christianity can be conceived of as a form of bhakti yoga centered on Christ.

If this approach speaks to you, or if it is a part of your spiritual heritage that you wish to preserve, it may help your meditation greatly to incorporate such elements. Herbert Benson found that the positive effects of meditation are more profound when people incorporate their own religious faith into it. So perhaps you will want to find a way to do this.

Start an Inspirational Bookshelf

A lot of books dedicated to help you live more spiritually will insist on the absolute necessity of finding a teacher. Whenever I read a book that says this, I think, "Then why do I need this book?" If the teacher will tell you what you need to know, you may only get confused with different styles if you read books, too.

It is quite possible to make progress on your own. Good teachers are not always available or accessible. However, guidance is important.

One thing that you can do is start a special collection of books that you find particularly helpful and inspiring. Some of the books you keep on your inspirational shelf may come from among those listed in the back of this one. Some may be scriptures. And perhaps this book will be there. You can keep coming back to these books many, many times, because you are not reading for new information so much as for guidance and inspiration. Sometimes the twenty-fifth time you read a given passage, it speaks to your exact situation more than it ever did before.

Guidance is vital. But be open to the fact that the universe can provide it in many different ways.

How Do I Know Which Approach to Follow?

We have provided you with a lot of alternative methods here. It is probably not wise to try to use them all. So you have to choose. How do you know which ones you should try? Ultimately, no one can tell you the answer to this question. This is fortunate, because you must trust your own instincts about which practices attract you, and which do not. Consider these questions. How do you decide:

- which pair of shoes to buy?
- which book you will buy in the bookstore?
- which route you will take to work?
- which person to marry?
- which career to follow?

Ultimately, you know that nobody else can give you the answers. Others may have useful things to say about these decisions, but anything others have to say is provisional. You know that you have to make up your own mind about what feels right, try that out, and see how it goes. In China and Japan, they advise you to ask your belly concerning major decisions, meaning, look deeper than just your abstract reasoning.

However, if you feel confused by too many options, here is a place to start. Try it for a while and then modify it according to your own experience.

∾ PRACTICE ∾

Basic Meditation

1. Find a comfortable, quiet place.
2. Sit in a manner that allows you to be relaxed but also alert. Sitting up straight avoids drowsiness and, according to many traditions, aligns centers of spiritual energy. Place attention on the body, letting it find its own natural straightness and stability.
3. Let yourself settle in and center down. Start with being aware of what is around you, using all sense modalities: what you see, hear, smell, touch, and taste, if applicable. Gradually tune inward by focusing on your breath, breathing gently in and out, experiencing each breath as a quiet and simple pleasure, becoming one with it, making no effort to change or alter your breathing in any way, but just experiencing it. A *slightly* greater amount of attention to the out-breath can be helpful.
4. Trust the process. Don't try to make anything special happen, or worry whether you are doing it right. Whatever happens is right for you now. Be present with whatever happens. Meditation is nothing special—just a time to *be*.
5. Ultimately, there are no distractions. If your mind wanders to things other than the breath, then just be aware of it. When you can, return to the breath. Tell yourself: "Thinking, thinking." Smile at your busy brain.
6. Continue for a comfortable period of time.

Enjoy Your Practice

All of us have probably known someone who "found religion" and became more difficult than ever to be around. Perhaps they pray or meditate for long periods, but it seems that instead of this opening them up and making them happy, they become all the more rigid and anxious. This is a sign that they are pushing too hard. Do not let this happen to you. Proceed down this path with joy. It is true that the first fifteen or twenty minutes are the hardest and that you often reach the best part of your meditation only after that. So there is good reason to lengthen your meditation time. But still, five minutes of meditation with the right attitude is more helpful than five hours with the wrong attitude.

The reason to meditate is to enjoy it. Forget about it being good for you. Forget about enlightenment. Smile. Enjoy this wonderful time. And as you learn to enjoy just sitting, you can learn to enjoy the other moments of your life—just driving, just talking on the phone, just doing paperwork, just preparing dinner, just cleaning up, just eating, and so on. You learn to enjoy meditation ultimately in order to enjoy your life. Bringing the meditative attitude into the rest of life is the subject of our next chapter.

Practice for Weeks Three and Four

Because establishing a regular practice of meditation is so important, we suggest you spend two weeks just doing that. This is in fact only a minimum period of time, but at least you can make a beginning.

1. During week three, practice sitting meditation for at least ten minutes once a day. Then during week four, add a second sitting of the same length—for example, sitting once in the morning and once in the evening. Remember to keep it enjoyable and not struggle.
2. Every day, reread a little of this chapter to help you keep the right attitude and spirit. In this way, you can keep us with you as you take your first steps in formal meditation practice. By the end of week four, you may have read the chapter two or three times.
3. There is always a way to enter and encourage the meditative state. Experiment during this period with the different methods in this chapter during your meditation periods:
    - Mantra meditation (p. 58)
    - Breath meditation (pp. 59, 60)
    - Remember, you are not trying to force peaceful feelings but to work with what is ("Peace Is the River," p. 49)
    - "Practice Mere Recognition" (p. 61)
    - "Encourage Yourself" with coping thoughts (p. 65)
    - "Use Gathas" (p. 66)
    - "Dwell with a Word or a Phrase" (p. 67)
    - Begin with breath, then body awareness, then awareness of thoughts and feelings (p. 67)

- "Practice the Four Immeasurable Minds" (p. 69)
- "Go from Sound to Silence" (p. 71)
- "Go from Motion to Stillness" (p. 71)
- Practice inner light meditation (p. 71)
- "Take a Break" (p. 72)
- "Take Refuge" (p. 73)
- "Walk the Path of Devotion" (p. 74)

You don't need to try all of these. Just experiment with those that have the most intuitive appeal.

4. In addition, try a little walking meditation (p. 72). Use it as a way to take a break from your work during the day whenever you need to.
5. Continue the moments of mindfulness practice you began in week two (p. 42).
6. Begin collecting books for your inspirational bookshelf (p. 74).

Week Five

BRING MEDITATION INTO YOUR LIFE

The activity of a contemplative must be born of his contemplation and must resemble it. Everything he does outside of contemplation ought to reflect the luminous tranquility of his interior life.

—Thomas Merton, *New Seeds of Contemplation* (1961)

The Dalai Lama said, "I believe that the very purpose of our life is to seek happiness. . . . Whether we believe in religion or not . . . we are all seeking something better in life. So, I think, the very motion of our life is toward happiness."

This is a simple but nonetheless profound truth. We are all seeking happiness, though many of the ways in which we are seeking it are dead ends or are even destructive. The reason to learn to live more mindfully ultimately has nothing to do with becoming outwardly pious. It has everything to do with becoming happy—with becoming liberated from suffering.

As you taste the peace of meditation, a yearning arises. It is a yearning to experience this peace in daily life, not just while sitting in meditation. It is wonderful to experience joy, peace, and restfulness during sitting, but the ultimate purpose of meditation is to experience peace and joy all day long.

Meditation and daily life are two aspects of one reality. As you experience more peace and joy in daily life, your meditation deepens. And as your meditation deepens, you experience more peace and joy in daily life. Once you learn how to sit for at least a few minutes in quietness and peace, it is only natural that you begin to look for ways to bring this into the daily round. The fourteenth-century German mystic Meister Eckhart wrote, "Take heed how you can have God as the object of your thoughts whether you are in church or in your cell. Preserve and carry with you that same disposition when you are in crowds and in uproar and in unlikeness." In other words, take that state of being from the meditation cushion to work with you. Take it with you when you drive the car. Take it into every aspect of your life.

Change the Channel

Sometimes when you meditate, you switch attention from one thing to another. You may focus on your breathing, on your body, on sounds around you, or on the mantra or gatha you are saying inwardly. Once you learn to do this, the next step is "channel-changing" meditation. This is the meditation of daily life.

Imagine you are a television set or a radio, with a tuner for switching channels from one program to another. In sitting meditation, you set your tuner on your breath. In walking meditation, you set it on the soles of your feet, feeling the peaceful contact with the earth with each step. When you then go about the rest of your day, you just continue to switch the tuner to what is happening here and now. There are unlimited numbers of daily life meditations to practice. After walking meditation, you switch your channel changer to "making-breakfast meditation." After that, you switch channels to "eating-breakfast meditation." Then you do something called "driving-to-work meditation." Then comes "work meditation," "coffee-break meditation," and so on. Each activity of daily life becomes the object of your meditation. You do each thing with awareness, breathing in and out, deeply present to each activity, not rushing into the future, not worrying about the past.

This principle is not hard to understand. But it may take a while to begin to practice it effectively. We are so used to living in a half-awake state, doing everything in a nonmindful way. Only a small portion of our attention is on what we are doing, while the rest is off worrying about the future or stuck in the past. We live most of the time in a cloud, in a dream. To overcome this tendency, we need practices that will help improve the clarity of our reception. When you are deeply present all day long, you are a Buddha! You are one who is awake.

The techniques used to become more mindful in daily life don't have to be done in a heavy, compulsive, or serious manner. In fact, they should be done in a spirit of play, like a child skipping rope or playing jacks. Meditation itself, so somber and serious-looking on the outside, is best approached in a spirit of lightness, ease, and happiness. The purpose of meditation and other mindfulness techniques is to enjoy your life, to notice the glint of sun reflected from even the humblest puddle of water, to appreciate the bird outside your window. When you pursue these practices in a spirit of self, you feel you are doing something oh-so-serious and important, another project of self-improvement. You can easily become frustrated as you worry that you are not making enough progress. When you pursue mindfulness practices in a no-self way, you know it is a kind of play, to be approached with joy.

It is unrealistic to expect that you can rush around all day, hating what you are doing, continuously infected with negative thoughts and feelings, and then expect to sit down to meditate and suddenly feel peaceful and happy. You can't do it. There is a close relationship between meditation and life. With these practices of mindfulness, you come to see that living deeply means to meditate all day long. By working with dreams, as we discuss in chapter 6, you even extend awareness into what happens while you are asleep. All of this is so that you don't miss it—so you don't miss your life. The most terrible fate of all is to discover, in the moment of death, that you have never been fully alive. So start today. Begin your "channel-changing meditation" right now, right where you are. Approach it playfully. Have some fun, and gradually become more fully alive and aware.

Saturate Your Life

Picture a dry sponge in a sink below a dripping faucet. If you leave that sponge in this position in the morning, by evening it will be quite full of water. There will be no part of the sponge that is not fully saturated.

With our meditation and other mindfulness exercises, we are slowly saturating our lives with moments of mindfulness, till all of life becomes transformed and mindful. This process is a little difficult to initiate. But then it gains momentum. At first, if you are trying to learn to clean your kitchen more mindfully, you have to make a determined effort to slow down and come into the present. The first ten times, perhaps even the first one hundred times, you have to make a special effort to clean the kitchen mindfully. And many, many times, you will slip into worrying about the future or regretting the past. But at some point, the momentum switches in your favor. You begin to generate so much mindfulness energy, that it pulls you back into the present moment whenever you drift away. Now when you clean the kitchen, you feel the pull of mindfulness, whereas before you felt the pull of forgetfulness. Living more mindfully in daily life is a matter of slowly saturating mindfulness into all aspects of living.

Slow It Down a Notch

Haste is a bedeviling force in modern life. It is very difficult to be mindful when you are rushing. Becoming mindful is an act of conscious resistance to all the forces of unconsciousness that continually assault us, infecting us repeatedly with ideas that we cannot be happy now because there is something that we lack. The thing we lack may be the right job, the right relationship, more money, a hot tub, a large-screen television, or just about anything. The first act of resistance to all of this is to *slow down*.

We say this is resistance, but that is a misnomer in one sense, for slowing down is not a struggle. Most of us do not need another issue to struggle with in our lives. We are simply suggesting that you begin cultivating an awareness of when you switch to autopilot and begin rushing about. And then when you become aware, just see if you are able to turn it down a notch.

We are so conditioned toward rushing into the future that you may wonder if slowing down is possible. "Slow down?" you may say. "I have to hurry up! I have thirty hours' worth of stuff to do every day as it is. My only hope is to work more quickly, more efficiently, so maybe at the end of the day I can find a few moments to relax."

This does not work for a number of reasons. First of all, *speed breeds speed*. Whenever you are rushing (even if you think you do so to prepare to relax later), you are learning to rush, not to relax. You become a person who rushes, and rushing merges into your identity. When you finally reach the time to relax, you are still rushing inside. When you finally sit down and take it easy, you are still occupied with all the things you have to do. Everything you see around you only reminds you of more tasks to do and errands to run.

Have you ever noticed that our labor- and time-saving devices don't always save us time? I appreciate my computer, and I would not want to trade it in. But this morning I had to check my e-mail before I could begin to write. Then my utilities program informed me that my antivirus definitions were out of date. Another message told me that my hard drive needed to be defragmented. By the time I'd done all these things, at least an hour and a half had gone by. The computer may save me time, but it is not an unmitigated gain.

A concentration on efficiency produces an energy in your body and mind that pulls you continually into the future. You can sense this sensation in your body—a tension in the neck and shoulders, a pulling, prickly feeling in the belly, a leg that jumps up and down when you sit. Speed only breeds speed. Often it is not even efficient.

We get into some ruthlessly vicious cycles. Rushing around all day, our brains and bodies do not shut down so easily at night. We don't sleep well. Because of this, we leave ourselves a minimum of time in the morning, trying to squeeze out a few more drops of precious sleep. But then we must hit the ground running to make up for the few extra moments of sleep. We calculate it so that, if we move without stopping, perhaps wolfing down a bite to eat and a few slurps of coffee over the kitchen sink, we can make it just about on time. And heaven help us if we then run into a traffic jam on the freeway! By seven thirty in the morning, many of us have been rushing for an hour or two, and we are already behind.

Of course if you take this suggestion to slow down seriously, some things will change. You might want to get up a little bit earlier, not only so you have time to eat mindfully or even to meditate, but also so that you are not fighting the battle of minutes and seconds once you are in the car. This becomes possible because as you move more in the direction of peace and ease, of taking time and not rushing, you rest more deeply. When you rest more deeply, it is easier to move through the day in a peaceful way. There is a deep paradox here: The more we rush, the less time we have. The more we slow down, the more time we have. Rushing constricts time; moving more slowly opens time up. I think you will see that this is true.

When you have the chance, it is helpful to slow down radically. This is wonderful to do. If occasionally you can learn to move at about half speed, your mind will begin to settle into the present more deeply. However, on a busy workday morning, it is wonderful if you can slow it down just about 10 percent—enough perhaps to give yourself a sense of some small luxury—enough to eat a real breakfast in peace or spend a little while in meditation. Throughout the day, turn down the speed just a notch or two. You may discover the paradox that while speed creates speed, a more relaxed pace creates time. You make fewer errors and have to do fewer things over when you are not rushing, and in this way actually save some of the time you fear losing. For example, if you are rushing on the highway, anxious to shave a few seconds or minutes off your travel time, you are far more likely to be ticketed or to have an accident. Then you are confronted with a major loss of time, to say the least. What's more, rushing elicits aggravation and resistance from other drivers, which slows you down anyway and leaves you frustrated. If you are trying to type too rapidly, you make many errors. Going just a little bit more slowly actually saves time by increasing accuracy.

However, don't justify slowing down because of efficiency. Slow down because it is a way to treat yourself lovingly. Slow down because otherwise you miss your life.

The pace of modern life is killing us. We are continually exposed to the toxins of stress, speed, pressure, and negative thoughts and emotions from both ourselves and others. These things are often more powerful and destructive than the environmental toxins we worry about. Slowing down is a wonderful act of subversion and resistance. It is an act of joy and a powerful practice. It is a practice to engage in with a sense of calm and ease. You can breathe in and out, and tell yourself from time to time, *"All I need to do in this moment, is breathe in and out, and do* this *(whatever you are doing)."* You will know when you are practicing correctly because you will feel joyful and peaceful, light and calm.

∼ PRACTICE ∼

Visualize Slowing Down

Sit comfortably on your meditation cushion or chair. Close your eyes and breathe in and out for a few minutes. After getting centered, bring a gentle awareness to one of the aspects of your life that has seemed a bit too harried. Perhaps it is your morning routine. Perhaps it is dinnertime. Or maybe it is the early part of your workday.

Pick the part of your life that you would most like to slow down a notch, and visualize what this might look like. Sense what it feels like.

Open your eyes and take out a notebook and pen. Write down both what you visualized and what it felt like. See if you can identify three minor changes in this aspect of your life that will bring you greater calmness. Write them down.

∼∼∼

Radical Medicine

If you have difficulty slowing down or letting go of some of the things you tell yourself must be done each day, ask yourself this bracing question: *"What will happen with these matters when I am no longer alive?"* Let this question sink in. The truth is, all of the things that we rush around doing, that we imagine are so essential, will have to fend for themselves when we are gone. It is doubtful that the world will fall apart because we are not there to do them.

Learn the Art of *Wu-Wei*

In Chinese Zen, there is a practice called *wu-wei*. Although it means "not doing," it does not mean doing nothing. It is about a certain kind of awareness, a certain attitude toward the doing. Often, when we do something, our mind is elsewhere. Brushing our teeth in the morning, we are thinking of the next thing we have to do, and the next thing, and maybe even the next thing after that. Brushing teeth in the spirit of *wu-wei* means coming back to the present. It means being aware of brushing our teeth, instead of rushing through it just to get it done. It means doing it for its own sake, not for the sake of accomplishing the task. It is letting the doing happen on its own, as though we are doing nothing at all. The more we do things in the spirit of *wu-wei*, the more empowered we become to enjoy every moment of our lives.

The ancient Chinese sage Chuang-tzu described the spirit of *wu-wei* in the now famous ox-cutting passage. The emperor Wen-hui was amazed at the skill and grace of his cook in carving an ox. The cook explained:

> "What I care about is the Way [Tao], which goes beyond skill. When I first began cutting up oxen, all I could see was the ox itself. After three years, I no longer saw the whole ox. And now—now I go at it by spirit and don't look with my eyes. Perception and understanding have come to a stop and spirit moves where it wants. I go along with the natural makeup, strike in the big hollows, guide the knife through the big openings, and follow things as they are. So I never touch the smallest ligament or tendon, much less a main joint.
>
> "A good cook changes his knife once a year—because he cuts. A mediocre cook changes his knife once a month—because he hacks. I've had this knife of mine nineteen years and I've cut up thousands of oxen with it, and yet the blade is as good as though it had just come from the grindstone. There are spaces between the joints, and the blade of the knife has really no thickness. If you insert what has no thickness into such spaces, then there's plenty of room—more than enough for the blade to play about in. That's why after nineteen years the blade of my knife is still as good as when it first came to the grindstone.
>
> "However, whenever I come to a complicated place, I size up the difficulties, tell myself to watch out and be careful, keep my eyes on what I'm doing, work very slowly, and move the knife with the greatest subtlety, until—flop! the whole thing comes apart like a clod of earth crumbling to the ground! I stand there holding the knife and look all around me, completely satisfied and reluctant to move on, and then I wipe off the knife and put it away."
>
> "Excellent!" said Lord Wen-hui. "I have heard the words of Cook Ting and learned how to care for life!"

The psychologist Mihaly Csikszentmihalyi describes an experience similar to that of Wen-hui's cook, which he calls "flow." Flow is an experience of optimal functioning, of being in the groove in such a way that what you are doing occupies your entire attention as you act with ease and skill. A musician might experience flow, for example, on a magical night when all the prior practice comes together into a moment of musical grace. Or you can experience flow playing tennis or Ping-Pong, no longer worried about winning or losing, just caught up in perfect concentration—arm, racket, and ball blending into one wave of activity. Csikszentmihalyi's research testifies that flow experiences have more to do with happiness than material wealth does.

Where do you experience flow? How can you arrange to do more of those kinds of things?

Begin and End the Day Intentionally

The beginning and ending of the day are times when we are sensitive to external influences. At the start of the day, the mind is fresh and impressionable. What we think about at the beginning of the day sets a tone for all that follows. You can take advantage of this fact by allowing yourself a little time for meditation and inspirational reading. This can make a distinct difference in how your day unfolds. If you do not start the day with mindfulness, with a clear intention to cultivate joy and peace, just how will this happen? Right at the beginning of the day, consider how you will cultivate joy. As the Psalmist wrote, "This is the day the Lord has made, let us rejoice and be glad in it."

Similarly, if we are to be peaceful and happy people, it is important that we get a good night's rest. At the end of the day, we are more affected by things because we are tired and our mental and emotional resistance is at low ebb. So what we put into our minds in the period just before sleep is very important if we want to have a restful night. Again, a little meditation, quiet reading, or listening to peaceful music will help set up a good night's rest more than a stimulating movie or a scary novel.

Harry's Dilemma

A client named Harry phoned one day. He'd been having difficulty sleeping and wanted to know what he could do about it. He had already tried some nonprescription sleep aids, and they did not help. I went through my standard list of things to help with sleep problems, making sure he was not napping during the day, consuming a lot of caffeine, watching television in bed, or lying in bed tossing and turning—all of which can contribute to sleep disorders. Harry had not been doing any of these things. Then I asked what he had been doing in the hours before bed. It turned out, there was a big push on at Harry's work. He was going all out from seven in the morning till eleven at night, when he would fall asleep exhausted, only to wake up two hours later, unable to get back to sleep for the rest of the night. I told him the obvious: He needed to slow down for at least a few hours before he went to bed. He seemed reluctant. I explained: As long as you are doing the same thing, you cannot expect a different result.

Find Bells of Mindfulness

One very useful technology of change comes from Buddhist monastic tradition. Periodically through the day, a monk strikes a large, resonant bell or gong. At the sound of the bell, people in the monastery stop what they are doing or saying, come back to their breathing, and return to themselves. On a retreat with Thich Nhat Hanh at a California university, we experienced an interesting variation on this. The university clock struck bells at fifteen-minute intervals throughout the day. We were instructed to take advantage of this by using the clock as a bell of mindfulness. We must have looked a sight to people on campus as we all suddenly came to a halt!

You do not, of course, need to make a spectacle of yourself to practice this way. Whenever you encounter a bell of mindfulness, you can unobtrusively return to yourself and your breath. You don't need to act like you are playing freeze-tag. Practice intelligently. Don't stop in the middle of crossing a busy street. If you are alone and it is safe to do so, you can close your eyes and give yourself a refreshing pause in your activity. Otherwise, you can practice this in such a way that you are the only one who knows what you are doing.

But what do you do if you are not on a retreat or in a monastery? Where do you find bells of mindfulness in everyday life? If you are alert and a little inventive, you can find bells of mindfulness everywhere. Thich Nhat Hanh recommends two in particular: red traffic lights and telephones. This is a fun way to practice, and it turns something that is otherwise stressful into a source of peace and calm. Whenever you come to a red light, see it as an opportunity to rest, to breathe in and out and practice a moment or two of meditation. Likewise, when the phone rings, let it ring for a little bit. Take the time to enjoy two or three slow breaths in and out, telling yourself, "in, out, in, out, calming, smiling." Then slowly, without hurry, move toward the phone to answer it. Never pick it up before the third ring. If the answering machine comes on before you get there, so be it. This is not rude to the people who call. In fact, they will appreciate that you are answering the phone mindfully, ready to be calm and clear and understanding.

THE EXPERIENCE (TOM)

I had been working with the practice of red traffic light meditation for some time. One day, I pulled up to a red light, and prepared with anticipation for a few moments of calm, conscious breathing. Before I could do so, however, the light changed to green. I actually felt disappointed. I smiled. I knew my practice had grown a little deeper.～

The simple practice of converting red lights and ringing phones to bells of mindfulness takes a little getting used to. For a while, you may feel some of the old resentment come up at the red light, and some of the old feelings of anxiety at the phone call. "Why do I always get the red lights?" "Who is calling me? Is something wrong?" But changing this does not take a long time. By deconditioning yourself from those old reactions of annoyance, you have already made a substantial change. It is a way of reminding yourself that this is your life, that it is happening right now, that your peace and happiness in the present moment matter more than whatever future goal you imagine yourself to be rushing toward. You actually come to enjoy red lights and ringing phones.

With a little creativity, you can go further. There are bells of mindfulness everywhere. When your alarm clock goes off in the morning, don't move right away. Take three breaths in and out. Remind yourself of your intention to make this a happy, peaceful, wonderful day. *This day is not disposable.* It will never come again. So start it off with deep breaths and clear intentions. Throughout the day, anything that slows you down (and might otherwise be experienced as an annoyance) can become an opportunity to practice mindful breathing: waiting for the tea kettle to boil or the microwave bell to ring; waiting for your computer to boot up; the sound of the buzzer for the laundry; the ring of your pager. Whenever you shift tasks during your daily work, consider that a bell of mindfulness, too. And instead of rushing to the next thing, breathe a few conscious breaths. The seconds this requires are well worth it. Get creative about this and find your own best way to integrate the bell of mindfulness practice into your own life and situation.

Ask: "Where Am I?" "What Am I Doing?"

These are wonderful questions to pose to yourself from time to time throughout the day, in order to bring yourself back from the fog of worry and regret into the clarity and peace of the present moment. You can ask yourself these questions whenever you encounter one of your bells of mindfulness, or whenever you feel you have lost contact with the present moment. The answer should be simple and clear: "I am sitting here, breathing in, and breathing out, placing a stamp on this envelope . . . writing this check . . . talking to this person . . . driving my car." Or better still, don't answer at all: Just let the question pull you into the present moment.

Allocate Attention to Centering

For many of the things we do during the day, it is possible to operate on two levels simultaneously. In fact, we do this all the time. While we are driving to work, for example, we worry about what will happen that day. Doing our exercise, another part of our mind is off worrying about what we will do when we finish.

Cognitive psychology provides models to help us understand what happens when we operate on two or more levels. Imagine that you have a certain quantity of attention. Whatever that amount is, we will call it 100 percent. You allocate some of this attention to what you are doing and some to what you are thinking about. If you are driving your car and also thinking about what you will get your partner for a birth-day gift, you may be using only 20 percent of your capacity for at-tention on driving, and the other 80 percent thinking about the gift. However, if you suddenly find yourself in difficult traffic, you shift these proportions dramatically. Suddenly 100 percent of your attention is on driving. We do this kind of sharing and shifting of cognitive ca-pacity all the time. You may find, for example, that you are happily driv-ing along with some favorite music playing loudly, until the traffic situ-ation becomes more demanding. Then you find yourself wanting to turn down the music; you need to allocate more attentional capacity to your driving.

We can use this quality of multiple attention in a helpful way. While you are driving, you can be interiorly working with a favorite mantra or gatha. Some of the best of these may be ones that you invent. How about, "Breathing in, I am here. Breathing out, I know I am driving my car." Or if you have a more religious bent, you may be reciting a mantra like, "Driving in the presence of God." In other words, you are using this capacity for divided attention in a new way—one more to your ad-vantage. Why should some of your attention always be on things that worry you? You might as well use some of that attentional capacity for thoughts that are nourishing and healing.

Of course, driving is an important task, and we do not want you to be off in the clouds somewhere as you drive. But generally, if you do it cor-rectly, you will be more calm and aware—not less. It is more dangerous to be distracted by all the worry and anxiety that normally has you in its grip than to be calming yourself in this way.

Some tasks do not permit attention on two levels. When you find yourself in heavy traffic, you may need to bring all of your attention to your driving. Likewise if you are reading, depending on the difficulty of the material, you may need to concentrate, bringing all of your atten-tional capacity to the text. If you are doing something potentially dan-gerous, like putting food into a hot oven, you need all of your attention on what you are doing. Sometimes the best way to practice is simply to be fully concentrated on the task at hand. But you may enjoy, when it is possible, having a background of mantras, gathas, or prayers going on with part of your mind as you are doing routine things.

Cultivate a Balanced Lifestyle

There is an important principle in psychology called a balanced lifestyle. This means that each day should have as many things in it that you are looking forward to as there are things that you have to do but would rather not do. In practice, this may be difficult on busy working days. But it is a good idea to make sure there are at least some enjoyable things even on the busiest of days.

Mindfulness takes this a step farther. Everything we have to do has enjoyable aspects. Tasks become easier once you find the fun in them. It is a matter of acknowledging the positive aspects of each experience.

The Experience (Tom)

Today is a day for painting the house. The enormity of the job weighs on me a bit as I get out my materials. Then I remember: This is house-painting meditation. I breathe in and out, and come back into the present moment. I realize that there are many wonderful things about painting the house. I enjoy being outside on this beautiful fall day. Getting out the paint, scrapers, rags, dropcloths, brushes, and ladders is a kind of calming ritual, like lighting a stick of incense before sitting meditation. It is fun to dip the brush in the paint and cover the side of the house with it. I smile, breathe in and out, and enjoy each moment. When I start worrying about other things, or thinking about how large the task is, I recognize these thoughts, smile to them, and gently come back to the paint, the brush, the side of the house, and my breathing in and out.⌒

Examine Your Environment

You do not have to be a feng shui specialist to know that the quality of the environment in which you spend your time is a major consideration. Take the time to notice your home and work environments as mindfully as you can. Just see, to begin with, what these places are like—as someone would who was seeing them for the first time. If you do this deeply enough, you will see ways in which your environment itself sows seeds of happiness or unhappiness in you.

Perhaps, to have a feeling of inner peace, you need less clutter around you. Or maybe, if you are too much of a perfectionist about order, you need a more relaxed environment, allowing a few things to be out of place, giving a feeling of creative chaos. Perhaps you need a little music in the background, especially music that helps you feel peaceful and happy. Maybe you need more color on your walls or a flower on the table. Maybe you need a peaceful statue of the Buddha or the scent of incense. Maybe photographs of people you love would help. Perhaps you want to get some paper and paint some mindfulness reminders to hang on the wall where you see them when you first open your eyes in the morning, such as "I vow to live deeply and peacefully every moment of this day," or "Peace is always available."

You may be able to do more things at home in this regard than at work. And even at home, unless you live alone, you must be careful not to make changes in the environment that create disharmony with others. See what you can come up with. While it may be important to visit beautiful places when you can, it is doubly important to make the everyday places beautiful.

∾ PRACTICE ∾

Change Your Environment

After you have begun to notice your environment more clearly, meditate on the question: "How can I make this place one that evokes peace and happiness?" Spend time with the question. The first answers that come to you may or may not be the best. Sometimes the best ones will only come as you let your unconscious mind live with this question for a period of days or weeks.

∾∾∾

Let Your Peace Return to You

Behavioral psychology does not study just behavior, but also the environment in which behavior occurs. It is of no use to study the behavior of organisms without looking at the environment they inhabit. It makes no sense, for example, to say that the mouse ran three feet forward, then went one foot to the right, and began chewing, unless you also know that the mouse was in a T-maze with a piece of cheese at the right end of the T.

When Buddhism talks about no self, it means that there is no separate self apart from our context. We cannot expect to be in a destructive environment with extremely difficult people without it affecting us. If you find yourself in a very destructive work environment, it may not be enough to bear it stoically. Perhaps you should get out. *Nothing is worth the sacrifice of your peace and joy.* You may think you are suffering for others' sake, but when you lose your peace and happiness, you not only add to your own suffering, but you increase the suffering of those around you. For if you let yourself become miserable, then others have to deal with a miserable, unhappy person.

In the New Testament, when Jesus sends out the twelve, he talks about how to deal with people who are unreceptive. He counsels them to stay in one house and adds, "As you enter the house, salute it. And if the house is worthy, let your peace come upon it; but if it is not worthy, let your peace return to you." If you are in an environment that overwhelms your peace and well-being, do everything you can to "let your peace return to you." And if it is bad enough, find a way to leave that place or situation.

Stay in Charge of the Task

When we wake up in the morning, our minds are filled already with things we have to remember to do that day—errands to run, work to do, household tasks, and so on. The ultimate intention behind these tasks is happiness. We do these things because we believe we will be happier if we do them than if we do not. Even if, upon waking, we feel reluctant to go to work, it is important to know that the reason we go to work is ultimately for the sake of our own happiness. We work for many reasons, but at least one of them is in order to have enough money to live a decent life so we can be happy. We run errands and do chores for the same fundamental reason.

Sometimes, however, the tasks themselves take over, far beyond what is good for our happiness. This can occur in two ways. For one, sometimes the things we do no longer serve our happiness, but we continue to do them because we have always done them—out of habit. If your job, for example, makes you miserable, it may no longer be contributing to the sum of your happiness. It may be time to pull yourself out of your rut and look for something else to do to earn a living. And how many parents are busy chaperoning how many kids to how many organized activities, without questioning whether these things contribute to anyone's happiness? A kind of automaticity takes over that keeps us doing whatever we do without even posing the question.

The second way in which the task takes over has to do with what happens once we start a task. We may start to paint the house because we believe we will be happier if we take care of our property in this way. Sometimes, however, once we start a task, a drivenness to get to the end of it takes over. At this point, we want to finish the job, no matter what. You are no longer within yourself, deciding to do something or not do something because it contributes to your happiness, but now the task has taken over. At this point, the task adds to your misery rather than to your happiness.

∼ PRACTICE ∼

Ask: Who's in Charge?

When you undertake any task, ask yourself repeatedly, "Who's in charge?" Every so often, stand back for a minute, return to your breath, and ask if continuing this job right now is the best thing to do. If you have a tendency to have to bring a task to completion before stopping, even past the point where it is good for you, you may wish to take a radical countermeasure. For a period of time, practice not finishing anything at the first pass, at least as much as is practically possible. You can do this by finishing the task the next day, or more simply, by just pausing for five minutes to breathe when your task is almost finished. This is like the stimulus control strategy dieters are taught. Since eating is often triggered by the presence of food (rather than the more appropriate stimulus of hunger), it is helpful to leave a little food on your plate (despite those parental voices that lectured to the contrary). In this way, you are breaking the automatic, conditioned response of eating in the presence of food. Similarly, you can overcome letting the task be in charge of you instead of you being in charge of it by not finishing.

Of course, if you are the kind of person who never finishes anything, but brings things to 90 percent completion and then never gets back to it, you might skip this particular practice.

~~~

THE EXPERIENCE (BEVERLY)

It's Monday morning and I was out of my office all day Friday at a seminar. I arrive early so I have time to get organized for my day. My e-mail loads for about ten minutes and announces that I have twenty-eight messages. Friday's mail is sitting on my desk and my cell phone rings even though it is only 7:30 A.M. Several minutes into my workday I already feel the calm from my morning meditation period leaving. And there is a nagging thought starting to emerge that I need to hurry up or nothing will get done.

And then I laugh at myself. Habit energy! I sit comfortably in my chair and take some centering breaths. And I remember there is no such thing as multitasking. Instead of hurrying, I need to slow down. One thing at a time.

I move my mail off my desk onto my table and go over a list of priorities for the day. I decide to spend about twenty minutes responding to my e-mail. I pick up one of my projects and allot two hours to developing a first draft of my report to the board of directors. I enjoy working on the report, and pretty soon, I am in the flow.~

Devote a Day to Mindfulness Practice

One thing that can help you generate more energy in your mindfulness practice is to have a day that you devote to mindfulness. Ideally, you are learning to live deeply and mindfully every day. However, it is all too easy to get pulled out of our intention to be mindful. Our lives are too demanding, too stimulating, and the quality of our mindfulness is as yet too weak.

A day of mindfulness is a day that you set aside to move more slowly and calmly. You resolve that, for this day especially, you will not do anything just to get it done, but will do everything for its own sake. In other words, you make the bed to make the bed, not to get it done, and not in order to get to the next thing. You might spend more time than usual lingering over your morning coffee, not missing one sip. Take a luxuriously warm shower, enjoying every moment. Spend more time in sitting meditation and walking meditation. Play peaceful music. Write to a friend. Pause frequently to practice a few moments of mindful breathing. Write in your journal. If you work in the garden or do chores around the house, do them as if you had all the time in the world. If you become driven by tasks, practice leaving some unfinished. You may wish to practice "noble silence," eliminating all or most all of your talking for the day or part of the day.

The day of mindfulness gives your mind and body the chance to slow down, to experience being rather than doing, to come into the present moment without always rushing into the future. It is similar to the Judeo-Christian tradition of the Sabbath—a time to rest and replenish.

If you take this practice seriously, you will understand why rabbis struggled so much with the question of what was allowable and not allowable on the Sabbath day. In the Jewish tradition of the Sabbath, one is supposed to refrain from work—meaning anything that disrupts the natural flow of life through the artifice of human effort. This sounds simple enough at first. But if you take it seriously, what, exactly, constitutes "work"? Is it work to cook your breakfast? To get dressed? And if you have employees (servants in those days), is it okay to let them work? What if they are not Jewish? Does that change the situation? Can Sabbath rules be lifted if there's an emergency?

Both the day of mindfulness and the Sabbath traditions aim at giving you a day of rest. But on a day of mindfulness, you can do work. Simple manual tasks are best. Let your intention be to do each task with ease and grace, taking your time, aware of each movement, enjoying every aspect. You work as though not working (*wu-wei*). You do each thing as though it is the only thing to be done all day long—as though it were the last time you will ever have the chance to do it. If you vacuum your house, you vacuum in order to vacuum, not just to get the vacuuming done. If you empty the dishwasher, you empty the dishwasher in order to empty the dishwasher, not to get to the end of it so you can go on to something else. Also, you can choose any convenient day as your day of mindfulness, instead of the designated Sabbath.

However, as with the Sabbath traditions, questions arise. Is it okay to watch television or take in a movie on a day of mindfulness? How about

reading a novel? Playing a computer game? Getting caught up on a little work you brought home from the office?

Theoretically, all of these things could be done mindfully. But with
some experience, you come to know which of these things will pull you
away from the spirit of the day, and which will not. Perhaps the idea of
entertainment in general is a little questionable. But it also makes some
difference whether you are watching a movie about Gandhi or a scary
sci-fi thriller.

There's a certain tension in the stomach that develops when you are
doing a task to get it done rather than for its own sake. The best answer
is to find your own way, trying things with mindfulness, noting if they
pull you out of your center or not, if they help you feel peaceful or give
you the frantic energy of doing and achieving. Don't fool yourself that
you can do things mindfully that really bring you away from the spirit
of mindfulness.

∼ PRACTICE ∼

Things to Do on a Day of Mindfulness

- When you wake up in the morning, breathe and smile. Create a
  gatha to use that sums up your intention for the day, such as
  "Dwelling happily in things as they are."
- Slow down. Do everything at half speed.
- Spend more time than usual in sitting and walking meditation.
- Intersperse brief periods of mindful breathing throughout the day.
- Linger over your coffee or tea, enjoying each sip.
- Enjoy a deliciously warm shower or bath.
- Eat meals slowly and in silence. Enjoy every bite.
- Read inspirational literature or scripture that deepens your mind-
  fulness practice.
- Write out favorite passages from inspirational literature, taking
  your time, breathing mindfully.
- Do things you might normally do, such as cleaning your house or
  weeding the garden, but do so without rushing, without trying to
  get it done. (If this is hard, practice by intentionally leaving things
  not quite finished until you can do this more easily.)
- Listen to beautiful music.

- Write a letter to a friend. Breathe in and out as you do so, seeing your friend's face, sensing your connection.
- Attend a worship service or meditation group.
- Sit outside and be aware of the fresh air, the blue sky, the trees, and the flowers.
- Visit a beautiful place. Take a walk there or eat lunch there.
- Have a conversation with a friend in which you practice mindful speaking and listening.
- Be mindful of all little human activities, like brushing your teeth and using the toilet. Do them in a spirit of grace and ease.
- Breathe in and out at red traffic lights, when the phone rings, when the timer sounds. Gently refuse to be pushed around by such things.
- Practice doing one thing at a time (instead of putting the coffee on while the computer boots up, for example).

≈·≈·≈

Connect with Your Tradition

If you wish to connect mindfulness practice with your religious heritage, connections are not hard to find. Mindfulness is found in some form in all religious traditions, but it is not always emphasized in the same way. From the Jewish tradition for example, we have already quoted the Psalmist on rejoicing in the day God has made. We could point out, as well, that following all 613 *mitzvoth* (good deeds) requires mindfulness. You have to be aware and present in order to follow these in a conscientious way.

In Christian teaching, Jesus makes it quite clear that we should come into the present, what the theologian Paul Tillich called the "Eternal Now." In the Sermon on the Mount, he said, "Therefore, do not be anxious about tomorrow, for tomorrow will be anxious for itself. Let the day's own trouble be sufficient for the day." The Christian monk Brother Lawrence and many others taught the "practice of the presence of God," which teaches that God is to be encountered in the here and now. The modern mystic Frank Laubach, known for his promotion of literacy, describes his own practice of the presence of God. After quoting a favorite hymn about abiding each moment in God, he concludes, "It is exactly this 'moment by moment,' every waking moment, surrender, responsiveness, obedience, sensitiveness, pliability, 'lost in his love,' that I now have the mind-bent to explore with all my might."

Whatever your religious heritage, there are many points of contact for bringing meditation practice into your life, once you look for them.

Not What It Seems

Mindfulness is a powerful inoculation against the pressures and toxicities of modern life. Just as it is important to practice meditation joyfully, and not with a sense of heaviness or duty, so it is also with daily life meditation. Use these devices with a light spirit. If a sense of heaviness or compulsion enters any element of the practice, then try it differently, approach it with a different attitude, or do something else. You are just learning, as the Buddha taught, to dwell happily in things as they are, not trying to change anything, not even trying to change or reform yourself.

We live in a world where theoretical physicists discuss time travel, parallel universes that interact with our own, and whether the space in the atom is truly empty or is filled with something like bubbles called quantum foam. Even by starting with the materialistic assumptions of modern science, and then looking deeply into the world, things are not at all what they seem. If matter is not what it seems, what then is human life? Such disconcerting questions can be frightening. But they can also teach us to relax a little more, giving up the ideas and categories with which we habitually view life, and come to a deeper vision.

Practice for Week Five

1. Increase your meditation now to fifteen minutes twice a day.
2. Continue to practice a few minutes of inspirational reading each day—in the morning if possible.
3. Add a second moment of mindfulness (p. 42).
4. Practice walking meditation at least once or twice this week.
5. Try the exercises and suggestions in this chapter:
   • Visualize slowing down (p. 85)
   • Practice radical medicine (p. 85)

- Practice *wu-wei* (p. 85)
- "Begin and End the Day Intentionally" (p. 87)
- "Find Bells of Mindfulness" (p. 88)
- "Ask: Where Am I? What Am I Doing?" (p. 90)
- "Allocate Attention to Centering" (p. 90)
- "Cultivate a Balanced Lifestyle" (p. 92)
- "Examine Your Environment" (p. 92)
- "Let Your Peace Return to You" (p. 93)
- "Stay in Charge of the Task" (p. 94)

6. Practice a day of mindfulness (or at least a part of a day) (p. 96).

5

Week Six

LOOK DEEPLY AT YOUR LIFE

At the level of the ego, we struggle to solve our problems. Spirit sees that struggle *is* the problem.
— Deepak Chopra, *The Way of the Wizard* (1995)

At the core of our being exists a pure mirror, untarnished and unsoiled by the impressions that fall upon it from the outside world. Like an inborn immunity, this part of us remains consistently whole, innocent, and healthy—even while enduring the numerous involvements and entanglements of this world.
— Pir Vilayat Inayat Khan, *Awakening: A Sufi Experience* (1999)

Appreciate What Is

The film *Shadowlands* is the story of the author C. S. Lewis and his surprising love relationship with an American woman named Joy. Lewis is a stuffy Cambridge don, unused to complications—particularly complications of human relationships. Just as he is coming to recognize his love for Joy, she contracts terminal cancer. During a remission, they drive into the country to a place called the Golden Valley. Lewis had a picture of this valley in his study. In childhood, he had imagined this to be a picture of heaven. As he and Joy share a beautiful day in this valley, in the time between the suffering they had already experienced and the suffering yet to come, Lewis finds a quality of happiness he had not known before. He says to Joy, "No, I don't want to be somewhere else anymore. Not waiting for anything new to happen. Not looking around the next corner, no next hill. Here now. That's enough."

To enter such a moment deeply is to enter the kingdom of heaven, the eternal now, the Buddha land of the present moment. While suffering can drive us to despair, it can also teach us the preciousness of here and now. For this reason, suffering is considered a "holy truth" in Buddhism. For when we examine suffering and its causes deeply, it leads to nirvana. It leads to bliss, just as this beautiful moment together for Lewis and Joy, a moment of heaven, was the result of wisdom gleaned from suffering.

Suffering teaches: This is your life. This moment is precious. Don't miss it. Don't miss the blueness of the sky, the delicate green of the first leaves of spring. Don't even miss the tinny roar of a neighborhood adolescent's motorcycle. Don't miss anything.

For this reason, Buddhist monks and nuns remind themselves daily that they will grow old, that they will get sick, that they will die, that everything they love will change. They consciously remind themselves that there is no possibility of escaping these realities. For if you forget, you will miss it all.

At first, this may seem like a negative practice. It runs counter to the superstitious feeling that entertaining negative possibilities will magically bring them about. But this is not the case. In fact, psychology has taught us that not facing things is often more dangerous than facing them. The reality we deny still hurts us in the same way that denying the reality of a wall doesn't prevent it from hurting when we walk into it. It is our repressed feelings that cause the most trouble.

Consider Sean. Sean thinks of himself as a nice person. And in many ways he is. He calls his mother on Mother's Day and sends his girlfriend flowers on the monthly anniversary of their first date. He coaches Little League in the spring and soccer in the fall. But Sean does not know that underneath he is seething with resentment toward many people in his life. He "forgets" to return phone calls. He always arrives late. Sometimes he acts as though the other person were not even there, or worse still, speaks with a slightly sarcastic tone that hurts people around him more than he knows. He maintains his belief in himself as nice in part by repressing hostile, angry feelings, yet these very feelings seep out and infect his relationships with others. If Sean can become conscious of these feelings, though this is not pleasant, and though it will challenge his one-sided view of himself, he can learn to take care of them, and not let them control his words and actions. Facing things that are negative or that make us uncomfortable is often helpful.

Similarly, the practice of reminding ourselves that old age, sickness, and death are an inevitable part of the human condition is in actuality a positive practice. There are two fruits of this reminder: *nonattachment* and an *awareness of the preciousness of each moment of life*.

∼ PRACTICE ∼

Practice the Five Remembrances

Many Buddhist monks and nuns practice remembering these five facts every day. In this way, we are not surprised when they occur. We are ready. And we do not need tragic events like those of September 11, 2001, to wake us up.

1. I am of a nature to suffer ill health. Ill health cannot be avoided.
2. I am of a nature to grow old. There is no escape from old age.
3. I am of a nature to die. There is no escaping death.
4. Everything and everyone I love is of a nature to change. I cannot hold on to anything or anyone.
5. My deeds (karma) are my only true possessions.

This week, at the beginning of your morning meditation period, spend a few moments remembering each of these points. Take it in deeply rather than by rote or mechanically. Let it contribute to your joy in being alive, even on a very normal, seemingly unexciting day.

One caution with this practice: It may not be advisable to practice this when you are sad or depressed. Skip it until you feel more solid.

∼∼∼

Touch the Preciousness of Life

Because life is limited, it is valuable. It is not possible to have day without night, male without female, birth without death. When you embrace the brevity of life, you do not need to despair. Quite the opposite can be the case. You can reach a perspective that this is not just another day, but it is a gift to enjoy. You can resolve that you don't want to miss one minute of it. You know that health is valuable only because you have experienced its temporary loss. When you know that someday health will be gone forever, you don't want to miss one moment of good health. Even if life is not all that you want, and even if your health is not all that you want, you know from this perspective that there are still many positive things right now.

Practice Nonattachment

Nonattachment is important because we easily lose perspective. There is a kind of stickiness about our normal awareness. Whatever momentarily occupies center stage in our conscious attention takes on cosmic proportions. A feeling develops that whatever is occupying us now is of supreme importance, and it *must* go well and smoothly, and turn out the way we want. Since inevitably, not everything in life goes smoothly and turns out as we wish, this feeling sets up a background of frustration and disappointment in our lives. In extreme cases, it can even generate despair.

Notice the term used here is *nonattachment* rather than *detachment*. This is important. The term *detachment* evokes a sense of a blasé, noncaring attitude toward life. This is not what we mean at all. In fact, when you become more mindful, far more of your life becomes enjoyable. However, losing a sense of proportion about things robs us of vitality. When it is supremely important that each thing go just as we would like, we are locked on target for disappointment. When we insist on receiving only the good we think we need and no other, we cannot receive the actual good the universe is trying to place in our hands.

Take the example of Sam, a client of mine. One day Sam called me on the telephone, very excited. He had been in a relationship with a woman for some time that, while wonderful in some ways, also had significant problems. Sam was excited because his partner had finally agreed to get therapy to deal with her part of these difficulties. Sam wanted me to see his partner for psychotherapy. I felt a conflict of interest in seeing both Sam and his partner individually. I knew that even if I succeeded in being present to each of them without siding more with one or the other, they would always wonder whether I wasn't taking the other one's side. When I offered referrals to other therapists I have confidence in, Sam insisted that I alone could be helpful to his partner.

If Sam could have been less attached, he could perhaps have come to the point of view that if indeed therapy was important for his partner, then what was important was finding her a good therapist. From this point of view, there would be many ways to get what he needed. But Sam was locked into what felt like the *only* way to meet this need. And for that reason, his partner would miss a helpful experience.

Psychology provides a helpful trick in this regard. The trick is to substitute the word *prefer* in your thinking in place of *must* or *have to*. I *prefer* to get the job offer, win the baseball game, or have good weather for the picnic. But when I feel these things *must* go the way I want them to, I lock myself in. My own desperation may then even work against me. For example, the thought "I have to get this job!" creates feelings of pressure and anxiety. A much more useful thought is something like "I strongly prefer to get this job, but I know that if I don't, I can find something else." Then you can relax a little. And if you are relaxed, you will probably do better on the interview and other application procedures. Desperation breeds more of the same.

∼ PRACTICE ∼

Change Must *to* Prefer

Take out paper and pen. Draw a line down the middle of the paper. Breathe quietly in and out for a few moments. Then review things in your life that you feel have to be a certain way for you to be happy. In the left-hand column, list these things. Your list should include both small, day-to-day concerns like "I must get the garden planted this weekend" and more serious matters like "I must get that job I interviewed for" or "I have to find a good relationship."

When you have completed your list, spend a few moments looking it over. Feel the tension in your body and in your consciousness as you take in all these musts. Now in the right-hand column, write a rebuttal to each of these, beginning with the phrase "I would prefer . . ." For example, "I would prefer to get this job, but if I don't perhaps something better will come along." Or: "I would prefer to have a partner, but if that doesn't happen, my life can still be worthwhile and happy." Be sure the statements you write are true and not unreasonably optimistic.

Now quietly read your list of preferences as you breathe. Notice the difference between giving yourself the little space created by the word *prefer*. Note how this affects your body and consciousness.

～～～

Just Ease Your Grasp

Nonattachment is not a matter of fooling yourself. You are not pretending you don't have any wants or needs. You are not pretending to be a saint or a guru, above it all and unconcerned. You acknowledge the outcome you wish. But you leave the door ajar. You give yourself a little space. You ease your anxious grasp on life.

When we lose perspective, we develop a black-and-white attitude. There seems to be only one way to go about things. There seems to be only one way to take care of our needs. When we view things with more detachment, with an awareness that this, too, will pass, we can adapt to what is. Then we find many ways to get what we need.

When you know that good health is temporary, you appreciate it when you are healthy. When you know that life is not forever, this can inspire you to enjoy every moment. Problems seem smaller, and you become fearless and patient. The highway construction that makes you late, the phone call that comes at an inopportune moment, or the breakdown of your refrigerator are not the major crises they pretend to be when you are caught up in them.

Follow the Eightfold Path

The basis of the Buddha's teaching is an acknowledgment of suffering and a way out of suffering. Suffering is important to recognize, because the process of looking deeply into suffering teaches us the way out of it. In itself, the fact of suffering is not news. The news is that there is a way out of it. At the heart of this teaching is a pragmatic attitude. There are no unnecessary adornments or speculations or moralisms—just a matter-of-fact teaching that if you do these things in this way, you will get this result. If you cling to a desperate hope that someday suffering will end, but you go on living, thinking, and perceiving in the same old way, this is obvious nonsense. It's like the man who complained to his doctor that whenever he banged his head against the wall, it hurt. The doctor's obvious advice: Stop doing that! To end suffering, you must do things differently.

Recall that the fourth noble truth in Buddhism is the eightfold path: right view, right thinking, right speech, right action, right livelihood, right mindfulness, right diligence, and right concentration. The Pali word *samyak*, here translated as "right," does not mean right in the moralistic sense so much as in the sense of complete or effective. In other words, this is how to live effectively if you wish to become enlightened. Three of these (view, thinking, and concentration) concern mental and perceptual habits and orientations and are directly connected with mindfulness. Clearly if your view of life is erroneous, if your thinking is distorted, and if your concentration is weak, it will be difficult to practice mindfulness. At the same time, by living more mindfully, you are already beginning to improve these aspects of the path. The other four (speech, action, diligence, and livelihood) concern what we do in daily life. If you speak in a harmful, unskillful way, if you act in a way that brings harm to yourself or others, if you earn a living in a way that creates suffering, or if you do not put enough diligence, or energy, into your practice, you will not be able to live mindfully. Mindfulness does not mix with wrong speech, wrong action, or wrong diligence.

To give one example, say you are an advertising executive responsible for a campaign to encourage teenage smoking. You have a problem in the area of right livelihood. Only those heavily invested in tobacco companies can still maintain that smoking is harmless. So it is clear that if this is your job, you are doing harm. If you are living mindfully, it is inevitable that you become aware of this. Mindfulness makes it difficult to maintain your rationalizations. If you are mindful, you are concerned about the consequences of what you do. Since you are causing suffering, this will weigh on you and prevent you from being peaceful and happy. Eventually, one of two things will happen: Either you will get another job, or you will become less mindful. Such work and mindfulness are incompatible. If you do such a job mindfully, the stress in you will build until you either deny or rationalize the situation, or find another job.

∾ PRACTICE ∾

Practice Mindfulness of Livelihood

All work contains a mixture of positive and negative effects. The Vedas, ancient scriptures of India, teach that evil clings to action like smoke to fire. There is no such thing as work that has no negative consequences.

Breathe quietly in and out, and consider:

- What are the positive effects of my work?
- What are the negative effects of my work?
- What effects of my work are mixed?

Stretch yourself a little. If you are a therapist, you might think you only do helpful work. But the money it costs to see you affects people's lives, even if you do your work perfectly. And most likely, you do not always do it perfectly. If you are a teacher, you may think you do only good. But the grades you give out can have negative effects on students. Even an overly positive grade can have negative effects if it puts the student in a false position.

Continue these reflections as you move through your work day, just noting compassionately what you observe, without judging or reacting.

It is troubling to become aware that the work we do is harmful to others. Because we have family and financial commitments, it is not always possible to just walk away from our employment, even if we would like to. The situation is complicated, too, because we know that if we leave our job, someone else will do it—perhaps someone with less conscience. What is more, there is no job that is perfect and that could not be said to bring some harm to someone in some way. It is always a matter of *relatively* right livelihood and of doing *relatively* little harm. Since there is no perfect job, it is always a matter of moving your work life a little in the right direction, changing how you do things where you work, changing your job if you must.

∾∾∾

Practice Right Action

Right action isn't just about large decisions and important actions, but is also about behavior that might normally be considered minor. One dharma teacher taught that right action is about how you use toilet paper. This may shock our Western sensibilities, but the Buddhist attitude does not divide the world into areas that are considered holy and important versus those considered worldly or trivial.

In light of Joko Beck's teaching that "chop wood, carry water" needs to become "make love, drive freeway," consider the topic of running a red light. If you are in a great hurry, if you feel great urgency about getting where you are going, it is easy to rationalize running a red light—especially if it is only a matter of a second or two. You tell yourself that you know there is a pause before the signal for the other traffic changes to green. You glance around and are confident that there are no police to give you a ticket. And you just can't afford that extra minute or two the waiting might cost you.

If you look at this situation more deeply, it is not hard to find the potential for harm. At a minimum level, there may have been a police car that you did not see. And if you get ticketed, this will cause you suffering (a fine, points on your license, increased auto insurance rates). This is the level of traditional, authority-based morality: Anything is right that does not bring me into conflict with authority. If I get away with it, it must be okay. But the consequences at this level are minor compared to those at other levels, such as those that can follow from having an accident. At the least, an accident involves harm to a major piece of property. At the most, it may involve the loss of health or even life. If you are living mindfully, you cannot rationalize this away.

There is more to gain from this simple example. If you look still a little more closely, you may ask, What is the cause of this situation? How did I get myself to the point where I was in such a hurry that running the light seemed worth the risk? Such a line of inquiry may lead you back to getting up in the morning and hitting the snooze button a few too many times. You calculated just enough time to get to work, leaving none to spare. So you were rushing desperately from the moment you sprang out of bed. A feeling of rushing while driving is always dangerous. By looking deeply into the problem of running a red light, you see a need to allow yourself more time, so that you will not have a feeling of rushing while you drive, so that you will not be tempted to run the light, so that you will not take such a risk. You come to see that allowing yourself time to get ready for work at a more leisurely pace is not trivial, and is not just about being more relaxed for your own well-being, but also affects all the other drivers who are on the road with you.

If you live mindfully, you experience the incompatibility between certain actions and mindfulness. In fact, if you are mindful—if you are cultivating calmness and joy in the present moment—you probably will not even have the impulse to run the light in the first place. But if you are living in an unmindful or forgetful way, is it any wonder that you do not feel peaceful when you sit on your meditation cushion?

Right speech is obviously an important aspect of living mindfully. We will deal with this in chapter 8, where we discuss interpersonal aspects of mindfulness.

Be Aware of What You Take In

Right consumption is part of right action. This is of great importance in a consumer-driven society. Every day we are bombarded with media messages. The very air about us is replete with radio and television waves. It is all but impossible to get away from them.

You cannot find greater peace and joy in life if you continue to expose yourself to things that are harmful, agitating, and disturbing. As the Buddhists say, "Because this is, that is." If you eat things that are not good for you, this will affect your physical health. If you consume television and radio, books, magazines, newspapers, and movies with negative content, this will affect your emotional and spiritual health.

Action based on this awareness need not be heavy-handed, moralistic, or joyless. You *certainly* do not have to feel it is your duty to impose your view of these things on other people. Mindful consumption is simply self-defense. Some psychological research confirms the commonsense point of view that exposure to negative media has negative effects. If you watch a film depicting violence, you become more prone to aggressive behavior afterward. On the other hand, if you watch a film about caring and empathy, this has a positive effect. In one study, a film about Mother Teresa caring for the sick elicited elevated immune functioning in those who saw it. Compassion is good for you.

When you become mindful, you notice how what you take in to

yourself affects you. A conversation, for example, can be highly toxic. You may notice that being around some people leaves you depleted or feeling a little sad or upset. Seeing an advertisement on television for something you want but cannot afford can leave you feeling cheated or deprived.

We offer no rules for mindful consumption. We will not say you should not eat meat or drink alcohol, or that you should avoid violent movies, or any other form of prohibition. To do so only results in an authority-based morality. And given human nature, authority-based rules lead to rebellion as much as obedience. Great spiritual teachers have differed on these points, some prohibiting, some proclaiming freedom from prohibitions.

We want to foster a mindfulness-based morality. The best course is to let your own mindfulness be your guide. Feel the effects of what you consume. If you know that something has a negative effect, but you still cannot give it up, be gentle and patient with yourself. Practice mindfulness of the consequences of harmful consumption until you find a readiness to change. (Our book *Mindful Recovery* offers help for those recovering from addiction.) You may decide that some of the traditional prohibitions of spiritual teachings make sense for you. Or you may decide that they do not. But let this grow out of your own insight, with knowledge of yourself and your life context. Otherwise your spiritual practice can become heavy and joyless.

∾ PRACTICE ∾

Practice Mindful Consumption

Notice carefully what happens whenever you take something into yourself, whether into your body as food and drink, or into your consciousness. Areas for observation include:

- Watching a movie
- Eating a meal or a snack
- Drinking a glass of water or juice
- Drinking coffee or tea
- Drinking an alcoholic beverage
- Buying something on impulse
- Buying something you have saved for

- Seeing or hearing a commercial
- The sights and sounds as you drive across town, and so forth

While observing these inputs, notice:

- What your mood is like before you take in this experience
- What your mood is like a short time after and a longer time after
- What your body feels like before, during, and after
- How your body and your emotions may interact

Devote at least one day to this practice, noticing without judgment everything you can possibly become aware of about it, bringing mere recognition to the act of consumption and its consequences.

Lower Your Threshold of Pleasure

By adolescence, if not sooner, we have received millions of messages persuading us that we need more and more. We come to require ever higher levels of stimulation to be happy. These messages make hungry ghosts of us, leaving us perpetually discontented in the most prosperous society in the history of the world.

Mindfulness lowers the level of stimulation that we need to reach in order to have fun. By living mindfully, you are training yourself to require lower levels of stimulation. You can come to enjoy just making your coffee, just sitting in your backyard in the fading light of day, just talking with a friend.

Our society teaches us quite a different lesson. The popularity of cocaine and other stimulant drugs is no accident. In fact, cocaine is a great metaphor for this process. The cocaine addict becomes used to a very high level of stimulation. Once adjusted to this level, anything below it seems flat and dull. Similarly, if you often watch action-packed films, full of violence and tension, movies dealing with the subtleties of human life will seem boring. Drinking soft drinks, you lose your appreciation for water. Watching television, you come to find reading difficult. By continually doing things that involve a high level of stimulation, you lose your taste for anything below this threshold.

Mindfulness reeducates your sensibilities. Be patient with yourself through this process. It may take a little while. But when you can watch a leaf falling with awe and wonder, the time taken to retrain your sensibilities and lower your threshold of pleasure will have been well worth it.

Give Up the Struggle

Without knowing it, many of us are addicted to struggle. We are often unaware of this because we attribute so much to outside factors; it's our jobs that keep us running, our busy families that won't give us a break. However, even when we finally do get a chance to relax, it is easy to observe that a lot of this pressure is generated internally. When we finally get to sit on our back patio, all we see around us are things to do—the walk needs sweeping, the garden needs weeding, the lawn needs mowing, the trees need pruning, and so on. Our minds are still racing, because it is the pressure inside that really keeps us hopping and struggling.

Part of what keeps us addicted to struggle is that our society reinforces us for being busy. We all talk about how busy we are. When someone asks us to do something we are not terribly interested in, we say we cannot do it because we are so busy. When was the last time you heard someone say, "Boy, I wish I had more work and responsibility! I've got way too much time on my hands!" Being busy is a status symbol: It shows what important people we are. Cell phones and pagers proclaim our importance to the world, declaring to all that we cannot afford to be out of touch for even a minute.

If we were to give up this idea of being busy, we would have to face the naked truth of life as it really is, apart from the mythology of self-importance and struggle. A myth, it has been said, is something everyone believes and no one seriously questions. Part of the American myth is that success creates happiness, and the sign of success is being busy and hurried. To be successful, you must struggle and work hard and sacrifice. And if you keep struggling, one day you will be happy.

If there is some truth to the idea that hard work brings success, it certainly is not always the case. Look around you. Is it always the most hardworking people who have the most success? Some people are lucky. Many others have worked very hard, but still have not achieved much success. It is obviously not always true that working hard brings success. You need talent. You need to be working at the right thing in the right way at the right time and place. You need luck.

And if the relationship between struggle and success is not always that more of one brings more of the other, it is clearly not true that success brings happiness. Success is a wonderful thing, but it may be more true to say that happiness creates success than the other way around. Happier people *feel* more successful. And because they are happy, others enjoy being around them, which helps tremendously no matter what your career is. Struggle perpetuates itself. You can see this, for example, with people who achieve wealth through scrimping and saving. They may no longer need to scrimp, but it has become such a habit, that they continue to bemoan every penny spent. When will they enjoy what they have?

Inevitably the drama of struggle fails us. And since we are so used to living this drama, when things are quiet we at first feel a terror of emptiness. We quickly find things to get us busy again, to reinvolve ourselves with the struggle, to convince ourselves we are important and push this emptiness away. However, when we come into the present moment—when we learn to enjoy the simple things we do every day—we no longer need the drama. And the emptiness we feared reveals an underlying luminosity.

∼ PRACTICE ∼

Challenge Your Busyness

For a day or two, practice being aware of how often you say how busy you are. Notice your intentions behind it. How often do you say it to get out of something you don't want to do or to make an excuse? How often do you say it with a background of self-importance? How often do you say it because you simply are busy and overwhelmed? How often do you say it for some combination of these reasons?

When it is not a matter of simply being busy and overwhelmed, correct yourself internally. For example, you might say to yourself: "I said I was busy, but what I really mean is that other things are more important than what this person just asked me to do."

Be sure to practice in a kind and accepting way, just noticing, sympathizing with whatever need you have to hide behind your busyness in some way. *Understand* why you do this.

~~~

Protect Yourself

There are some jobs and professions that, by their nature, bring one into contact with a lot of human suffering. Therapists, doctors, nurses, criminal lawyers, social workers, and others experience a lot of difficult people and human suffering every day. Should they quit their jobs because of the toxic atmosphere? Perhaps. The important thing, however, is to monitor the effect these things have and seek ways to protect oneself. To a certain extent, professional training provides a shield against some of this. However, it is unfortunate that the professional shield often comes with a cost. Many professionals cope with the difficulties of their work by ensconcing themselves in a protective layer of arrogance or white-coated professionalism.

There's another way. If you are strong enough in yourself, a spirit of compassion can protect against these toxins, without the layer of insulated professionalism. To cope with such difficult things, *more* compassion, rather than less, may be the answer.

Compassion must be linked with clear, accurate knowledge of yourself, your role, your abilities, and your limitations. Our society reinforces us for putting up a false front, for pretending to be more capable and knowledgeable than we are. Such pretense creates stress. If you know that the situation before you is beyond your capacity to help or change, but you are trying to pretend that you can, that becomes an awful burden. No wonder you may then feel a need to detach and pull back.

To be compassionate, you must also practice equanimity. Equanimity practice is often linked in Buddhist traditions to compassion. For you must recognize that you cannot control all circumstances in which others find themselves, and you cannot control their choices. You must be willing to let things be and accept life as it actually is. If you cannot do this, then practicing compassion becomes overwhelming, and you will tend to just numb yourself to others' pain rather than open to it.

If you are in a helping profession, recognize what you can and cannot do to help. Know and accept your limits.

Be Free to Be Yourself

Thich Nhat Hanh teaches this gatha: "Breathing in, I see myself as space. Breathing out, I feel free." Being free, especially in the sense of being free to be yourself, is essential. You must be free to be the person you are and are meant to be. You must be free to blossom in your own special way. The goal is not to become the same as that other person whom you admire; the goal is to become the person you and you alone can become.

The Jewish teacher Martin Buber once said that when he got to heaven, he would not be asked why he was not Moses. He would be asked, he said, why he was not Martin Buber. For the real tragedy is not that we did not live up to someone else's vision of life, no matter how wonderful, but that we do not live up to what we ourselves can be.

Insist on yourself, and watch out for collectivism in religion, spirituality, or philosophy. We caution against any "ism" that substitutes authority for the responsibility of doing your own thinking and reaching your own conclusions.

In the West, the dangers of self are obvious: selfishness, arrogance, competitiveness instead of cooperation, aggression, and violence. But a literalism about no self is at least as dangerous. In fact, the Buddha said the clinging to no self is even worse than clinging to self. Clinging too hard to no self brings despair, nihilism, or collectivism. It also leads to correcting others whenever they use the word *self*. So don't get caught on either edge of this dangerous sword—self or no self. But use both effectively to cut through delusion.

The world has had some bitter lessons about collectivism. The Holocaust in Nazi Germany is one such lesson. The tragic consequences of cult involvement such as the Jim Jones mass suicide in Guyana or David Koresh in Waco are others, and show that a cloak of religiosity is no protection against destructive collectivism.

We need one another, and having a community of people with whom you meditate and share spiritual practice can be helpful. Sometimes it may make the difference between being able to maintain a spiritual practice and not being able to. But we also need the space to be ourselves.

Healthy spirituality, though enhancing our relatedness to others, is ultimately noncollective. The heart of spiritual teaching is to put you in touch with the Buddha within. The moment you are mindful, the Buddha is born in you. And Buddha always thinks for himself. Buddha allows enough space between himself and others so both he and they are free. When you become the Buddha you are meant to be, the world will not have seen anything quite like it before. The Buddha taught us to be islands unto ourselves. In the parable of the sower, Christ warned against not having roots in ourselves. And while Jesus was one of the most other-centered people who ever lived, he was yet not primarily other-centered, but primarily God-centered. And for this reason, he was continually retreating from the overwhelming needs and demands of the crowd to go off to a quiet place to pray, either alone or with his closest friends. Some might call this action selfish or "navel-gazing," but without it, you will not have the capacity to help. Similarly, psychology teaches us the danger of being insufficiently individuated—of being only a part of the "undifferentiated family ego mass," as the family systems therapist Murray Bowen expressed it. We must have the space to be ourselves. The preciousness of the individual is the West's gift to the East and to traditions like Buddhism, the highest fruit of Western spirituality.

More than fifty years ago, Krishnamurti was already teaching that the age of the guru is past. We also believe this is so. We must cease to project the best that we are onto others instead of claiming it as our own. As the abuses of power of so many teachers, political leaders, ministers, gurus, and others testify, we need to connect directly with our own wisdom.

Ralph Waldo Emerson, in a journal entry dated November 1842, put it this way: "Each man being the Universe, if he attempt to join himself to others, he instantly is jostled, crowded, cramped, halved, quartered, or on all sides diminished of his proportion."

Avoid Roadblocks

Precepts and commandments in spiritual teachings are designed to be a gift, but often come to feel like a burden. In the West, they can elicit our rebellion, as we stand up for our own freedom and our own insight.

To understand this dilemma in a new light, imagine it from the perspective of an enlightened person. If you were such a person, people would inevitably come to you for guidance. They would ask: How should we live? So how would you, as an enlightened person, answer them? It would pose a dilemma, because you would know of course that reality is so much more rich and complex than any rules or guidelines could ever take into account. You would know that rules and precepts tend to elicit argument and rebellion from human beings. So you might be tempted not to answer at all, knowing that anything you could say would be inadequate, would be too simplistic, and could not possibly begin to cover all the kinds of situations and difficulties people could encounter. And indeed, some very spiritual people decided to do just that; they taught nothing at all. Even the Buddha did not feel he could teach anything at first, for how could he possibly explain enlightenment to those who had not experienced it for themselves?

But in the end, for the sake of compassion, the Buddha spoke. He tried to show the way. He gave teachings. He gave precepts to guide our behavior, knowing full well that these ultimately and inevitably would be inadequate. Despite the danger that people would misunderstand and misapply the teachings, being loose when they should be strict and being rigid when they should look more deeply, he spoke. And to most teachers—or at least to those who have left a record for us—this was the best conclusion. Risk the inevitable misunderstandings. For in the end, some guidance is better than none at all.

Many people lose their attraction for the spiritual life when they encounter a lot of rules. Some of these rules—especially since many come down to us from other times and places—do not seem to fit their insight about what is appropriate here and now. They do not want to give up things that bring them joy. They want to be free.

When you encounter this kind of tension, you must proceed very carefully. You do well to consider the teachings and traditions that have been laid down, not dispensing with them too casually. But if the rules feel like a heavy burden that removes the joy of the spiritual life, you may be better off not to follow them until or unless you come to see their necessity for yourself.

When you lose your way and start to question, return to simple precepts. Remember that you are walking in the direction of being able to live happily and peacefully in the present moment. Or remember to see the universe as full of life and intelligence.

See Everything as Alive

The missionary Albert Schweitzer's phrase for this central insight was *reverence for life*. We would add that you should not be too restrictive about what you consider living and what you consider not living. In fact, you should see everything as alive.

In biology, scientists are hard put to describe the difference between living and nonliving things. When you consider simple organisms, such as a virus for example, it is hard to say whether it is alive or not. Ultimately, it is one of those dualities into which we split reality that does not really hold up, revealing what Buddhism calls the emptiness of concepts.

In the study of comparative religion, the attitude of viewing things as alive is denigrated as animism—the belief that rocks and trees are alive or contain a spirit. This is supposed to be a primitive attitude. But consider the alternative. To us, everything is dead. We live on a dead planet, treating it as dead rather than living, destroying it ruthlessly, and with it, destroying ourselves. If that is animism, then we could use a good dose of it.

∾ PRACTICE ∾

Choose a Living World

For at least one day, practice seeing everything as alive. If you see a tree, greet it silently: "Hello, tree, I see you. I am here." Do this several times. Each time will be deeper than the first. Each time will increase your joy. Do this also with people, with animals, as much as possible with whatever becomes an object of your awareness. Do this also with objects you do not normally consider alive, such as a rock, a desk, your car, your meditation seat.

Notice how this practice affects your consciousness. Your world becomes more alive, and as your world becomes more alive, you do as well.

∾∾∾

Practice for Week Six

1. Increase your meditation time to twenty minutes twice a day.
2. Continue daily reading.
3. Practice walking meditation when you can.
4. Continue with two moments of mindfulness (p. 42).
5. Practice the exercises in this chapter:
    *   "Practice the Five Remembrances" (p. 105)
    *   "Change *Must* to *Prefer*" (p. 107)
    *   "Practice Mindful Consumption" (p. 113)
    *   "Challenge Your Busyness" (p. 116)
    *   "Choose a Living World" (p. 121)

PART III

⊷o⊷

The Path

In this section, we turn to areas where psychology is uniquely help-ful. Psychology has special strengths in working with emotions and dreams and in the skills for working effectively with our relation-ships. Journaling is also a very psychological kind of technique. Still, as always, spiritual understanding and practices are intertwined with psychology in this section, helping us nourish the proper attitude and understanding that empowers us to carry out what psychology has to teach.

To find mindfulness at every step on the path requires assistance in dealing with two special areas: negative emotional states and relation-ships. If we are unable to deal with negative moods, with our anger and our sadness, we will run from the present moment rather than build a home there. Similarly, we must be able to learn the skills to take good care of our relationships. If our relationships need healing, we will also need healing, and we will not be able to live mindfully.

Mindful living requires a good relationship with ourselves. If we do not like ourselves, we cannot come home to ourselves. To be able to come home, we must face the truth of who we are and work with it in a loving, accepting way. Dreams can help us to do this. Through dreams, the practice of mindfulness can be extended even into Somnus's noc-turnal realm. Journaling can help us bring awareness and attention to our daily life.

Week Seven

WORK WITH DREAMS

The dream is its own interpretation.

—The Talmud

When we set out to live spiritually, we can make a number of wrong turns. One of these is attempting to repress our nature rather than mindfully transforming it. We can avoid this by working with dreams. By their nature, dreams remind us of those aspects of ourselves most in need of attention and mindfulness. If we repress our anger, for example, we may dream it nonetheless, witnessing horrible things happening to the people we are angry at in our dreams. If we are willing to listen to such dreams, we allow this anger to be more conscious. We can work with it mindfully instead of repressing it, so that the energy of that anger remains part of us and provides us with needed vitality and enthusiasm for life.

The true nature of the spiritual path is not avoidance or repression but transformation. Transformation requires contact with the raw material—all of it. No evasion will do. This is why suffering lies at the heart of the Buddha's teaching. Suffering is a sure teacher, calling our attention to what needs healing. The world does not make us suffer, but our grasping and avoidance do. Whether we cling to impermanent things as though they were permanent, or try to avoid painful truths, we hurt ourselves. We suffer.

As we put these insights into practice, we develop a more refined notion of what is worth grasping at and what is worth turning away from. Before, we grasped at fleeting pleasures. Now, we grasp at enlightenment. Before, we sought immediate gratification; now, we try to hold onto a vision of ourselves as spiritual. This is almost as bad and nearly as pointless.

In the preface, we pointed out that this problem has been called "spiritual bypassing." People try to avoid real-life issues on the emotional/psychological level by trying to be so spiritual that they transcend them. This does not work. It does not work because avoidance does not work. No matter how many hours a day you meditate, if you use meditation to avoid your life rather than to live it, you will continue to be plagued by the same issues.

Spiritual Bypassing: Tim's Story

Tim was a respected meditation teacher. He meditated four hours a day, every day, and went on many retreats involving days on end of continuous meditation. While he was an accomplished meditator, and while I had respect for his abilities in this area, it was clear that he used meditation as a form of spiritual bypassing. Tim came to my office because of an intense fear of flying. He had been able to avoid this problem until now, but at this point, he was confronted with a chance to expand his teaching to a national level. He very much wanted to do this, but it would be impossible if he could not board an airplane.

Tim's life was presenting him with a teaching, with a possibility of facing an old fear. I knew that there were other areas that Tim was also avoiding, but I never got the chance to explore these with him. When the behavioral treatment we began forced Tim to confront his fear, he quickly dropped out of therapy, opting instead for another intensive meditation retreat.

"People will do anything, no matter how absurd," wrote Jung, "in order to avoid facing their own souls. They will practice Indian yoga and all its exercises, observe a strict regimen of diet, learn theosophy by heart, or mechanically repeat mystic texts from the literature of the whole world—all because they cannot get on with themselves and have not the slightest faith that anything useful could ever come out of their own souls." And while we do not agree that all these practices are absurd, they are absurd if used to avoid dealing with our own lives. They are absurd if we imagine that all wisdom resides somewhere out there rather than in ourselves and our own experience.

Look to Your Dreams

Using dreams as a tool to better understand our unconscious wishes and desires, our disappointments and yearnings, is a major contribution of Western psychology. This is an area where the West has excelled in helping people uncover and unravel those hidden signposts, life struggles, repeating patterns, and fears that often get in our way. Working with dreams can help you to get to your inner core, your life purpose; it can lead you to glimpse your true soul.

Many Buddhist traditions do not emphasize working with dreams. There seems to be a feeling that working with dreams is to involve oneself increasingly in *maya*—in illusion. But there are exceptions. Some Tibetan traditions practice a form of dream yoga, with the rationale that if we can learn to see through the illusion of our dreams clearly and mindfully, then we will be able also to see through the illusion of the waking dream as well, and ultimately, be able to deal with the difficulties of the *bardo* realm—the transition realm after death. But this is the exception among Buddhist traditions.

Many spiritual traditions value dreams. In the Bible, Joseph helps the pharaoh by interpreting his dream of fat and lean cattle to mean seven fat years followed by seven lean ones, and thereby prevents catastrophic starvation. Another Joseph, the father of Jesus, is warned of Herod's plot to murder Jewish children, and he saves the day by fleeing with mother and child to Egypt.

Whatever these spiritual traditions say, in modern culture, we are in great need of the counterbalancing dreams provide. We are disconnected from our deep, unconscious, and supraconscious selves. Our culture is desperately one-sided. We have become far too rationalistic, scientific, and technological. It is precisely in such a culture that dreams take on great importance. For while our rationalism is clearly valuable, it has come at a greater cost than we imagine. In his usual complex and discursive prose, Jung put it this way: "Modern man does not understand how much his 'rationalism' (which has destroyed his capacity to respond to numinous symbols and ideas) has put him at the mercy of the psychic 'underworld.' He has freed himself from 'superstition' (or so he believes), but in the process he has lost his spiritual values to a positively dangerous degree. His moral and spiritual tradition has disintegrated, and he is now paying the price for this break-up in worldwide disorientation and dissociation."

Working with dreams heals the split, returning us to our own soul and its wisdom. As the Jungian analyst Robert Johnson put it, "if we don't go to the spirit, the spirit comes to us as neurosis." In less fragmented cultures than ours, this may not be so necessary. In our world, it is vital.

Respect Your Dreams

Many volumes have been written about dreams. It is beyond the scope of this book to discuss the various theories and complexities of working with dreams. Fortunately, however, you do not need to become an expert on dreams to benefit from dream work.

The main practice we suggest is simply to bring mindfulness to your dreams. The act of respecting your dreams by writing them down in some detail, telling them to someone, or in any way giving them your attention and respect is already valuable. Do not worry too much about trying to interpret your dreams fully. A dream is never fully interpreted. But just by paying attention, you are already building a bridge between your conscious and unconscious selves. If you are overly rational and logical, as are so many in our world, dreams will put you in touch with the source of myth and feeling. Or if you happen to be very emotional, through dreams you touch aspects of yourself that view things from a much cooler, levelheaded perspective.

THE EXPERIENCE (TOM)

Dream fragment: *A workman comes to my home. He has received orders to install a telephone line.*

The symbolism is not hard to understand. A new kind of intrapsychic communication capacity is being established. This is exactly what happens when we allow ourselves to be aware of dreams. ∾

A dream is an excellent subject for meditation. When you meditate on a flower, you are not attempting to analyze the flower as a botanist might, naming and classifying it precisely, detailing its anatomical structures and their purposes. You are simply *being with* the flower, allowing the flower to be deeply present to you and you to it, in such a way that you appreciate the flower and become one with it. Treat the dream the same way. Enter into the dream world, be with it. It is more like trying to taste a dream than like trying to figure something out. A few minutes spent doing this is useful, though of course you can meditate longer and attempt greater depth if you wish. The attitude is one of *respecting* rather than dissecting the dream. This is the main thing and the most important thing, even if you do nothing else.

Remember Your Dreams

From sleep research it is clear that we all dream every night. Most, though not all dreaming, occurs during the phase of sleep in which our eyes move rapidly from side to side, called, appropriately enough, rapid eye movement or REM sleep.

If you do not remember your dreams or do not remember them often, it is usually enough to formulate a clear intention to begin to do so. It helps also to strengthen this intention by taking some action to show the unconscious that you are serious. Set a pad and pen on your nightstand, and jot down whatever you remember *immediately* upon waking. If you think you can put it off until after you shower and dress, you may discover that the dream evaporates in the meantime. So jot it down right away. If you do not have time to write the dream out in full, then just note enough to give your memory a handle on the dream so you can recall it later in more detail.

If you don't remember your dreams, record whatever you find yourself thinking about when you wake up, since this may relate to what you were dreaming. If you only remember parts of a dream, record whatever fragments or images you can remember, even if they seem silly, absurd, or meaningless at first. The conscious mind uses labels such as silly or absurd to reject perspectives foreign to it. But sometimes a silly fragment of a dream that you almost forget turns out to be very important. "The stone which the builders rejected has become the head of the corner," said Christ. Psychologically, this means that the very elements of ourselves and our experience that seem to lack value can often prove to be the most valuable in the end. This is especially the case with dream contents. Note carefully those discrepant, odd little details. By respecting this material in its entirety, you are sending a signal that you are ready to listen and learn.

Another way to help you remember dreams and also to dream more vividly is to make it a practice to meditate at least briefly before going to sleep. Breathe in and out calmly as you review the day's events, letting them settle down. Ask that you have wise and helpful dreams. Ask to remember them.

Understand the Alternative View

Freud called dreams the royal road to the unconscious. And dreams are a powerful tool for getting in touch with aspects of ourselves that normally remain hidden. One of the things that makes dreams a royal road is that they have built-in safeguards. If you are not ready to confront certain unconscious contents, then you will forget the dream.

While you may encourage yourself to remember your dreams, you should not force the process. If you have tried unsuccessfully to encourage dream memory, back off a little bit or take a break from doing dream work for a couple of weeks before gently trying again. Do not try to override the safety feature.

Freud believed dreams always contain a hidden wish. The wish is hidden in such a way that you have to decode the dream to find it. He was especially fond of finding hidden sexual wishes in dreams—which may tell us more about Freud and his time than it does about dreams. While it is sometimes true that dreams contain wishes, and while it may be worth inquiring into what wish a dream may contain, it seems forced to try to view every dream that way. Similarly, while sexuality is a vital and important aspect of our humanity, it is overly reductive to view every dream in this light.

To understand how a dream might represent a wish, consider that the outcome of the dream plot may in some way be desirable to you, even if it is something you would normally say was not desirable or even awful. For example, a young woman client was overly close with her mother. She said her mother was absolutely wonderful, and she never voiced the slightest negative feeling about her. One night she dreamed that her mother died in a horrible auto accident. This dream contained the young woman's aggression and hostility to her mother, of which she was totally unaware. At first, she resisted this interpretation fiercely. But eventually, she came to accept it, and with her acceptance, she came to a more realistic view of her mother. Her relationship with her mother improved, becoming less one of dependency and enmeshment, and more realistic and mature.

Jung felt that dreams try to communicate their meaning clearly and directly. He repeatedly quoted the Talmud, that "the dream is its own interpretation." We find this assumption more helpful. The symbolic language of dreams is a natural one. Intriguingly, people have sometimes been able to understand dreams under hypnosis that they do not understand otherwise. It is true that when we are awake, we do not always understand the symbolic language that dreams speak. But if a dream's purpose is to help us get acquainted with ourselves, to move us in the direction of wholeness, why would a dream then disguise itself?

Jung's view is both broader and more compelling than Freud's. The main thing to understand about dreams, according to Jung, is that *dreams are a complementation or compensation for conscious attitudes of the dreamer.* In other words, our conscious awareness is often one-sided in some way. One-sided awareness causes problems in our lives if it is not corrected. Dreams provide this correction to the limitations of the conscious point of view. Thus a man who underestimates his father may have a dream in which his father is twenty feet tall. A woman who rigidly denies validity to anything spiritual may have dreams full of numinous symbols and images. One can only understand these images, however, with reference to the conscious attitude of the dreamer. Dreams may also complement our conscious attitudes by representing an unacceptable wish, but that is only one way of many.

In trying to understand a dream, the first thing to ask is, *How is the content of this dream different from the way I usually see things, or from the way I have been seeing things lately? In what way does it correct some kind of one-sidedness in me?*

This is an important principle. If you have a dream, and you think that you already know what it means, you are probably wrong. This is not because the dream is trying to disguise its meaning, as Freud maintained, but because we tend to interpret dreams in terms of what we already believe. The challenge of working with dreams is to be open to a different point of view—one that, in its own way, is as valid as the way we usually see things. If you have a tendency to see yourself in a critical light, beware of interpreting dreams as critical. You are probably just seeing them in terms of the same old conscious attitude. On the other hand, if you tend to see the world in self-aggrandizing ways, take a closer look at dream images that seem only to duplicate this point of view. Try to be open to another way of seeing things.

The mythologist Joseph Campbell said that myths are public dreams and dreams are private myths. This means that dreams come from the same place in us that myth comes from. They originate in the part of us that thinks, not in terms of Aristotelian logic and rational syllogisms, but in terms of *story* and *symbol*. Jung's work with dreams shows that they often bear close relationship with myth (and myth with dreams, for that matter). To mention just one example, the circle is a universal symbol of wholeness or completeness. Understanding this, one becomes alert to round objects in dream material, using this knowledge of the general meaning of the sacred circle or mandala as a background against which to understand our own individual dreams.

THE EXPERIENCE (BEVERLY)

Some years back, I had received a promotion to a position that was to turn out to be an improvement, but a job that I would ultimately leave within a short period of time. But I was temporarily very pleased.

However, I dreamt that I was riding on the tail of a kite, along with my supervisor and my coworkers. I was flying high, but was certainly in a precarious position. This dream was clearly warning me to be careful of my inflated happy feelings about my new position. The dream was correct. ∽

Become Aware of the Symbols

Dreams speak the language of *symbols*. When we begin working with dreams, we have to learn this language. The meaning of dreams seems concealed or hidden only because we don't know the language. The circle, as mentioned above, is a universal symbol. But many symbols are more personal. An example would be the woman who dreams she is drowning while her husband is trying unsuccessfully to take her photograph. In other words, the dream is saying something like, "I'm in a struggle for my life, I can't breathe, and he doesn't get the picture."

Jung made a helpful distinction between symbols and signs. A sign is something that just stands in the place of something else, as the word *lake* stands for the body of water. When we say the word *lake*, we know clearly what is intended. A symbol, on the other hand, can never be fully explicated or understood. We can say, for example that the word *God* is symbol of wholeness and transcendence. But we have not thereby expressed everything that *God* means. God is ultimately ineffable.

Because of the symbolic nature of dreams, you should not approach dream interpretation allegorically, as though each element stood literally and specifically for something else. Since symbols do not simply stand in the place of some other thing, it is not usually helpful to try to decode a dream by looking it up in a dream book. For one thing, the meaning of a symbol is something that points beyond itself, as the word *God* does not literally point to an old man with a beard up in the sky, but something transcendent and ineffable, beyond comprehension. For another thing, as in the drowning woman's dream, the symbols may also be personal rather than universal. To understand such symbols, you need to know a lot about the dreamer's life and situation—variables that no dream book can capture.

To keep from getting lost in working with a dream, always remember that a dream *complements* your conscious attitude in some way. A dream tries to give you an alternative point of view, one that completes what is lacking in your conscious awareness. In some way, every dream is a challenge. If you interpret a dream only in terms of what you already know and believe and understand, look more deeply. Remember that dream language is symbolic, not literal. It is not a matter of substituting one thing for another thing. For this reason, the meaning of a dream retains a "something like this" or "as if" quality. It is not literally saying that the husband cannot take a photograph, but something like, "He doesn't get the picture; he doesn't see."

Dreams and Mindfulness

Working with dreams is a powerful way of bringing mindfulness to aspects of ourselves and our lives that we may not otherwise acknowledge, bringing new vitality and wholeness. We suggest approaching dreams as a mindfulness practice rather than as an intellectual puzzle. While the meaning of some dreams will become clear, some will remain mysterious. Whether dreams are understood or not, it is helpful to work with them, to hold them in mindful, meditative awareness as you would other important parts of your life and experience. If you try too hard to figure dreams out and press that knowledge into the service of your conscious self, the unconscious may retreat before the violent, grasping attitude of such an approach. But if you approach dreams with gentleness, patience, persistence, and respect, they will bless you.

How to Work with Dreams

Here are twenty ways in which to work with dreams to understand and integrate their message. When you work with a dream, you might like to review this list and try a few of these approaches. You will probably never want to do all of them with one dream.

1. Maintain a receptive attitude: *Respect, don't dissect*. This is essential. Take a meditative attitude. Do not try to force meaning to emerge. Do not try to decode anything. Just hold the dream in awareness and see what comes. If you try to force an interpretation, your effort will be frustrating and, most likely, incorrect.

2. In working with your own dream or another's, first say, "This is a wonderful dream." This is not an empty ritual, but a way of cultivating the proper attitude. To contact dreams is to contact the deep wisdom in us. Jung said: "Together the patient and I address ourselves to the 2-million-year-old man that is in all of us. In the last analysis, most of our difficulties come from losing contact with our instincts, with the age-old unforgotten wisdom stored up in us. And where do we make contact with this old man in us? In our dreams."

3. Write the dream down in detail. This is already a gesture of respect for the dream. Also, those odd little details and aspects that

don't quite fit often contain important meanings. If you have a dream about your mother, but the color of her hair is wrong, this is important. It may mean something like, "This dream is about my mother but not literally her; it is about her and also more than her." Or it may be about both your mother and whomever you think of when you consider that hair color, or about women in general, or about motherhood in general.

4. Associate to each element in the dream. After writing out the dream, list each element in the dream—the setting of the dream, the characters in the dream, the basic elements of plot, and any objects in the dream. For each element, ask yourself, "What does this bring to mind?" Record your thoughts. Often it will not be the first thing you think of that unlocks the meaning. Or describe what that thing is as if you were describing it to someone who came from another planet. For example, if a dentist appears in a dream, ask: What is a dentist? You might answer, Someone who drills, someone who pulls teeth, and so on. Notice if any of these associations and descriptions bring the feeling of rightness, of "Aha!"

Keep coming back to the dream itself, rather than associating to your associations. For example, if there's a dog in the dream, and this makes you think of that time you were walking on the beach with your dog, don't then go on to ask what that walk on the beach makes you think of in turn. Keep coming back to the original dream element. What does the dog make me think of? What else does the dog make me think of? What is a dog? And so forth.

5. Meditate on the dream. Hold the dream as a whole, or some aspect of the dream that feels important, in your awareness. Breathe in and out, just being present to this, exploring what it feels like, not trying to figure anything out. Welcome whatever comes. If nothing comes, welcome that.

6. Retell the story in general terms. For example, if you have a dream about having dinner with Ted Kennedy, this becomes, "I'm sitting down to eat with a powerful person." If you dream that you leave your purse somewhere, and you associate "purse" with personal identity, since it contains your wallet and identification, you can retell the story as, "It's as if I left my identity behind somewhere." In what way might your life be like that?

7. Give the dream a title. Doing this after you have written the dream out in full can help focus you on what stands out most about the dream. It also provides a convenient handle for the dream when you look back through your dream journal, without having to read the whole dream again every time.

8. Ask: In what way are things something like this with me these days? What part of me or my life is this like? See what comes up. Wait a bit with the question. Don't force it.

9. Beware interpretations you already know. Remember, a dream should challenge you in some way. Why would the unconscious send a message about what you already know?

10. Consider the conscious awareness of the dreamer. A dream is a complement to consciousness, so start with how things are feeling to the dreamer consciously these days. How does the dream point at something different from that?

11. Beware of interpretations that are overly self-serving or overly self-punishing. If you tend to excuse yourself too much from responsibility, or if you see yourself in grandiose terms, you may tend to interpret your dreams the same way. Consider the possibility that the dream may contain a message that shows you in a more realistic light. Conversely, if you tend to view yourself in too critical a manner, beware interpretations that just continue this trend. Be alert for something different. For example, if someone dreams of a voice from the heavens saying "Thou art Zeus," it makes a difference who the dreamer is. If the dreamer is shy and self-critical, the dream may mean that he underestimates himself. He is more powerful than he knows and even has divine attributes. On the other hand, if the dreamer is overconfident or arrogant, the dream may reflect a dangerous inflation that could bring the dreamer into great difficulties.

12. Pay attention to the body as you work with your dreams. You may be able to feel in your body what the dream is about long before you have an intellectual, verbal understanding of the dream. When your ideas about the dream are at least partly right, the body sense of the dream will ease and loosen, letting you know you are on target. Sometimes you will sigh a little and feel a slight release of tension when you touch on something important and have had a shift in your insight.

13. Consider the dream in the context of a series of dreams. It is common not to have an immediate understanding of what a dream means. But some dreams are obviously connected thematically. As you look back through your dream journal, using the titles to guide you, you can trace the development of the symbols in the dream. For example, a client had a series of dreams about the rock star Bruce Springsteen. His associations suggested that he represents a certain youthful, vital, rebellious energy. When he dreamed of having dinner with Bruce, but being at another and rather distant table, the dream was telling him something like: "I am too far from my youthful energy. I need to connect with it in some way." But if in another dream, the Springsteen element were in charge, then given what he stands for to this person, he should be careful. The rebellious, adolescent part of us is wonderful in many ways, but it is not always the best part to allow to make major decisions!

14. Tell someone your dream. Writing down a dream is powerful, but telling someone else can be even more so. Sometimes you don't understand a dream at all, but as you begin to tell it, you have an "Aha!"

15. Work actively with the dream. Sit with paper and pen and reenter the dream atmosphere. Feel the story. See if the dream seems to want to continue in some way. If it does, let it. Record what happens. Try to let the dream unfold without making it go a certain way.

Or focus on an important character in the dream. Just be with her, breathing in and out, feeling her presence. Let her speak and write down what she says. Ask questions and record the answers. Interact with her in full accord with your normal, waking attitudes and perspectives.

You might draw the dream. Paint a significant object or person or scene. It does not matter if you have no artistic talent. In fact in some ways, if you don't, all the better. For then you may have more of those fortunate accidents that reveal more than you initially are aware of. Some say that if a dreamer starts moving his hands while describing a dream, this means that the dream wants to be drawn.

Sometimes when you are stumped in working with a dream, the minute you start to work actively with it, you get a feeling of understanding. Working actively is one of the most important things to do with a dream, and will often be more helpful than trying to figure a dream out intellectually.

16. Change your body position. Doing so helps us change our mental perspective. If you feel stuck, move to another chair. Or lie on the floor. Or think about the dream as you go for a walk. If you have a dialogue with a dream character, sit in one chair when you are speaking, and sit in another when the character speaks.

17. Ritually enact the dream message in some way. Robert Johnson cites the example of a man who is warned in a dream about his unhealthy penchant for fast food. The fast food is not only literal, but also symbolic of activities that do not nourish the dreamer. To enact the dream ritually, he bought his favorite fast-food meal, and buried it in the back yard, symbolically putting it away from himself.

A ritual enactment should be a small, symbolic act. If you dream about India, you do not need to spend your life savings to go there. Perhaps read something about India or talk to someone from there.

If a dream indicates you should be in contact with your inner child, you may want to finger paint, play on the swings at the park, sit on the floor with your old dolls or erector set, and so forth. Just see what feels right.

18. Ask yourself what your dream may be about. Could it be about:
- something that happened yesterday?
- the place the dream occurs in? the story? the characters?
- some aspect of me? which?
- my body or my health?
- childhood issues?
- personal growth? spirituality? issues of meaning or faith?
- an unacceptable wish of some sort?
- sexuality?
- work or career?
- relationships?
- money?

19. Take the bodily shift into your body again and again. For example, if you contact a part of yourself in a dream that is self-assured, and you want to feel more like that in waking life, imagine what it would be like to be that person—what it would feel like in your body. See if you can call up that feeling several times as you work with the dream, and again at different times during the day.

20. Learn about mythology, religion, and other sources that might be useful for understanding dream symbols. Jung called this process *amplification*. And while few of us can be expected to have the sort of encyclopedic knowledge that Jung had in this area, whatever you can learn is helpful.

Be Patient with Your Dream Work

Above all, approach dream work with patience. You can get better at it. But you must not be in a rush. Since it is like learning a new language, you know you must go at it one step at a time. With more and more experience of the language, you will of course increase your ability to understand. Jung estimated that he worked with two thousand dreams a year for the many years of his career. It is from this broad experience that he was able to interpret dreams so well. As you gain experience with dream material, you will get better at it, too. Take the attitude that to remember and record a dream and work with it in some way is already a wonderful practice, even if you do not yet have much intellectual understanding of the dream.

Although it is best to work actively with dream contents, dream theory can prevent us from getting lost. You can benefit from the work of those who have studied dreams extensively. Below we outline some universal themes and ideas from Jung's work that can help orient you.

Identify the Archetypes

An archetype is a primal pattern. Jung used the word to indicate dream characters and situations that are universal to human beings. He wrote: "The archetype is an inherited tendency of the human mind to form representations of mythological motifs—representations that vary a great deal without losing their basic pattern. There are, for instance, numerous representations of the motif of the hostile brothers, but the motif remains the same."

Think of an archetype as a kind of container, to be filled in by individual experience. Take the mother archetype, for example. This is a universal theme. As Jung sees it, we are born with a tendency to experience life in terms of such categories. The categories, however, must be filled and activated by our personal experience and history. So while we all understand the category of mother, it makes some difference whether our actual mother is loving or distant, warm or cold, blonde or brunette, or if we have no direct experience of mothering at all. Archetypal aspects refer to that which is universal, which is common to all human beings. Individual experience colors in the archetype. Just as it makes a difference whether you fill a gallon jug with water, wine, or Kool-Aid, so individual experience will influence how we perceive and deal with archetypal material. However, the general shape of the liquid will be the same, always being that of the jug, regardless of what fluid it contains.

Jung felt there are as many archetypes as there are typical human experiences and situations. One could, for example, talk about the archetype of fording a stream. In practice, however, Jung only identified archetypes that he discovered to exist with great regularity in dreams. So in a practical sense, archetypes generally refer to a limited number of types of characters and situations.

Encounter the Characters of Your Dreams

At the beginning of a play, there is a list of all of the characters who appear in it. Some of the more common and important archetypes resemble just such a list of characters. Especially relevant here are the archetypes of anima, animus, shadow, and wise old man or woman.

These archetypes are strong psychological forces. They are in themselves neither good nor evil, but both and neither. These personalities are *numinous* and *autonomous*. That is to say, these characters have a divine, awe-inspiring quality. When you encounter them in anything close to pure form, you know they are not to be trifled with. They have potential to bless and heal, but also to harm and lead astray. And even though in some sense they are aspects of us, it is best to think of them, from any practical perspective, as separate beings. At least you should not imagine that you can control them. They are forces of nature, and they should be held in the kind of respect with which you regard an ocean storm, a hurricane, or a bolt of lightning.

Anima and Animus

Jung believed that we all, both men and women, have qualities that could be labeled feminine and qualities that could be labeled masculine. A man in any given culture learns to accept those parts of himself that fit his masculine role, and to repress those aspects that, because of their feminine character, do not fit his conscious identity. These repressed aspects are forced into the unconscious, where they coalesce around the archetype of the anima. Similarly, in women, unacceptably masculine traits are repressed and coalesce in the unconscious around the archetype of the animus. (The word *anima* is Latin for soul; *animus* is the masculine form.)

When a man begins to remember his dreams, one of the first figures to appear is the figure of the unknown woman, the anima. The anima can provide important guidance. Contact with her moves a man in the direction of wholeness, of androgyny in place of one-sided masculinity. Likewise, being in touch with the animus brings a woman into completeness, helping her become whole by integrating her masculine aspects.

Integration of a woman's animus or a man's anima into conscious awareness is very important. To understand why, take the case of romantic love from a Jungian perspective. In the ancient Greek myth, human beings were once round (read: "whole, complete") but were split in two by a jealous god. Ever since then, we have been looking for our soul mate, our other half, who will complete us and restore us to wholeness. The popularity of books about soul mates demonstrates the power of this mythic point of view. From a psychological perspective, a man falls in love by projecting his anima onto a woman. A woman falls in love by projecting her animus onto a man. The real person is scarcely seen or known, so captivated are we by the anima or animus. This is a very important experience in the Western world, because it is one of the few doors that remain open to us for the spiritual experience of ecstasy.

However, falling in love in this way brings problems in its train. No flesh-and-blood human being can live up to a numinous archetype. No flesh-and-blood man can fully incarnate the animus, as no flesh-and-blood woman can incarnate the anima. This means that when we fall in love, disappointment lies in wait for us down the road unless we can successfully negotiate the transition from seeing the beloved archetypally to having a solid, human, nourishing, realistic, and down-to-earth relationship.

As a therapist, I hear the relatively candid and uncensored thoughts and feelings of men and women about each other. I am amazed at the disappointment and bitterness of women regarding men and of men regarding women. Since romantic love is one of the few ways our culture allows for spiritual, ecstatic experience, it takes on great importance in our lives—more importance, in fact, than it can actually bear. This raises expectations for relationships to an ever higher degree of impossibility and absurdity. This split between our expectations and reality can only be healed when we withdraw the projection by coming into relationship with our own anima or animus, allowing those we love to be real people, with faults and foibles, rather than gods and goddesses who magically make everything easy and wonderful.

One of the most important practices in dream work is getting acquainted with your animus or anima. Once these figures appear, you can foster a relationship with them by working with them actively, talking with them, and drawing and painting them. Such work heals the split in ourselves so we in turn can heal the split in our relationships, ending the bitterness of overexpectation.

Become Acquainted with Your Shadow

The shadow is a part of ourselves that we view from a conscious perspective as weak or inferior and that we therefore push out of awareness into the unconscious. The shadow is not evil per se, though sometimes we think of it that way since it is incompatible with our ideals and aspirations. Shadow figures generally appear as a person of the same sex as the dreamer.

Sometimes the shadow appears in a dream literally as one who follows or "shadows" us as we move. The shadow generally exhibits qualities that contradict our cherished views of ourselves. If consciously we take pride in our intellect and learning, our shadow may appear as a drooling idiot. If we take pride in our physical appearance, being thin and beautiful, the shadow appears as someone who is misshapen, deformed, fat, or ugly.

When the shadow appears in our dreams, we usually are not pleased at first. In fact, we are often disturbed by such visitations. We may want to interpret such a figure as pertaining to someone else, someone we have conflict with or dislike in some way. But actually, a visitation by the shadow, however disturbing, is something to embrace. Integrating shadow aspects into our conscious awareness is very healing. For one thing, the psychological energy we have used to repress acquaintance with this aspect of ourselves is liberated. Coming to terms with the shadow frees creativity and vitality. And as the process of integrating shadow content unfolds, the shadow itself undergoes positive transformation. In *Beauty and the Beast*, the Beast is revealed as the prince he really is when Beauty loves him. Such transformations happen often in dreams when we accept parts of ourselves that we previously rejected.

In Buddhist legend, Mara is the evil tempter, the spirit of illusion, who tried to prevent the Buddha from achieving enlightenment. Significantly, even after the Buddha's awakening, Mara continued to visit him from time to time. Do you know what the Buddha did when Mara came to visit? The Buddha greeted him as an old friend and invited him in to tea!

Contact Your Wise Old Man/Wise Old Woman

The first things to surface in dreams are aspects of us and our lives that are difficult or disturbing in some way. This is usually the first layer to become conscious, because these are the aspects that need to come to the light of conscious awareness to be healed and integrated before anything else of value can happen. Unfortunately, this means that many people give up on dreams or dismiss them as nonsense, since these images are disturbing.

But for those who persist, treasure awaits. One such treasure is the figure of the wise person—generally of the same sex as the dreamer. When such figures appear, you will naturally want to seek more contact with them. You can talk to them and benefit in many ways from their wisdom. They are, in fact, your own wiser, inner self.

Work with Your Dream Characters

Once you have learned about anima, animus, shadow, and the wise old man or woman, you may be tempted to feel that you have said something important by labeling these dream figures when they appear. "Oh, I know what this is—it's just my anima up to her tricks!" But don't do this. Remember, these are forces of nature. If a funnel cloud is coming your way, you would not just say to yourself, "Oh, that's just a tornado," and then go about your business! These characters are to be dealt with, interacted with, respected, and, as much as possible, understood and valued for the gifts that they bring.

Jung made the mistake early in his explorations of considering such dream figures as infallible, crediting them with a wisdom in all ways superior to that of the conscious mind. He later revised this opinion, concluding that the perspective of the conscious self and that of the unconscious are of *equal* importance. Each has an important role to play in the ecology of the psyche.

We can benefit from Jung's experience. While unconscious figures may dazzle us with their wisdom and insight, we should not abandon our conscious viewpoint quickly. If Madame Anima advises you to take a course of action that runs contrary to the moral point of view of your conscious self, do not be too easily persuaded. When you dialogue with her, fully represent your conscious feelings and reactions to her point of view. The conscious mind is a precious gift of evolution and should be respected as a fully equal partner in such exchanges. The process of moving toward wholeness works best when both the conscious and the unconscious mind do their full part.

Look beyond the Personal

While on the one hand, it is absurd, given the personal nature of dreams, to think that you can profitably work with them by simply looking up their contents in a dream book, on the other hand, since dreams do come not just from our individual selves, but also from that in us that is collectively human, there are some regularities in dream symbols and motifs.

Look for Circles and Squares

Be alert for round objects and square objects in dreams. These might not be immediately obvious or emphasized in the dream material. For example, a hat may be a representation of a circle. A city laid out in a square shape may be a similar symbol, or a square-shaped peanut-butter-and-jelly sandwich.

Jung used the Sanskrit term *mandala* in describing such dream symbols. Mandalas are common in Eastern spiritual practices. A mandala is a sacred circle or square that demarcates sacred space. These are healing symbols in dreams, representing wholeness, the harmonious tension among and integration of opposites. Such symbols often emerge in dreams when we are under stress, and represent the possibility of resolution of the conflict in a new pattern of wholeness and well-being.

The circle tends to indicate unconscious wholeness; the square generally represents a more conscious wholeness.

Explore the Transformation of Dream Characters

Aspects of ourselves that we deny and run from come back at us with increased energy. For example, if you are pursued in a dream by an aggressive dog, this may represent part of yourself that you have disowned and that needs to be reclaimed and integrated. As you interact with this part by speaking with it, arguing with it, forming an alliance with it, or fighting it, you bring this aspect into a new relationship with your conscious self. Often this aspect then transforms in future dreams into something less threatening. For example, I once had a dream about being pursued by a crocodile. After working with this material and interacting with it actively, in subsequent dreams the crocodile changed itself into cuddly, cute, friendly little puppies that ran playfully after me.

In fairy tales, when the princess kisses the frog, he is transformed into a handsome prince—his true nature or Buddhahood. Transformation is the "kissing frogs" aspect of dream work. When we embrace the aspects and energies of ourselves that we find least acceptable, they become handsome princes, revealing their true nobility and beauty.

Jung studied medieval alchemy for what it revealed about processes of psychological transformation. Ostensibly aimed at transforming base materials into gold, Jung saw in alchemy a symbolic representation of change, transformation, and wholeness that was less about literal gold and more about the transformation of ourselves. Alchemical symbols emerge in dreams when we are undergoing transformation. For example, if the color gold or yellow occurs, this may symbolize the culmination of a transformative process. Since gold was viewed as connected with the sun, symbols and images directly and indirectly connected with the sun may have similar meaning. Crocodiles, for example, were worshipped in Egypt as divine beings connected with the sun god Ra. Of course, not every instance of the color gold will have this meaning. But you should be alert to such a possibility.

Look at the Meaning of Journeys

Life itself is a journey. When we think of journeying, it may evoke older images of people on pilgrimage, setting out on foot for distant, sacred places. In such a context, the meaning is clear to us. We can sense the meaning of such a theme. Be prepared, however, that the unconscious may borrow more modern versions of this motif. Instead of setting out on foot with a pack on your back and a wooden staff in your hand, you may dream about taking planes and trains or driving in your car.

Explore Water as the Boundary
of the Unconscious

Water is the source of life. We are made mostly of water and we are born out of water. The rite of baptism, for example, connotes birth as a spiritual being.

Water in dreams also often stands for the boundary between conscious and unconscious aspects. This is probably one of the reasons the Egyptians revered crocodiles, since they dwell on the boundary between water and air, and can live on both water and land. Towns along the shore have a similar meaning. The sea or ocean tends to mean the unconscious; a river connotes movement of energy, as in the "stream of life."

Find Hidden Puns

Sometimes when you record a dream or describe it to someone, it becomes clear to you that dreams often employ visual or verbal puns. For example, I worked with a man whose wife had died. He was quite angry with her for leaving him. In a dream, his deceased wife smeared feces all over his bathroom walls. The meaning of the dream "clicked" when he described his wife's death as a "dirty trick" she had played on him.

Transform the Animals

Animals represent instinctive energies that are necessary to maintain vitality and creativity. If we get overly civilized or restrained, our dreams may try to heal this imbalance by connecting us with animal figures. If the animals in a dream are threatening, developing a relationship with them can transform them into less threatening images. Eventually they may become human, showing that we have "humanized" this energy or taken it up into our human life in some way.

Schools, Tests, and Exams

Sometimes we revisit schools we attended, or we have dreams of taking tests or exams, perhaps not feeling prepared for them. Behind such images is that sense that life itself is a form of education, with its own tests and exams. Such dreams indicate that, from the perspective of the unconscious, it is not mere words when we say things like, "Life is a learning experience."

Trees as a Symbol

Trees are a rich symbol. You might think, for example, of the Tree of Life in the Garden of Eden. The appearance of a tree in a dream may indicate a new life or a rebirth. Eating fruit from a tree may be a reference to the "forbidden fruit" on the Tree of the Knowledge of Good and Evil. This may refer to sexuality, but it can also be much broader—an expansion of conscious awareness.

Children: A Dream's Symbol for New Beginnings

Children may, of course, simply be themselves, particularly if they are children who are important in your daily life. But they can also symbolize anything new or young in our lives. For example, a child of five may symbolize a business venture or marriage or anything else that is about five years old. If an unknown five-year-old appears in a dream, ask yourself what began in your life about five years ago.

Cross Rivers and Borders

Such symbols show entering a new area or phase of life, a transition. Ask yourself in what way you have entered new territory in your life, whether internally or psychologically or externally.

Recognize the Divine

Whatever one's beliefs about God's existence, God is a psychological fact, an archetype. That is why all cultures have some notion of a god or gods, which they in some cases even arrived at independently. From a Jungian perspective, the archetype of God is the equivalent of the archetype of the self, of all that we are, of wholeness.

The psyche is polytheistic. Dreams show many divine and quasi-divine beings as having psychological reality.

Of course, symbols always have to be understood contextually—in the context of what is happening in the life of the dreamer. But when such universal symbols appear, it is worth considering whether the symbols have a collective, universal meaning.

Value Synchronicity

Western science focuses on causal relationships between events. Jung's work with dreams, on the other hand, led him to believe that some events are connected in a different but equally meaningful way—in an acausal way. In *Memories, Dreams, Reflections*, Jung relates that a solid walnut table suddenly split with a deafening crack. It was difficult to explain this, since it was a summer day in a relatively humid climate, and the old table did not split at a joint or crack. Two weeks later, a parallel event occurred. A bread knife that had recently been used and put away in a cupboard suddenly and loudly split into several pieces. Jung took it to a cutlery specialist, who told him the metal was sound, and someone must have been pulling his leg. Jung does not attempt to explain these events, except to say that their co-occurrence was not accidental.

Jung has been criticized for such ideas. To scientists, such things sound like hocus-pocus. To spiritualists, Jung's objective analysis does not make enough of such occurrences. But when you work with dreams regularly, synchronicity becomes a familiar experience. Not too long ago I had a dream about a particular kind of a plant held in a horizontal position. I drew it the best I could in my dream journal, but did not recognize the plant and could make nothing of its appearance in my dream. That evening on the news there was a piece about cocaine traffic in Colombia. It included an image of a man holding a coca plant in his hand in a horizontal position, the same plant in the same position in which I had drawn it that morning. Immediately, the dream image clicked. I showed the image to Beverly to ask her what it reminded her of, and she, too, was reminded by my drawing of the image we had just seen on television. If you are aware, you will have many such things happen.

The subject of synchronicity raises more questions than it answers. An individual experience like that of the coca plant could perhaps be explained in other ways. But when such events occur fairly often, they become increasingly difficult to explain away or rationalize. Whatever such things ultimately mean, they at least indicate that there is a kind of knowingness in dreams that goes beyond our normal ways of knowing. We are interconnected with the world in ways beyond what we can logically understand.

Know Yourself

While the dream world operates under very different principles than our waking life, and while it can be a strange, confusing, and even at times terrifying realm, it can also bless and guide you greatly. If you do not know your dreams, you do not know yourself.

Practice for Week Seven

1. Continue to practice meditation (twenty minutes twice daily), mindful moments, daily reading, and walking meditation (chapter 3).
2. Begin to record and work with your dreams, using the suggestions and ideas in this chapter. If you do not always have the time in the morning to work with a dream, at least jot some quick notes to jog your memory. Then record it more fully later in the day.
3. Continue to practice a day of mindfulness (chapter 5).
4. There's a lot of information in this chapter. If it is largely new, you may want to read it several times as you work with your dreams this week.

Week Eight

TRANSFORM NEGATIVE EMOTIONS

The highest form of worship is simply to be happy.
—Anonymous Hindu saint

Sadness and Worry: Barbara's Story

Barbara was devastated. She hadn't seen it coming. She thought everything was fine. In fact, since everyone had praised her work, she had begun to wonder when she would get a raise.

But today her boss said he had to let her go.

The company was not doing well. Since she had been the most recently hired, she was the first to go. He appreciated her; he promised extremely good references. They would send her four weeks' pay.

Barbara was stunned. On the drive home, she struggled to take it in. The company had seemed to be doing well. All the trappings of success were there. The office suite was impressive, the furnishings custom designed. Everyone wore the best clothes. Yes, she had noticed that the number of clients had dropped off. But since she had only been there four months, she thought this was probably just the natural ebb and flow of the business. And about a month ago, her boss had a pained look when he said her paycheck would be a couple of days late. But she believed him when he explained it was just a banking error and that it would be straightened out.

By the time she reached the door of her apartment, the difficult news had grown into a full-fledged disaster. "This is horrible!" she told herself. "It took me four weeks to get a job last time. And even then, I felt lucky. I may not even *find* another job! What if I end up on the street?" As she stared blankly into her empty refrigerator, her vague premonition of doom became utter certainty. She was convinced that she would never find work again. She envisioned herself homeless, pushing a shopping cart with her few possessions around the dirty city streets.

Barbara closed the door of her refrigerator and opened the large bottle of red wine on the counter. Several glasses later, as she sat dazed in her living room, no food in her stomach, the day's disaster became proof positive of her worthlessness. It did not matter that this didn't make any sense. "I'm just no good at anything," she thought. She continued to sit and drink as the winter light faded in her dark apartment. When her best friend called, she let the machine answer. Mercifully, at some point, she just fell asleep.

Learn the Lessons

Barbara deserves our sympathy. Being suddenly terminated from employment is hard to bear. And while her reactions were not constructive, they are thoroughly understandable. Her job was important to her, and losing it would hurt financially. She faced the prospect of weeks, perhaps months, of job hunting.

And yet while we sympathize, it is also easy to see that Barbara did not do much that evening to help herself. Long before her firing, she had refused to notice the negative signs at the office. She had indulged herself in expectations of quick salary increases that raised her hopes unrealistically and made her termination feel like that much more of a fall. As the news slowly sank in, she nourished her own hysteria. What was a bad situation now became a total disaster. Instead of taking care of herself by talking with her friend, she shut herself off and ignored the phone call. Worse still, she engaged in a mild self-poisoning by overindulging in wine.

We all may be overwhelmed from time to time. We all may sometimes make it worse by refusing to do constructive things and choosing destructive things instead. To criticize ourselves for these tendencies is not helpful; nor do we want to criticize Barbara. But what can we learn from her experience?

For one thing, Barbara focused on the external problem without realizing her immediate need for self-care. She worked herself into a state of near panic. She cultivated and exaggerated the negative elements of her situation. For example, she convinced herself that the difficult task of finding work would be all but impossible. She also cut herself off from positive elements, such as a nourishing meal or a call from a friend. And at least to this point in the story, she did not do anything to change what could be changed.

Reflection on this pattern tells us a lot about what helps when something triggers a negative emotional state. The things that help us cope with negative situations and the emotions they elicit are quite different from the things Barbara did. First, we need to recognize that we are suffering and that we need to take care of our emotions. We need to find a way to calm body and mind. We need to reflect and look deeply into the causes of our suffering. We also need to find ways to nurture ourselves and take constructive action.

Let's take a look at these elements.

Recognize the Need for Self-Care

Like many people, Barbara focused on the external situation. Since there was nothing she could do about it at the moment, this just made her more upset. The more she did this, the more upset she became. The more upset she became, the more she lost perspective. She continued to work herself into a negative mood, telling herself that she may never find work and may end up homeless.

When your house is on fire, the first thing to do is put it out. It is not a good time to stand around and complain or try to figure out what happened and who's to blame. When your emotions are on fire, you need to take care of them. Only then will you have perspective on what happened and what you need to do about it. Once you take care of the fire, you have already faced the hardest part.

You cannot deal all at once with a problem like finding work. There are many steps involved, and they have to be executed over a period of time. But if we take the first step of caring for our emotions, we will be able to find our way, one step at a time.

Calm the Feelings

We have talked a lot already about the importance of the breath. Both Buddhism and behavioral psychology use the breath for self-calming. Whenever you breathe in and out with awareness, you come back to yourself. Most of the time, mind and body are separated. The body is here, but the mind is off elsewhere, worrying, planning, ruminating, and scanning for trouble. When you breathe mindfully—even for just the span of one breath—you achieve oneness of body and mind for that period of time. Help is already there, just one conscious breath away.

It takes determination, however, to do this in the face of trouble or disappointment. Your relationship with your breath is like a relationship to a friend. If you have ignored a friend for a long time, you cannot expect her to be there for you when you suddenly need her. For conscious breathing to be a help to you in times of distress, you must have practiced it in times of relative calm. If you have practiced in the calm times, it will be there for you when you need it in the difficult times.

Calming yourself is not denial. In fact, it is the opposite. When sad feelings come up, you welcome them into your awareness. You just refuse to cultivate panic. Instead, breathing in and out, you calm these feelings, so that you can integrate them into your awareness. Hysteria and panic actually shut down and restrict awareness and therefore accomplish much the same thing as denial or repression.

Barbara was experiencing a significant change in her life through the loss of a promising position. It is not that she should be happy about this, or indifferent to her own distress. The goal of spiritual practice is not becoming insensate. But neither should she make it worse by working herself into a state of panic or hysteria. She may be thinking: "I've lost a job I was counting on. I feel sad and distressed. I am very disappointed that I will have to look for work again." All of that is realistic and reasonable. Breathing in and out, calming these thoughts and feelings, she can accommodate to this loss, and ready herself for the steps that will be needed to cope with her new circumstance.

There is no problem with acknowledging our disappointment, frustration, sadness, or anger when something happens that triggers these emotions. These are part of life, and even advanced Zen masters and spiritual teachers must contend with them. The problem arises when something else gets added. Often we go on to tell ourselves something extra and quite unnecessary—something perhaps a little like this: "I'm sad about this loss. *And it is absolutely terrible and horrible! This must not be so!*" In this way, we cultivate distress rather than calm and perspective.

What is it about us that loves to indulge in self-torture? There are certain moods in which we all but gleefully cultivate the rottenness of our own negativity. It may taste bitter, but at least it is our own bitterness, and we sit down to it, clanging knife and fork at the banquet of our own despair. Something hurtful or even tragic has happened. That is bad enough. That is *difficult* enough. But then we make this all so much worse. We cultivate thoughts of how unbearable it all is, how unfair. When we think like this, our bodies tighten and our breath becomes shallow. Our thoughts and feelings turn dark and despairing. In some cases, our despair even reaches the point of suicide.

You don't have to do this. You can be sad—even extremely so—without losing yourself in despair. And the first step, the key to all this, is to come to the breath.

When pain or loss strikes, first recognize that the immediate problem is not to fix the external situation, but to take care of your emotions. Come back to your old friend the breath. Breathe in and out. Do not fight with the sad feelings or struggle against them. It is enough at first just to avoid cultivating them or making them worse. Breathe in and out, and feel and experience the sadness.

Every experience of sadness connects with every other experience of sadness we have had. This means that sadness never comes as a stranger, but always as an old friend. Smile to your old friend. Calm the feelings. Investigate. How is it with this old friend of yours? What is your body like when you feel sad? How does your breath change? What happens to your mind? Breathe gently in and out, with full awareness, accepting and calming these feelings, and sadness need not become despair.

THE EXPERIENCE (TOM)

This is the second time I've written this section. Right in the midst of the first attempt, my computer froze. Zap! Several pages of unsaved work were gone. As self-pitying emotions welled up, I knew what I needed to do, especially since I was writing about negative emotions. I recognized my need to take care of my feelings, even before I tried to fix anything. In this way, I took care of myself before the emotions got out of hand. I practiced some conscious breathing, then calmly returned and started rewriting. No big deal.

I also began saving my work more often. ∾

Look Deeply at the Root of the Problem

While becoming calm is the critical first step in dealing with a negative mood, there is a second step. To heal pain, we must look deeply into it. How did this pain arise? What is its origin and cause? And how did we create or encourage it?

To gain this kind of insight, you must have calmness in yourself. Calmness and looking deeply are intimately connected, for it is impossible to look deeply if you are not calm. At the same time, if you are calm, you already begin to see more clearly.

Psychologists talk about three aspects of negative moods: what we feel (emotions), what we think (cognition), and what we do (behavior). Each of these influences the other:

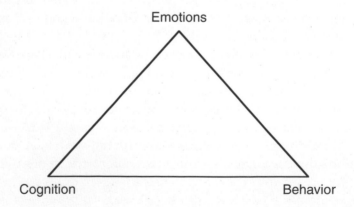

Our emotions influence our behavior and our thinking. Our thinking influences our emotions and our behavior. And our behavior influences our thinking and our emotions. While we cannot cause ourselves to instantly snap out of negative emotions or moods, there are two ways we can influence our emotions: by what we think, and by what we do.

Look Deeply at Your Thoughts

Looking deeply in a Buddhist context means seeing the pattern of how we distress ourselves. We distress ourselves because we try to make the impermanent permanent. We live as though our jobs, relationships, health, and life itself were permanent. For this reason, we suffer when something happens that reminds us of life's impermanence.

Psychology can also help us to look deeply. Cognitive treatment of depression, for example, is based on the premise that depressive thinking is always in some way distorted. In general, depressive thinking tends to exaggerate negative aspects and minimize positive aspects.

The psychiatrist David Burns, in his book *Feeling Good: The New Mood Therapy*, enumerates the following types of depressive distortions in thinking:

1. *All-or-nothing thinking.* This involves seeing things in a black-and-white manner. If your report card has an A in every subject but one, you feel like a failure.
2. *Overgeneralization.* You see one negative event as a never-ending pattern of failure and defeat. For example, you burn the dinner, then tell yourself, "I never do anything right."
3. *Mental filter.* You dwell on one negative detail to the exclusion of any positive aspects. For example, you look at a lovely landscape, but what you think about the most is the single beer can lying on the ground.
4. *Disqualifying the positive.* You find some way to insist that positive aspects are not as real or as important as negative ones. Barbara did this by discounting her employer's genuine appreciation, his offer to be a positive reference, and the four weeks' pay he sent her.
5. *Jumping to conclusions.* You make negative assumptions about things you could not really know for sure. Especially mind reading (assuming someone else is thinking or feeling something negative with-out checking it out) and fortune-telling (predicting negative events as though you had an infallible crystal ball). Barbara engaged in fortune-telling by assuming that it would take her a long time to find a job (it could happen tomorrow) and that she would

become homeless. Of course it might take a long time. But she also might find a job right away. Both traditional Buddhist teaching and cognitive psychology emphasize the uselessness of fortune-telling.

6. *Magnification (catastrophizing) and minimization.* You see things out of proportion, enlarging the importance of negative aspects, shrinking the importance of positive aspects. Barbara's labeling the whole situation as "horrible" is an example.

7. *Emotional reasoning.* Because you feel it, that must be the way things really are. Because you're sad, everything must really be terrible. Because you're angry, someone must have done something to cause it.

8. *"Should" statements.* You try to motivate yourself with self-punishing thoughts, especially statements involving shoulds and musts. The psychologist Albert Ellis says "don't should on me" and avoid "mental must-urbation."

9. *Labeling and mislabeling.* This is a form of overgeneralization. If you make a mistake, you're a "loser." If someone cuts you off on the road, he's a "jerk." Both of these reactions ignore other aspects of the person in question. Barbara labeled herself as "no good at anything," ignoring many positive abilities. (Notice that all you need for this statement to be wrong is just one area of ability.) It is better to see a mistake as just a mistake.

10. *Personalization.* You blame yourself for an event not primarily under your control. Barbara blamed her termination on herself, when in reality it was based on the company's overall business situation.

Don't Make It Worse

What all ten of these ways of thinking have in common is some element of distortion in the direction of a negative perception. Dr. Burns maintains that in his experience with depressed people, he has never encountered a case where some distortion in thinking was not involved. The Buddha said that where there is perception there is deception. It is always good to be aware that there can be some element of distortion in the way we see things.

People who are vulnerable to depression also have a stronger tendency than others to engage in upward comparison. Thus a person with millions of dollars compares himself to Bill Gates and feels poor; a woman who is very beautiful compares herself to supermodels and feels unattractive. Happier individuals engage in more downward comparison, seeing themselves as better off than many people. A woman who lives in a small apartment can compare herself to the homeless and still feel well off; and even a man with one leg can compare himself to those who have no legs. An added advantage to downward comparison is that it facilitates compassion, which in itself aids our mindfulness and deepens our spiritual presence.

Some pain and loss in life is inevitable. This is the first noble truth of the Buddha, the truth of suffering. We may try to forget or ignore this fact, but it remains the case. No matter how much recognition, success, wealth, or fame we achieve, suffering inevitably comes—at least as long as we try to fool ourselves that the impermanent is permanent. There is nothing new or startling about that, though it is a little startling how much we deny this reality. But what is truly startling is our capacity to make it worse.

If you are feeling sad, well-meaning people may tell you to just "snap out of it." Sometimes, you may even be able to do this. But if the sadness is deep, you will not be able to follow this advice. This is because we do not have direct control over our emotions. We cannot force ourselves to stop feeling sad, anxious, embarrassed, or ashamed any more than we can force ourselves to be happy, confident, peaceful, and at ease. Still, we are far from helpless in the face of such feelings. If we at least make the effort to calm them, that is already a miracle. Then if we can take the next step of looking into our thinking and see how we heap despair upon our sadness, we can go much further toward alleviating our pain.

Both Buddhism and psychology help us to be calm and to investigate our patterns dispassionately. So if we calm a sad feeling first, and then examine our thoughts, we can identify what we are telling ourselves about the situation that contributes to our distress. Cognitive psychology teaches that it is very helpful at this point to write it all down. Thoughts are fluid and elusive, and the act of writing gives us more of a handle on them. So write down what you are thinking. Go through the list above, and see how you are adding to your own pain unnecessarily. Then, as an additional step, cultivate more adaptive, constructive thinking. Mindfulness teaches us not to struggle with ourselves, so it is important that we do not do this in a way that creates internal warfare.

However, it is helpful to insert more positive, constructive thoughts into the stream of awareness.

Barbara's Story Continued

The day after Barbara was laid off, she was able to respond more constructively. She sat for a few minutes, breathing in and out, and was able to identify what she was telling herself that was increasing her pain. In particular, she found out that she was minimizing positive aspects and magnifying negative ones. She realized that she felt some relief about leaving this job. From the first, she had had misgivings about it being the right position for her. She also had exaggerated the financial consequences and the difficulty of finding work. She reminded herself of her strengths and that she always had been able to interview well and to find work, even if sometimes it took longer than she would have liked. She also discovered that by telling herself it was horrible, she was engaging in black-and-white thinking and magnifying the negative. Not everything about this was horrible. The break from work was welcome, even though she would have preferred to have a break without the threat to her financial security. It certainly was unrealistic to imagine herself on the street just yet!

Barbara wrote down what she was telling herself and identified the distortions in her thinking (minimizing positives and exaggerating negatives, all-or-nothing thinking, and so on). Then she went on to write some thoughts that were more constructive, without denying the reality. She wrote: "While this will be a financial setback for me, it is very unlikely that I will end up on the street. I may have to face the discomfort of calling my creditors and working with them on some late payments. And while that is no fun, it is not awful or terrible."

Barbara also noted that while her emotions did not shift dramatically in any immediate way, she already felt a little better. As part of her looking deeply, Barbara also worked with her dreams and identified a destructive pattern. She came to see that she had an unhealthy dependence that she did not like to admit, as though someone would somehow always rescue her. This prevented her from saving money so that she could take better care of herself in such emergencies. She vowed, as a practical step, that she would begin a regular practice of saving—even small amounts—as soon as she was employed again.

～ PRACTICE ～

Challenge Depressive Thinking

Take out a blank sheet of paper. Close your eyes, letting your body and your mind relax, and take a few conscious breaths. Turn the paper to a horizontal position, so it is wider than it is long, and draw three columns. Label them *Situation*, *Thinking*, and *Rebuttal*.

Now remember an occasion when you felt very sad, but that you at least suspect contained some element of exaggeration or distortion. In your mind's eye, allow yourself to reexperience the event. Bring it all back in detail. Recall what you saw, heard, touched, and if relevant, tasted and smelled. Recall what you were thinking or telling yourself internally. Notice how your body feels as you remember these details.

In the first column, describe the event that made you sad *objectively*. That is, write it in such a way that a person watching it from the outside who had no emotional investment in what was happening would agree with your description.

In the second column, record your thoughts. Now rest again for a few moments, breathing in and out consciously.

As you reconsider what you have written, can you see that there is no necessity between what you wrote in the first column and how you interpreted these events in the second column? Remember, where there is perception, there is deception. See if you can create a little space, a little wriggle room, between the event and your thoughts about it.

Now go through the list of ten distortions on pages 157 and 158, and try to identify those that apply. If you need help or get stuck, ask a trusted friend to give some input. Write the label of that type of thinking next to your thought.

Finally, in the third column, write a rational rebuttal. This should be a thought that simply makes sense, not something overly optimistic. Again, ask someone for help if you need it.

For example, Barbara wrote in her first column that she was laid off because of a downturn in the company business. Notice that this description is objective and does not include emotional language. In the second column, one of her thoughts was that she would become a homeless person. She labeled this appropriately as "fortune-telling," and then wrote in her third column: "I really don't know how this will turn out. While it is possible I could become homeless, that doesn't really seem very likely. For all I know, I could find an even better job, and quite quickly."

∼∼∼

Understand Schemas and Complexes

As we become aware of our thoughts and how they function to increase suffering, we detect patterns. Certain areas of our mental functioning are riddled with land mines and difficulties. We may discover that we are especially prone to particular kinds of distortions in thinking, such as fortune-telling or overgeneralization. Over time, we can cultivate new, more constructive mental habits.

There are other kinds of patterns we may see that exist at a deeper level than the errors in thinking noted above. Jung called these deep patterns *complexes*. Whenever one of these areas is triggered, we need mindfulness more than ever. A complex is a constellation of thoughts and feelings that represent a difficult area of functioning. A thirty-five-year-old man who lives at home with his mother and cannot entertain the idea of leaving her because "she would be all alone" may quite likely have a mother complex involving an unacknowledged dependency on her. A Buddhist term for this is *mental formation*.

A more recent term for a related idea is *schema*. This term comes from cognitive psychological research, in which it means a configuration or pattern of information. We have schemas about all kinds of things. For example, we have restaurant schemas, which tell us what to expect when we go to a restaurant. This schema is a distillation of our various experiences with restaurants. We know, for example, that the general pattern will be something like: Ask for a table, wait to be seated by the hostess, look over the menu, give our order to a server, eat, ask for the check, pay it, and leave a tip. All of this information is represented in the schema, a kind of neuronal pathway that connects this information as it is encoded in the brain.

Schemas are often helpful. They give us an idea of what to expect. They provide a sense of comforting predictability. Imagine if every time you went into a restaurant, you had to figure out what to do from scratch! Life would be very confusing and chaotic without schemas to organize our information about the world.

Some of the more important schemas are not about matters like restaurants, but concern our emotional well-being—who we are, what other people are like, and how we fit into the world. For example, people who grew up during the Depression years often have schemas of deprivation. It is not uncommon for such a person to feel deprived even with far above average wealth. And there is no convincing such a person otherwise, despite the objective reality. Or sometimes, attractive men and women see themselves as unattractive. They manage to maintain this belief by discounting positive information about their appearance and magnifying the slightest hint of negative information.

When a schema has been activated, you are looking at life through a particular lens or filter. Sometimes that lens may be distorted in a way that is maladaptive. Seeing yourself through schemas is like looking at yourself through a fun-house mirror; there may be some truth in the image, but it is so distorted that you can hardly recognize yourself. Often maladaptive schemas originate in childhood. It is as if we made some decisions back then about who we are and what the world is like, and no amount of contrary experience changes our conclusions. We maintain our schemas by ignoring and discounting information and experiences that do not fit them, while giving inordinate attention and validity to experiences that fit. In this way, schemas provide a sense of order and predictability, but at great cost. Both meditation and psychotherapy work by bringing attention to these patterns, which already begins to break them up.

See the World Afresh

Sometimes schemas are faulty. They also may limit the possibilities we see in new situations. The Harvard psychologist Ellen Langer's research demonstrates that increased awareness has profound effects on our creativity, our adaptability, and even our health, longevity, and well-being. One example of this involves seeing things in what she calls a "conditional" way. In one experiment, subjects were shown several ordinary objects. Some of them were shown these objects in the usual, unconditional way. "This is a hair dryer. This is an extension cord. This is a dog's chew toy." Others were shown these objects in a conditional way. This involved only the slight change of replacing the word *is* with the words *could be*. In other words, they were shown the same object but were told, "This could be a hair dryer. This could be an extension cord. This could be a dog's chew toy." Later, all subjects were put in a situation that required an eraser. Only those who had been told the objects "could be" something could recognize that the rubber chew toy could also be used as an eraser. This is the kind of fluidity of thought, the sort of capacity to change cognitive sets, that you find also in Zen masters.

Schemas do help to make our world more predictable and familiar, but they also prevent us from seeing other possibilities and acting creatively. Buddhism is full of stories about Zen masters who are not trapped in these categories of thought but find spontaneous solutions to problems that lie outside of traditional thought patterns. Thich Nhat Hanh recounts walking with a little girl who asked him what color the trees were. He told her: "They are the color that you see." In this way, he pointed to her own immediate experience instead of adding to her thinking *about* the experience.

The Zen master Po-chang had to find a leader for a second monastery because of his many students. To identify the best leader, he set a pitcher (or what could be a pitcher!) before his monks and asked them to tell him what it was without calling it a pitcher. When the cook kicked the pitcher over and walked out, Po-chang was impressed, and made him leader of the new monastery. While it is never quite satisfactory to translate such Zen accounts into a moral precept, perhaps you could say that the cook pointed to the reality of the object as a thing you could interact with by kicking it—not what one typically thinks of doing with a pitcher. The cook was able to see reality outside of the concept "pitcher."

Eleven Schemas

In their popular book *Reinventing Your Life*, the psychologists Jeff Young and Janet Klosko outlined schemas (which they call "lifetraps") and how to change them. Here are the schemas they found most important:

1. *Abandonment*. The hallmark of this schema is a sense of continual threat that the people you love will abandon you in the end, leaving you alone and isolated. People with this schema cling tightly to others, which, ironically, often causes them to feel smothered

and eventually withdraw. In this way, the schema actually creates the feared result.

2. *Mistrust and abuse.* This is a pervasive expectation that others will hurt or abuse you. In order to then protect yourself, you treat others with suspicion. This can manifest as either few or no relationships, or relationships that are superficial. You may not ever really open up to others. Some people with this schema seem to choose people who will fulfill it, perhaps as an effort to overcome their fear.

3. *Dependence.* Having been made unsure of your own competence as a child, you need constant support from people who you feel are more capable than you are. Since others can never fully understand your needs, there is usually a letdown at some point, triggering anger at those you depend on.

4. *Vulnerability.* You never feel safe. Disaster in some form is always just about to strike, whether legal, medical, financial, or in some other form. As a child, you were repeatedly taught that the world is an unsafe place. Parents may have worried excessively about your safety.

5. *Emotional deprivation.* You feel that others will never meet your needs for love and understanding. You may be attracted to people who are cold and ungiving, thus endlessly creating feelings of deprivation, or you may be that way yourself, triggering more of the same from others. You alternate between being angry at others and feeling hurt and alone.

6. *Social exclusion.* You feel that you never quite fit in with others. If you have this schema, you probably never felt part of a group of friends when you were growing up. Perhaps there was something different about you that you felt prevented you from being accepted.

7. *Defectiveness.* You feel that there is something wrong with you deep down, that if people ever really got to know you, they would reject you. Conversely, if others do seem to value you, you may think there is something wrong with them for valuing such a defective person as yourself.

8. *Failure.* You view yourself as not achieving as much as your peers. You maintain this schema by exaggerating your failures and minimizing your accomplishments, which in turn keeps the pattern going.

9. *Subjugation.* This is a pervasive sense that your own needs and desires are less important than those of other people. Either out of guilt (a sense that you will hurt others if you assert your needs) or fear (a sense that you will be punished for asserting your needs), you allow others to control you.

10. *Unrelenting standards.* This schema is essentially what has otherwise been called perfectionism. If you have this schema, you continually place achievement over happiness. You never feel that what you accomplish is quite good enough.

11. *Entitlement.* Individuals with this schema feel special. They feel that they should be able to have it all and to have it right now. Rules do not apply to them.

Bring Mindfulness to Your Schemas

Mindfulness can help us identify and alter our schemas. First of all, as we become more mindful, as we learn to calm ourselves and look deeply, we become more aware of these patterns. For example, if you have an unrelenting standards schema, you start to notice how hard you are on yourself. If you have a mistrust and abuse schema, you may begin to notice how unsatisfying your relationships are and how self-protective you feel around others, as though at any moment they would try to hurt you. Looking deeply, you may begin to see how these schemas were lessons you drew from childhood experiences. Finally, as you become more calm and mindful, you begin to notice inconsistencies between your experience and your schemas. If you feel that no one likes or appreciates you, you may gradually become aware that at least some people actually seem to do so. You begin to allow yourself to see and acknowledge experiences that do not fit the schema, and in this way, over time, you begin to develop a new, more realistic view of who you are and what the world is like.

Sometimes it can be difficult to identify your schemas. In their book *Why Can't I Get What I Want?* our friend the psychologist Charles Elliott and his coauthor, Maureen Lassen, describe how schemas can actually resemble their opposites. For example, a person with an underlying defectiveness schema may act as though he were supremely confident, doing this in an exaggerated, extreme way in an attempt to try to defend against his underlying pain. Or a person with a social exclusion schema may always insert herself in social situations in overly aggressive, intrusive ways to compensate for these painful feelings. So if you find yourself acting in such an exaggerated way, you might consider whether the underlying schema is exactly the opposite of what it might appear.

Two schemas that may be difficult to distinguish are emotional deprivation and entitlement. With both of these schemas, you often feel hurt by other people. In the case of emotional deprivation, you feel hurt because you continue to see and interpret life events as once again showing you that your needs are never met, seeing slights everywhere and neglecting to notice the occasions when your needs actually are given consideration. People with entitlement schemas can feel hurt, too, but for a different reason: They feel hurt because they expect too much from other people. People with both sorts of schema suffer a lot, and one is not more deserving of kindness or empathy than the other. But there is a tendency for those with an entitlement schema to be a little more angry than hurt. Also, those with entitlement schemas often act as though the rules don't apply to them. They may park in the handicapped zones or be the one in class who continually asks for special favors from the instructor.

As we become more calm and aware of the world as it is, our view of ourselves and of life clears. Mindfulness inherently breaks up the automaticity involved with such distortions. It helps us to distinguish between the world as it is and our maladaptive view of it.

∽ PRACTICE ∽

Identify Your Maladaptive Schemas

After calming yourself with mindful breathing, write down a list of key emotional events in your life—events that touched you for good or ill. Just give these events short titles, such as "The time I won that award," or "The day my father died." Now consider how these events affected you. If you recorded a death or the breakup of a relationship for example, did it leave you with a feeling that people always leave you? Then you may have an abandonment schema. Did you list the time you brought home a report card with all A's and one B, and your father said, "Why did you get the B?" You may have an unrelenting standards schema. At first, consider these as just guesses. To know if they are schemas, you must see that there is a repeating pattern—that people always seem to leave you, that you are always focused on minor mistakes you make rather than your overall competence, and so forth.

Find your own one-sentence way of expressing the schema. With therapy patients, quite often someone will deny having "abandonment" issues. This term just doesn't strike a chord. But if you put it something like, "I find myself always on guard for signs that people will leave me," they may resonate with this. To another person, these may seem very much the same thing, but for the individual there can be a world of difference in the shades of meaning. Say it your way, using your own words so that it connects with your experience and memory. Also, don't be limited to the list above. If you find another term for it that fits better for you, use it instead.

In the coming days or weeks, be alert for emotional reactions to situations that confirm your guesses. Breathe consciously and then let your attention expand to include the feelings in your body, your thoughts, and your emotions, in addition to the breath. Notice what triggered the schema. Persist in bringing kind, calm attention to the schema. This begins to change the pattern.

~~~

Nurture Yourself

When we are distressed, it is time to be especially gentle with ourselves. We need to take care of ourselves, to give ourselves more of the things in life that are nurturing and healing. In doing so, instinct is on our side. Animals crawl away to a quiet, safe place to rest when they are sick. They instinctively withdraw and allow themselves to rest so healing can occur. Human beings, however, do not always follow this instinctive wisdom. We rush around to doctors and pharmacies. Sometimes we even nurture the pain we feel, refuse to rest, and cut ourselves off from sources of healing.

Barbara, for example, refused to answer the phone call from her friend. If this had been a person with whom her relationship were less positive, this would have made more sense. In that case, she would have been protecting herself and her wounded animal nature. But this was not so. Her friend was someone who always did her best to listen deeply when Barbara was troubled. Talking with her could only have helped.

Barbara also overindulged in wine. There was at least a partial motivation to be kind to herself in allowing this. It was a way of cutting herself some slack and not depriving herself. However, this choice lacked wisdom. If she had been calm enough, she might have been able to see that alcohol, as a depressant drug, would in the end only intensify her negative feelings. And that is indeed what happened. While the first glass of wine helped her feel a little calmer, additional glasses only kept her lost in her spiraling negative thoughts and feelings. (For more about mindfulness as a spiritual path for dealing with addiction, see our book *Mindful Recovery*.)

Again, while we cannot control our emotions directly, there is a lot we can do about them. We are never helpless in the face of emotion. It is at least as false to say we have no influence over our emotional life as it is to say that we can completely control it.

Look Deeply at Your Behavior

In the behavioral approach to depression, *doing* is the way out. The idea is to see the behavior patterns that support a depressed mood, and change the pattern. Depressed people tend to stay isolated and inactive. They eat too much or too little, sleep too much or too little, and refuse to participate in fun activities that are inconsistent with their mood. Even if you are not depressed, you would begin to feel depressed if you were to do these same things. If you started eating too much or too little, sleeping too much, staying alone too much, and so on, you would get depressed also, no matter how temperamentally resilient to depression you may otherwise be. But the reverse is also true: If the depressed person can somehow participate in fun things anyway, often the mood shifts to match the activity. Getting yourself to engage in some enjoyable activity may go against the grain, but it can be very effective in bringing about a shift of mood. It is like jump-starting a car: The initial resistance of the motor to turning over must be overcome with a jolt of electricity. But once this happens, the motor can keep running quite nicely on its own. Similarly, once you break up a bad mood by engaging in a reinforcing activity or "pleasant event" (as these have been called), the mood shift can sometimes sustain itself without further effort.

Sometimes people try a reinforcing activity and, because the change is not dramatic or immediate, declare that it "didn't work." Such a view is of course part of the hopelessness of depression. Chances are good that when someone says this, one of three things is at work. First, the person may not have chosen an activity that is sufficiently reinforcing. It can sometimes be a matter of trial and error to find activities that will help. Sometimes things we think of as being fun are not really as much fun as we imagine, and some things we think are not fun actually are. For example, when I was a theology student and felt stressed, studying ancient Greek vocabulary always had a calming and soothing effect on me. This is not a task that I would have thought of as "fun," but it occupied just enough of my attention, without being too difficult, that it allowed a space for a shift in mood. On the other hand, in our culture, going to a party is supposed to be fun. But the truth is, especially if you are introverted by nature, parties may actually be more draining than helpful. The behavioral approach is empirical: That is, do not assume what will be helpful, but try and see which things really are. This attitude is quite compatible with Buddha-dharma (the pragmatic teaching of the Buddha).

A second difficulty is that sometimes the person may not have persisted long enough in the reinforcing activity. Even if you are doing something that you truly love to do, five minutes of doing it may not be enough to reverse a negative mood that has lasted for hours or days.

A third difficulty is that, while a change in mood has occurred, it is not total or dramatic. And since people who are depressed think in black-and-white terms, they may not notice a more subtle change. One way to overcome this is to rate your mood before you engage in an activity and then rate it again afterward. For example, you could rate your sadness on a scale of 0 to 10, with 10 being the worst imaginable sadness, and 0 meaning the total absence of sadness. Perhaps, before engaging in an enjoyable activity, you rated your sadness as a 7. Afterward, you rated it as a 5. You can conclude from this that the activity was helpful because it moved your emotions in the desired direction. If you were thinking more globally about it, you might have missed this change. You might have just said to yourself, "I feel sad" before beginning the activity and "I still feel sad" after it. Rating a level of emotion or mood in this way is a psychological device to help you be more mindful, so that you notice shades of gray and subtler shifts.

If your negative mood state has not reached clinical levels, it is relatively easy to change. Instead of a jump start, you may just need to turn the key to get the motor running again. The less intense the negative mood, and the shorter its duration, the less effort you will need to expend to change it.

One of the best things to do is some form of moderate physical exercise, or better yet, walking meditation. *Walking meditation is a wonderful way to nurture yourself and heal negative moods or emotions.* It is especially helpful if you try to keep your attention in the present instead of rehearsing negative thoughts. Walk with awareness of the many positive things around you—trees, grass, sky, flowers. Smile and breathe mindfully. While sitting meditation may also help, if you are upset, it is often more helpful to give your body something to do. Changing your environment and doing some physical activity calms the body directly. And you may be better prepared to benefit from sitting meditation after you walk than before.

∾ PRACTICE ∾

Twenty-five Healing Things

What are some of the things that you do for yourself that are nurturing and nourishing? It is impossible to prescribe these things for another person, because what is nourishing for one may not be nourishing for someone else. The best answers are sometimes the simplest.

You could take a slow, hot bath, doing this in a meditative way, keeping your attention as much as possible on the pleasant sensations rather than on your problems and worries. You might also try reading a little in one of your favorite meditational or inspirational books. Sometimes a good book—perhaps passages that you have marked or copied that were particularly helpful to you—can be the best of friends. I keep a notebook of favorite quotations for both writing and personal inspiration in difficult times. You might also call a close friend or family member who is good at listening and not too quick to offer easy advice, spurious solutions, or judgment. Or you might listen to a familiar, uplifting or soothing piece of music. Every so often, for example, I will listen to Beethoven's Ninth Symphony, and by the time I get to the "Ode to Joy" chorale in the fourth movement, I almost always have tears of joy on my face, no matter what mood I was in to begin with. Fix yourself a cup of tea or coffee, and breathe in and out and meditate on the experience. There is no end to simple, nourishing things that one can do.

On a piece of paper, list as many enjoyable, healing things as you can. Try to come up with at least twenty-five, but don't be limited to that number. Keep coming back to the list to review and add to it. Don't be too critical of your ideas; let them flow.

The next time you are a little out of sorts, take out your list and try a few things that appeal to you.

~~~

Send Yourself a Love Letter

It is a great victory, a true miracle, when you can respond to negative emotions in positive ways. Changing a negative mood is a greater miracle than walking on water or telepathy. Realistically, it is sometimes hard to motivate ourselves to do one of our healing things, however much we know we should. It may be all you can do to simply choose some form of *distraction* to at least help interrupt a negative cycle of worry or sadness. By distractions we mean things that are entertaining, but that may not be purely nourishing, or that may have limitations and difficulties attached to them. For example, a glass of wine (if you are not addicted) may be a form of distraction with some benefit. But there are difficulties. If one glass of wine becomes too many glasses of wine, the destructive aspects outweigh the helpfulness. Similarly, you may go to a movie, read an exciting novel, watch television, or go to the mall and buy yourself something special. However, each of these things has potential problems and difficulties. The movie or novel may take you away from your concerns for a while, but may fill you with disturbing images. Television, unless done selectively, may leave you bored and frustrated. Some research indicates a positive correlation between time spent watching television and depression: People who watch television more tend also to be more depressed. And buying yourself something may dig you deeper into indebtedness, causing more problems in the future. Still, as stopgap measures, these may be better than permitting a destructive spiral of thought and behavior to continue.

If you are prone to negative emotions and moods, it is best to prepare ahead of time. There are many ways of doing this. In addition to your twenty-five healing things list, you could write the following on an index card and promise yourself you will take it out and read it the next time you feel down:

I do not need to fix everything right now. All I need to do right now is keep bringing calm awareness to these negative emotions.

This is like sending yourself a love letter. You send it to your future self while you are feeling strong and calm. It's a message from the Buddha within.

You might wish to supplement this with some further instructions to yourself. For example, if you know you tend toward overgeneralization, you might tell yourself something like this: "Right now, you are probably seeing things in too black-and-white a way. Take a realistic view. What are the positive elements?" Or if you suffer from a deprivation schema, you may send ahead some thoughts to help you deal with that. For example: "Even though you are feeling deprived and sad, you may be missing some positive things that are available right now, such as . . ." (and then name a few that are generally true for you).

Take Care of Your Anger

Two women got angry at each other on the road one day. The anger escalated into a horrible episode of road rage. When it ended, one woman had shot the other in the head, killing her.

Road rage is always shocking, perhaps particularly so in this case since it is rare that women are involved. Both of these women were nice people, loved by their friends and families, and good workers. Now one is dead. And the other faces the prospect of life in prison.

Anger is a signal that we perceive something to be unfair. The sense of unfairness causes us to focus on the perceived external source of our troubles, which can lead to destructive action. Anger will come up in all of us from time to time. You cannot avoid it. The Dalai Lama admits that he feels angry sometimes, and so does Thich Nhat Hanh. But they know how to take care of their anger. And that is the most important thing. Unless we take care of this painful emotion, it becomes a destructive force. Far too often, that is just what happens. Psychology used to teach that expressed anger is good, and that the most important thing about anger is to not let it get bottled up. Bottling our anger was thought to be destructive; releasing our anger was thought to be positive. Many therapists still continue to teach this, having their clients scream or beat pillows or hit each other with Nerf "swords."

Psychologists have learned more about anger since then. And as is generally the case, we have discovered that anger is a far more complex phenomenon than the simple "let your anger out" model would imply. For one thing, the consequences of anger depend in part on who gets angry at whom. It is very different if you express anger at a young child than if you express anger at your boss and will have different consequences. For another thing, while there may be people who need help to feel and cope with anger, for the most part, when we beat pillows and so on, we are *practicing* being angry. We may feel some relief from the pleasant fatigue that follows the physical exertion, but it is not helpful in the long run. The next time we are in a similar situation, we only become angry more quickly.

We cannot stress enough that unattended anger is destructive. It may be that anger is a signal that we cannot do without, just as we cannot do without sensory signals of pain. But if we do not take care of this feeling, or worse still, if we fan it into flames, it will cause a lot of suffering.

The person who suffers the most from your anger is you. Anger puts your body on the alert. The hormones epinephrine, norepinephrine, and cortisol are released into the bloodstream, preparing you to fight or run, shunting blood away from maintenance processes like digestion and toward the large muscles, leaving you with a knot in the stomach. But while these hormones prepare us for an emergency, they come with a high price tag. Chronic release of these hormones has been implicated in hypertension and heart disease. And when the anger subsides, you are left exhausted and depleted.

We have known for some time now that there is a connection between coronary artery disease and a pattern of behavior called the type A personality. This type of person is characterized by a constant struggle to achieve, time urgency, irritability, anger, hostility, and impatience with anyone who gets in his or her way. While initial findings linked this personality with increased risk of heart disease compared to the more easygoing type B, subsequent studies have revealed the real culprit to be the hostility component. One major study found that men who were chronically hostile and angry were five times as likely as nonhostile men to develop heart disease and other ailments.

Another study of anger compared styles for dealing with an angry and arbitrary boss. Those who said they would express their anger by immediately protesting and then informing their union (the "anger out" group) had the highest blood pressure. Those who said they would just walk away (the "anger in" group) had somewhat lower blood pressure. Those who said they would try to discuss it later (the "reflection" group) had the lowest blood pressure of all. While one cannot say from a study like this one whether anger style determines blood pressure or the other way around, such findings are consistent with a mindful approach to emotions.

In their book *When Anger Hurts*, the authors Matthew McKay, Peter Rogers, and Judith McKay summarize the physiological costs of anger this way:

> It seems that it does not matter whether anger is expressed or suppressed. It's just plain bad for you. Chronic anger that is expressed is bad for you because it feeds on itself. It prolongs and supercharges all the associated hormonal changes. Chronic suppressed anger is damaging because it mobilizes the sympathetic nervous system responses without providing any release of the tension. The effect is the same as flooring the accelerator of your car at the same time as slamming on the brakes.

Angry outbursts hurt our relationships. If we have a lot of practice at being angry, we are difficult to be around. This not only hurts the people around us, but it hurts ourselves, as people withdraw from and avoid us. It can have devastating effects, too, on our ability to get along with others and make our way in the world.

Anger also prevents others from receiving whatever wisdom we have to offer. Young protesters of the 1960s, for example, had good points to make to those in power. But many of these protests were done in an angry, polarizing way. The effects of this anger and the counteranger it elicited are still with us today. By viewing people with other perspectives simply as legitimate objects of anger—as people who are somehow less human or less moral than ourselves—we only create more suffering. Protests conducted in an angry, self-righteous spirit do not help, whether the subject of the protest is the Vietnam War in 1968 or the meeting of the World Trade Organization in 1999.

Care Now: Decide Later

In essence, the same principles apply in working with anger as noted above: First notice that you need to do something to take care of your feelings. You need to touch your calmness. If you have been practicing mindfulness, you can develop enough facility to deal with most anger-provoking situations by simply calming these feelings and working with the breath. Psychology can also help us look more deeply.

In most situations, you do not have to decide what to do right away. You can take care of the anger first and decide later what to do about the situation that triggered it. You can always say something like, "I'll get back to you on that," or, "I'll have to think about it." For example, Jack's doctor recommended an herbal remedy only available in a store on the other side of town. He called ahead and verified that the store was open and that the remedy was in stock, but when he got there, it turned out that, while they normally carried this product, they were out. The person on the phone had not bothered to check the shelves. Jack felt his anger rise as the clerk asked if he would like them to call him when they got more in. Formerly, Jack might have given him a very hard time or sworn at him and then stormed out in a huff. But he remembered he didn't have to do that, and he didn't have to decide now. So he said, "I'll let you know." When he got home, Jack practiced mindful breathing with his feelings of anger and frustration for fifteen minutes or so and then felt much better. Only then did he consider what he wanted to do about obtaining the remedy.

When we examine angry thoughts, we find that they have a particular quality. For the most part, they are either thoughts about who is to blame, or shoulds. The fallacy behind angry thinking often involves an assumption that other people should do what *we* think that they should do—which means what furthers our own needs. This assumption is the culprit behind a lot of angry thinking. A more reasonable assumption is that *other people will try to seek their own happiness and avoid suffering according to their best available understanding at this point in their growth*—which is after all what we ourselves are doing. Once you look deeply into this more reasonable view, you will see that it is inevitable that sometimes people will act in a way that puts them in conflict with what we perceive to be our own needs. Conflict of interest then becomes normalized, and we can see this as natural, and calmly try to get what we need without hurting others.

Identify Anger Thoughts

It is helpful to review the kinds of thoughts that tend to feed our anger. McKay, Rogers, and McKay report eight kinds of such thoughts—four types of "shoulds" and four types of "blamers":

Shoulds

1. *The entitlement fallacy.* If I feel a need very strongly, others should take care of this need. (More helpful: Others have needs of their own to take care of. I am responsible for my own needs.)
2. *The fallacy of fairness.* My view is fair and correct. The other person's view is not fair. (More helpful: There is no objective standard of fairness. It is natural for conflicts of needs to arise.)
3. *The fallacy of change.* People should change for us if we apply pressure. (More helpful: Change is difficult. People only change when they want to change. Pressure sometimes makes it harder for people to change.)
4. *The letting-it-out fallacy.* This fallacy is based on the belief that others bear total responsibility for my pain, and that they therefore should be punished for their misdeeds. Therefore, I will feel better if I express my feelings of hurt and anger. (More helpful: I always bear responsibility for taking care of myself. Expressing angry feelings may damage my relationships, and I also may be cultivating a destructive habit of anger.)

Blamers

1. *Good/bad dichotomies.* Others are "bad" when they don't meet our needs. (More helpful: Other people are, like us, trying to find happiness and avoid suffering.)
2. *Assumed intent.* Similar to mind reading. For example, "She is trying to hurt me." (Actually, we never know for sure what other people are thinking, feeling, or intending.)
3. *Magnifying.* Using global terms like *terrible, awful, disgusting, always,*

and *never*. For example, "He's *always awful* to me." (The words *always* and *never* are usually wrong, since only one contradictory instance is required to refute them. For this statement to be true, it would have to be the case that he never once was anything but awful. If that were indeed the case, there would probably not be any relationship with him in the first place. Magnifying only makes a conflict of needs worse.)

4. *Global labeling*. "He's a jerk." Also: "neurotic," "insecure," "crazy," "useless," "stupid," "incompetent," and so on. (More helpful: Think of specifics. "I don't like the way she did *that*.")

∼ PRACTICE ∼

Work with Anger Thoughts

After doing a little conscious breathing to center yourself, think of two or three occasions on which you became angry. Then, on a sheet of paper, summarize what happened, trying your best to be neutral and objective in your description. Then think about what happened *inside*— what you were telling yourself or thinking. Write down these thoughts, and compare them with the list above. See if you can identify what kinds of *shoulds* or *blamers* you may be using. Then write a more reasonable way of seeing the situation. For example, instead of, "He was acting like a jerk," you might write, "What he said hurt my feelings, since I am sensitive about my looks." Instead of, "She always treats me poorly," substitute, "Sometimes I don't like the way she treats me." If anger is a difficult area for you, you might like to do this exercise repeatedly, gradually cultivating a new mental habit.

Transform Anxiety

Even if you do not suffer from depression or anger, many of us are plagued with worry and anxiety. The early twentieth century was dubbed the age of anxiety, and there is no indication that this is changing much as we move into the twenty-first century.

When you use breath meditation to calm the body and the mind and then look into your worries, you may notice some things about them. For one thing, worry can follow after worry in our consciousness, like waves breaking upon the shore. If you are prone to worry (and many of us are), they simply come one after the other, with rather short intervals in between. Also, the worries seem to have no sense of scale: A worry about a trivial matter can occupy us as fully and completely as a worry about a major matter. There is little difference in this regard between worrying about when the cable guy will come and whether your body will survive a serious disease. Each can, if we allow it, totally kidnap our consciousness.

When you start to see your worries in this manner, you are having an experience of *impermanence:* One worry simply follows another, and each one can grip us completely, regardless of its true importance. But after the wave of worry has passed, where is it? This insight begins to change how you relate to these waves of worry. They begin to seem less substantial and substantive. When you have this experience, you are already changing your relationship to your worries, and are beginning to transform them.

As always, such insights must become more than intellectual. They must sink deep into our awareness. To allow them to penetrate in this way, we can contemplate the truth of impermanence again and again as we watch our worries come and go, come and go. What follows is a powerful way to work with worry.

∽ PRACTICE ∽

Work with Worries

To contemplate a truth is to allow it to penetrate your awareness by holding the central idea in mind and turning it over and over gently, not trying to take it apart or elaborate upon it, but simply holding it in awareness. You may from time to time repeat some words to yourself that are central to the idea you are contemplating—especially when you lose focus—but this is only to point the way. You start with an intellectual idea, but the rest of the process is not intellectual.

To work with worry, fear, and anxiety, first calm the body and the mind with breath meditation for five or ten minutes. Then contemplate the following ideas in a leisurely way, turning the idea over in your mind, coming back to it when you wander from it, perhaps occasionally repeating key words and phrases:

- Worries come, worries go.
- Each worry pretends to be of great importance, but then disappears.
- Worries come and go; I am not this worry.
- I am not this body.
- I am not this span of life.
- I am not my career.
- I am not what people think of me.
- I am not my finances.
- I am not _____ (fill in whatever else you may overidentify with).
- If I am not these things, what am I?
- I am life itself.
- I am love.
- I am peace.
- I am joy.
- I am light.

~~~

Practice "Maybe It Will be Okay"

My morning walk involves crossing a few streets. Even though I walk early enough that traffic is not a problem, I noticed that cars seemed to come out of nowhere whenever I needed to cross a street and were scarcely to be seen otherwise. I began making jokes about it, as though drivers were hiding around the corners until they saw me coming and then quickly coming by as I crossed.

Mindful of this pattern, I determined to change my attitude. Whenever I needed to cross, I told myself, "Maybe it will be okay." From that moment on, it seemed as though cars almost never came by when I was crossing. Whether reality changed, or my perception changed, or whether those are really much the same thing, I cannot say. I can only say that it helped my morning walk to be more pleasant.

Whenever you find yourself worrying about something, try telling yourself: "Maybe it will be okay. Maybe it will work out."

And maybe it will.

Taking Responsibility

There is a golden thread running through this discussion of caring for negative feelings. That thread is: We need to take responsibility for these feelings rather than blame other people or circumstances. No one but us can do the work of calming and looking deeply, of changing and transforming. Thich Nhat Hanh expressed the Buddha's teaching on this matter this way:

> When a wise person suffers, she asks herself, "What can I do to be free from suffering? Who can help me? What have I done to free myself from this suffering?" But when a foolish person suffers, she asks herself, "Who has wronged me? How can I show others that I am the victim of wrongdoing? How can I punish those who have caused my suffering?"

Everyone who comes into my office for therapy nourishes the hope, sometimes secretly and sometimes explicitly, that I will be able to tell them how to turn their feelings off. Their feelings are painful, and they just want them to stop. But there is no way to do that. And what is more, our efforts to avoid feelings cause a lot of problems—at least as many as wallowing in them. But when you know how to take care of feelings, you become confident. You are no longer afraid.

Buddhism emphasizes that the Buddha was a human being. That is, he was someone just like us—just like we can become. To become like him, we need to be responsible for our own well-being.

When Do I Need More Help?

If a negative mood lasts more than a few hours or days, if it is intense and severe, and if it has begun to interfere with your work or affect important relationships, you may want to give yourself the gift of psychotherapy. Take a positive view of making this step. Therapy can assist us in becoming more mindful and aware. Taking care of our emotions can help us avoid major health problems down the road. And compared to that, the cost of therapy is trivial, not only financially, but also in terms of suffering.

One difficulty currently is that real therapy is becoming rarer because of the prevalence of managed health care. True therapy increases mindfulness. It gently helps you to be aware in a different way, so you can break old patterns. However, with managed care, therapists often feel a time pressure, since they know that they only have a limited number of sessions. Under such conditions, therapy can deteriorate into sessions of advice giving. And while advice can play a role in therapy, it should be more like the spice in the dish than the dish itself. True therapy is first of all a place of deep, calm, mindful listening. A therapist who does not listen deeply and at some length before diagnosing your problem or making suggestions for change may be of limited help. So whatever the limits of your medical coverage, look for a therapist who listens deeply, who seems to want to understand you more than diagnose you or dispense quick advice.

If you'd like more information on the topics covered here, see:

Depressive Thinking

Burns, David D. *Feeling Good: The New Mood Therapy*. New York: Avon Books, 1980.

Schemas

Elliott, Charles H., and Maureen Kirby Lassen. *Why Can't I Get What I Want?: How to Stop Making the Same Old Mistakes and Start Living a Life You Can Love*. Palo Alto, Calif.: Davies-Black Publishing, 1998.
Young, Jeffrey E., and Janet Klosko. *Reinventing Your Life*. New York: Dutton, 1993.

Anger

McKay, Matthew, Peter D. Rogers, and Judith McKay. *When Anger Hurts: Quieting the Storm Within*. Oakland, Calif.: New Harbinger, 1989.
Nhat Hanh, Thich. *Anger: Wisdom for Cooling the Flames*. New York: Riverhead, 2001.

Practice for Week Eight

1. Continue with the practices of a day of mindfulness, moments of mindfulness, reading, walking meditation, and dream work.
2. Increase your meditation time to twenty-five minutes twice daily, if you feel ready to do so.
3. Practice the exercises in this chapter:
   - "Challenge Depressive Thinking" (p. 161)
   - "Identify Your Maladaptive Schemas" (p. 167)
   - "Twenty-five Healing Things" (p. 171)
   - "Work with Anger Thoughts" (p. 178)
   - "Work with Worries" (p. 179)
4. In general, this week give special attention to your emotional life. Read this chapter at least twice. When negative emotions surface, recognize them. Don't try to push them away, but don't wallow or get lost in them either. Breathe in and out, making a calm, open space to experience them fully and clearly. Look into the roots of the problem. Do something to nurture yourself from your list of twenty-five healing things.

8

Week Nine

CULTIVATE HEALTHY
RELATIONSHIPS

It is essential to remember that every being we encounter is
someone who has been dear to us.
—Jeffrey Hopkins, *The Tantric Distinction* (1999)

Love is possible only if two persons communicate with each
other from the center of their existence, hence if each one of
them experiences himself from the center of his existence. Only
in this "central experience" is human reality, only here is alive-
ness, only here is the basis for love.
—Erich Fromm, *The Art of Loving* (1956)

R elationships test the heart. Not just our relationships with
our spouses, partners, or significant others, but all relationships.
The way we relate to our children, mother, father, and sib-
lings—the way we relate to friends, coworkers, the postal clerk—this
tells us more about who we are than the most powerful psychological test.

When we are angry or irritated with others, the heart is too small.

When that feeling of slight impatience arises because someone else is using the phone and we want to, or because someone pulls into "our" lane on the highway, life is giving us feedback. It is telling us that the heart needs to expand. It is telling us that we need to learn to accommodate others' needs without allowing our own peace to be threatened. When the heart is too small, other people seem to be a nuisance, and our life fills with tension and conflict. When the heart is large and ample, relationships are a joy and flow smoothly and peacefully. Good or bad, the quality of our relationships measures the adequacy of the heart.

Usually we approach it the other way. We think that the quality of our relating reveals something about the other person. If he is easy to be around, if we feel good in his presence, we think he is a good, decent person. If he causes us discomfort or uneasiness, if he challenges us in some way, we think he is a bad, difficult person. Or worse still, we play amateur psychologist, pinpointing exactly what is wrong with the other, how he is sick or pathological or has "issues."

Our primary need is not so much for a more sophisticated way of psychologizing, analyzing, and interpreting other people. Often this is just a more refined, intellectual way of blaming. We are already sufficiently skilled at that. What we need is a *change of heart*, a fundamentally new way of seeing the people with whom we share the highway, the office, and the bedroom.

Invite a Change of Heart

Now that you have been practicing mindfulness for a while, perhaps you will have noticed that you are happiest when you feel most connected with others, when you feel love. Some of our saddest moments, on the other hand, occur when we feel alienated—when our connection with others is disrupted by conflict or anger. The closer the relationship, the greater the unhappiness when this is so.

Our happiness has more to do with the people in our lives than we normally imagine in our individualistic culture. If we think of ourselves as separate, discrete selves, we may be misled to imagine that our happiness is a separate quantum, something to clutch and hold and defend. From the perspective of the small and separate self, happiness is a zero sum game: The more I have, the less you have, and the more you have, the less I have. Mindfulness refutes this assumption. When we are around happy people, we feel happier ourselves; when we are happy, we contribute more to the happiness of others by simply being a happy person than by any self-conscious effort to be helpful.

This is the perspective of no self. To take no self rigidly is as much a problem as to take self rigidly, since the world is neither self nor no self, but *this*—what you are experiencing this very moment. Yet when we embrace no self as a useful counterpoint to self, a new reality opens. We see that the reason to practice love and compassion has as much to do with this being good for us as it has to do with it being good for others or for the world.

All religions teach love. In the West, Judaism is one of the most ancient traditions to give importance to love of neighbor. And the glory of Christianity is precisely to elevate this principle to centrality. Buddhist teachings on this subject are particularly helpful in showing us how to put these insights into practice.

All teach the importance of the quality of our relating to others. Yet injunctions to love our neighbor echo with sentimentality and seem quaint in a world where the things that really count are money, success, fame, and fortune, and all their accoutrements. Those fortunate enough to still relate meaningfully to their religious heritage may yet find it difficult to put the practice of love foremost in their awareness and breathe life into it. More likely, they find an unsatisfying split between belief and practice in a competitive and hostile world.

Drawing on both the spiritual and the psychological, we will examine those practices that help open the heart and mind to others. Under the area of relationship skills, psychology has much to teach, while spirituality offers a crucial piece of the relationship puzzle by providing essential teachings on love.

Open Your Heart

Before you entrust seed to soil, you must prepare the ground. For a seed to take root and grow, the soil must not be too hard or compacted. It must contain enough space for the seed to spread its roots and enough moisture and nutrients to support the young plant's growth down into the earth and up toward the light. Without preparation, the seed will not grow.

Practicing relationship skills without first preparing the soil is likely to yield results that are stilted and hollow, or worse still, prove impossible to do at all. The intention to be loving, compassionate, and skillful requires the soft soil of an open heart to achieve significant results.

Buddhists refer to preparing the ground as "mental training." We often translate these practices as "meditation" or even "prayer," but Buddhism has no such terms in its vocabulary. The term *mental training* emphasizes above all changing *ourselves*. Western religious sensibility gives words like *prayer* an emphasis on changing external reality. This is not as absurd a notion as our materialistic culture often assumes. Dr. Larry Dossey and others have marshaled the scientific evidence that prayer does make a difference in recovery from illness, even when people do not know they are being prayed for. But the Buddhist emphasis is a little different. In Buddhist practice, one is not attempting to exert supernatural force upon the world so much as to align oneself more harmoniously with the world as it is, apart from our usual prejudices and conditioning. By expanding the heart with these practices, you change yourself. This is already a miracle.

Now that you have introduced meditation into your daily routine, you are already engaged in this process, already learning to open yourself to reality and become still, deep, and receptive. Perhaps you have already noticed changes in your relationships. Beyond general meditation practices, however, there are also practices specifically geared toward changing the way we relate to others. These are collectively called *metta meditation*.

Metta Meditation

The word *metta* (*maitri* in Sanskrit) means *lovingkindness*. This type of meditation or mental training aims to prepare our mental ground to be more open to others, more accepting and loving. The essence of this practice is easy to understand. But like all meditation practice, it requires patience and persistence. All beings, says the Dalai Lama, seek happiness. On this basis, taken in its most profound sense, one can see that there is no need to reject anyone, including ourselves; for we are all in the same condition, all trying to be happy, all trying to avoid pain. True, some of our efforts are shortsighted and misdirected. But if we can see these underlying intentions of seeking happiness and avoiding suffering behind all that we and others do, we hold the key to compassion. Compassion arises of itself when we look deeply enough to see in this way. We do not have to force ourselves to feel compassion; it is already there. It is our nature. When we remove, through mental training, the obstacles that cover our compassionate inner Buddha, our true self, then the Buddha of compassion incarnates in us, becoming concretely present and manifest.

One form of metta practice is simply to cultivate the awareness in daily life that all beings are seeking to find happiness and avoid pain. Throughout the day, you simply remind yourself of this fact. In moments when things are peaceful and calm, stop to remind yourself of this. See it in your actions. See it in the actions of others. Even more powerfully, see these intentions at work when someone irritates, disappoints, or hurts you. See if you can look deeply enough into others' behavior to find these primary intentions at work. Likewise with yourself, when you find yourself doing things that you do not fully approve of, remind yourself that you, too, are simply trying to be happy and avoid pain.

This awareness, remembered throughout the day, is already a powerful antidote to the fragmentation and alienation we described in the first chapter. You increasingly feel relatedness and connection with all beings. The aggressive driver, the rude person on the telephone, the discourteous clerk at the store—none of them are foreign to us as we see that each is attempting to be happy and avoid suffering, as are we.

The ancient sage Patanjali makes this promise: "Undisturbed calmness of mind is attained by cultivating friendliness toward the happy, compassion for the unhappy, delight in the virtuous, and indifference toward the wicked." Of particular note in this advice is how it differs from normal consciousness. Normally, we dwell only briefly on the positive in human beings, while being consumed by their negative aspects—their lack of understanding and insight. Reversing this trend is a powerful practice; the promise of peace is not overstated.

Develop True Self-Love

Formal metta meditation involves rehearsing a set of intentions toward yourself and others in an ever-widening circle of concern. The practice begins *with yourself.* The Bible tells us to love our neighbors *as ourselves,* and in this practice, we take the last clause seriously. Love for ourselves is the assumed basis for loving others. In ancient times, this hardly required explication. People then, as in traditional societies today, could not have conceived of the self-doubt and low self-esteem endemic in our modern culture.

But for most of us, self-love needs emphasis. The psychologist Erich Fromm clarified that the capacity for love and compassion is a single, undivided capacity. There is not one separate capacity with which we love ourselves and another with which we love other people. It is one capacity. The more loving, understanding, and compassionate we are toward ourselves, the more loving, understanding, and compassionate we can ultimately be with others; the more loving, understanding, and compassionate we are with others, the more loving, understanding, and compassionate we can be with ourselves.

This issue is muddled in our culture because we confuse *self-love* with *selfishness*. One of Freud's groundbreaking insights is that we display outrageously and excessively what we do not truly own. Our preoccupation with ourselves is not true self-love but its lack. Selfish behavior is not genuine self-love. It is shallow, hollow, and empty. It reveals an underlying, profound self-doubt and self-hatred. It is a symptom, which, like all symptoms, is a misguided attempt to find what is missing. It attempts to point us in the right direction—the direction of a deep, genuine, and grounded love of self.

The slogan of a selfish culture is that more is better. If one piece of pie is good, then two are better. At the same time, because of our neurotic split about food, if it is good to be a little thin, then it is even better to be anorexic. If one glass of wine is good, then the whole bottle is better. The effects of such behavior reveal an actual lack of self-love, as we destroy body and mind alike. Self-loathing is evident in the result, as we become overweight or starve ourselves or destroy our livers and brains in a flood of alcohol. *This is not excessive love for self and a lack of love for others, but altogether a lack of love, both of self and of other.*

So it is no accident that metta meditation has as its foundation the cultivation of genuine, solid self-love. The first person who must receive our love and understanding is us. And cultivating a true love of self, we at the same time deepen our capacity to love others.

Love Yourself and Then Others

You must begin with lovingkindness toward yourself. If you are upset and angry with someone, it will not do to try to force yourself to feel compassion toward him or her. The difficult emotions you experience testify that *you* are the one most in need of lovingkindness at that point. Begin with yourself. Send yourself oceans of love, patience, and understanding. Often, this will be enough, as the kindness toward self begins to overflow to those around you.

Metta meditation begins with self and then expands in progressively wider circles, each of which is a little more difficult, a little more of a stretch. From a base of genuine self-love, we gradually expand the focus of our concern. First we expand to those who are closest to us, such as our families, then to our friends, then to neutral individuals or acquaintances, then to enemies—those the very thought of whom causes us pain—and finally to all beings. This is a progression from easy to hard, in other words, based on the assumption that self-love is most natural and easy, then love of our families, and so on, with love of enemies and universal love the hardest. However, as we have discussed, in our culture it is not always to be assumed that we love ourselves in a true and genuine sense. So it may be easiest at times to water seeds of love by beginning with our partners, our children, or whomever we find it easy to feel loving toward, perhaps even the cat or the dog.

∿ PRACTICE ∿

Metta Meditation

1. Sit or lie comfortably. Spend a few moments centering yourself with conscious breathing.
2. Begin with yourself. Let a loving, accepting attitude arise toward yourself, toward your body and mind. Smile warmly to yourself. Aloud or silently, as you breathe consciously, say the following:

May I be happy and joyful.
May I have all that I want and need.
May I have ease of well-being.
May I be safe and free from harm or injury.

May I be free from anger, fear, worry, sorrow, and all afflictions of
   body, mind, and spirit.
May I attain the peace beyond understanding,
         liberation from all suffering,
               the bliss of enlightenment.

3.   Pause and breathe between each statement, letting the intent be-
     hind it be clear and vivid, not mechanical. Stay with each statement
     for at least a few breaths, and continue until you start to feel a
     change in your consciousness.
4.   When you are ready, move on from yourself to others. Changing
     the pronoun "I" in the statements above appropriately (you, he,
     she, they), extend the same intentions to:

     • the people closest to you, your family, your beloved
     • friends
     • neutral people or acquaintances
     • enemies or people the very thought of whom causes you pain
     • all beings

     As above, try your best to make the intention behind the words
     clear and vivid.
5.   Do not rush through this for the sake of some kind of complete-
     ness. It is best to take your time and proceed in a relaxed way, rather
     than trying to complete a list in order just to get through it. If
     you are the one most in need of healing during a particular session,
     you may spend the whole meditation period sending yourself
     lovingkindness.

   It can help to practice this systematically. For example, spend a
whole meditation period on yourself (or a week or a month of meditation periods), then move on to those closest to you for the same amount
of time, then to friends, and so on. Or if you prefer, include some of
each level within one sitting. But however you choose to practice metta
meditation, it is most important to remember to do it with true feeling
behind the words and not simply by rote.
   You might like to begin with the intentions as stated here. They have
the virtue of a broad and generous spirit. But of course, adapt them or
use others as you see fit. It is helpful to use the same intentions at each

level. Using the same words at each level impresses powerfully on the mind that all beings are ultimately seeking the same things.

Consider how you want to incorporate this with other meditation practices. For example, I often practice other forms of meditation in the morning, and then practice metta meditation at night. Or you may choose metta meditation in place of your regular meditation practice for a period of time.

~~~

Pinpoint Your Resistance

Subtle changes begin the moment you start this practice. Like a good, patient scientist, be alert for these, as well as for the more profound changes that take longer. Allow a period of time for regular metta meditation and see what happens to your mental state and, indirectly, to your relationships.

With certain individuals, you may notice some resistance to cultivating the same intentions toward them that you cultivate toward others or toward yourself. Of course, you expect this when it comes to working with enemies—those the very thought of whom causes you pain. More surprising, however, is when we experience it with ourselves. For example, when working with the statement "May I be happy and joyful," do you notice a slight twinge of doubt, as if it were not okay to wish this for yourself? Or you may balk a little at wishing yourself to have all you want and need, especially if you have a traditional Western religious background. "All I *need*, okay, but is it really okay to have all I *want?* Isn't that a little greedy?" But this is precisely the point as you stretch and extend your sense of kindness toward yourself and then toward others. Gradually, the resistance loosens, and you feel a greater openness, with fewer restrictions and limitations.

You might find it easy enough to pray for your own enlightenment, but when it comes to asking the same thing for Harry or Sally, you feel a twinge of reluctance. Imagine Harry and Sally being enlightened persons! This can be especially difficult with our enemies, finding it hard to acknowledge them as spiritual beings who are also seeking liberation from suffering.

Such resistance shows that the practice is hitting home. When these intentions penetrate your consciousness deeply enough, you will notice an increased ease in dealing with others, and may notice them responding to you differently as well. Others sense the change.

Simplify, Simplify

You might like to use the full statements listed above (or similar ones) for a while. These words focus our thoughts, which otherwise remain blurred, indefinite, and fluid. After doing this for some time—perhaps weeks or months—the words may sometimes feel burdensome. At this point, experiment with using fewer words, simplifying the sentences, or using no words at all. For example, when practicing metta meditation for yourself, imagine just resting in the presence of total love and acceptance, perhaps saying the word *love* to yourself. Likewise, with other people, you may find a wordless capacity emerges to just hold them in love. In practicing for all beings, you may want to imagine a light reaching out from your heart to all living beings. This can be more than sufficient without using words. When your intent becomes hazy or unclear, then return to the full verbal form.

As with meditation in general, there are many moments during the day to practice metta meditation informally. A therapist or doctor may pause briefly between seeing patients, for example. The mail carrier can silently voice an intention at each stop. It does not take a lot of time. You can find ways to practice metta meditation with each person you come in contact with in quiet and unobtrusive ways. Slowly, you may begin to see this change your interpersonal landscape.

Examine Your Relationship Skills

Part of the practical nature of Buddhism teaches that kind, loving intentions, while important, are insufficient. The pain we create for one another more often stems from ineptitude or lack of skill than from negative intent. The practice of mindfulness helps tremendously with this as we observe with full awareness how what we say and do affects others and how what they say and do affects us. When we can do this calmly and without excessive self-recrimination or blame, we gradually learn what is skillful and what is not.

No one wants to go to a physician, however kindly, who lacks the required skill to help. A surgeon who does not know what she's doing is a danger to the world, no matter how good a person she is and how positive her intentions. Similarly, it matters little that your auto mechanic is friendly if he is incompetent.

In personal relationships, we allow room for positive intentions. It is helpful to honor the positive intention behind someone's overly blunt remark. But skill is vital nonetheless. And the lack of it can create an animosity that, over time, robs us of our compassion and our peace. At that point, when we lose not only the ability but even the intention to be loving toward someone, it is difficult to get back on track.

Consider, for example, the profound animosity you find in some couples. If two people are together, presumably they came together out of love and attraction. So how does it happen that, months or years later, this love has degenerated into regular hold-no-prisoners, straight-for-the-jugular arguments or even physical violence?

Lack of skill accounts for much of this degeneration, ultimately turning love into hatred. This is a transformation we could live without. Perhaps because of our devotion to ideals of romantic love, we somehow expect that a good relationship should come easily, of itself, without effort, care, or attention. Instead of wondering how to care for our relationship, we view the relationship as a static, unchanging entity, judging it good or bad, as though that's just the way it is and there's nothing we can do about it. But no matter how strong the love is at the beginning, if a relationship is not grounded in a down-to-earth capacity to give mindful attention, being aware of what we say and how we say it—if there is no willingness to give some effort to everyday things like listening deeply and performing small kindnesses—the day will come when love is overtaken by hatred.

Last night I saw *Antiques Roadshow* on television. I watched a woman's eyes light up because the five-dollar article she bought at a garage sale was appraised at thousands of dollars. I wondered about the person who sold this piece so cheaply. What if he was also watching the show and saw that he had sold something worth so much for so little? Yet this is an everyday occurrence in our relationships. Through lack of skill, we give away our most precious possession for a pittance. We sell our most important relationships for practically nothing.

Skillfulness and preparing the groundwork together. One enhances the other. It does not matter how well you weed and water your garden if the soil is not prepared in a way that allows the seed to germinate and stretch into the light. Likewise, no matter how well you prepare the soil, if you do not take care of the young plants that emerge, your harvest will be disappointing. If you do not prepare the ground by cultivating lovingkindness, you will find it difficult to put your skills into practice. Without preparation, your anger and hostility may be too strong. Even if you say the right words, but by tone and gesture betray an underlying anger, then your words will ring hollow and false. It requires both processes working together—preparing the ground and regular care—metta meditation and skilled practice, to produce the harmony and everyday miracle of good relationships.

Listen Deeply

To listen deeply to another person is to give a wonderful gift. Since our culture values action and solving problems so much, we vastly underrate the healing power of listening. We think that to be helpful, we must say something, do something, offer advice, or solve the problem for the other person. "Good advice is often a doubtful remedy," wrote Jung, "but generally not dangerous because it has so little effect." Even when our advice is helpful, it is often not the advice per se that helps but the concern that the other person feels behind it.

Deep listening is the most important part of psychotherapy. But even therapists tend to assume that it is our words of wisdom, our wonderful advice, or our brilliant psychological interpretations that make the difference. And while these all have a place, it is less significant than generally assumed. Even our words of therapeutic wisdom may ultimately be more of value because the client feels cared for by them than because of their specific content. Those of us who practice therapy, valuing it as we do and as we should, must at the same time realize that the existence of our profession is at least as much a symptom of the lack of deep listening available in our doing- and solving-oriented world as it is a cultural advance. When we realize this, we will not be led astray; we will realize that we need to say less and listen more, with more depth, clarity, and calmness.

To listen effectively, we must create a space for the other's concerns in our hearts. We cannot do this when we are already full of our own thoughts, plans, worries, and goals. We cannot do it when we are planning what helpful advice to offer the moment the other person stops talking. We can only do this when we are still and calm enough to make this space available. That is why all our other mindfulness practices come to play in listening as well.

To listen to another person requires a willingness to *understand*. To understand means to *stand under*, to calm your mind enough to let your own concerns, reactions, opinions, judgments, and preconceptions take a place below the concerns of the other at least for a while. Understanding may even be more important than love, for if you understand, then you love. But if you say you love, but do not understand, you may be deluding yourself.

Put Beliefs and Attitudes Aside

Often when we say we are listening, we are actually just running the other person's words through the filters of our own beliefs and attitudes. One such filter is *agree/disagree*. With this filter on, we do not listen, we simply test the other person's words against what we already think is true. It matters little whether we agree or disagree. Even if we agree, we do not really hear, but we defend ourselves and our own view of the world, creating distance between ourselves and the other. For there's a perception that to let another person in may change us. And this perception is correct. To listen is in fact a willingness to be touched and changed by another.

A second filter is *pleasant/unpleasant*. If what the other person says creates a feeling of tension or unpleasantness in us, we want to defend ourselves from it; we want to push it away. Sometimes when we cannot help but blurt out our sage advice or judgment, it is because by doing so we are attempting to hold this discomfort at bay. It makes *us* feel better to say, "What you really should do is . . ." or "You're looking at it wrong. The truth is . . ." It reduces *our* discomfort to say such things. But it may not be so helpful to the other person. She may even feel, "You just don't understand!" For our offer of solutions or advice, while protecting ourselves from unpleasant feelings, can close us off from the reality of the other person. And if the other person disagrees with our advice, we can close her out still more by saying to ourselves, "See, it's her own fault! She deserves it. She won't listen!" For if we can persuade ourselves that the other person has brought misfortune on herself, we feel safe in the knowledge that we would not be so foolish under similar circumstances.

The filters pleasant/unpleasant and agree/disagree both create distance. If what the other says is pleasant, we may think we can let it in more easily. But often, though we feel more relaxed than with material we judge unpleasant, it has the same effect. We are not creating space for the other. We are so relieved the other is saying something nice, we don't listen with any depth.

It is risky to remove the filters and listen. We risk being affected, changed, and transformed. We risk feeling sadness or pain. It is not empty words to say listening is a gift. By listening, we risk letting in things we disagree with, which are unpleasant to hold in awareness. We can only allow this to happen if we have enough calmness, mindfulness, and solidity to allow those things a space within ourselves. We can only do this if our mindfulness has given us the confidence that we can let in the other's words and deal effectively with whatever they elicit in us.

∽ PRACTICE ∽

Observe Filters

For a day or more, pay attention to your mental filters at work when you listen to others talk. The key is often in your body. When we hear something we don't like or disagree with, or even if we have begun to anticipate that we are about to hear such a thing, our bodies tighten up a little, as though we were expecting to receive a blow. Be aware of this tension. Notice how it shuts down your awareness. Breathe into it and calm it. See if you can hold a little more spacious, calm attention for the one speaking.

∽∽∽

Become an Active Listener

Skillful listening is not just about keeping quiet, however. When we listen skillfully, the other person knows we are present. To listen skillfully, we need to *show* the other person that we are taking in what she says and making room in our hearts. This is not so much a matter of saying so directly, though that can be okay to do. You can say: "I am here for you. I am listening." It is far more important, however, to embody these words.

The face of the good listener is alive. When we listen well, our facial expression subtly traces every nuance of what the other person says. If she says something sad, there may come a faint mist in the eye of the listener—not overblown and melodramatic but detectable. If she says something funny, we smile. All of this happens naturally. The listener need only allow his face to be alive to the other person. A mechanical approach will not do.

Good listeners are active in a certain way. For example, a good listener may nod her head a lot and make a lot of listening sounds, such as "Uh-huh" and "Um-hm." When I first saw a video of myself doing therapy during my training, I was embarrassed to see how much I nodded my head. On camera, it looked overblown, exaggerated—not at all like the cool, suave therapists in the movies. But I could tell by watching the reactions of the client that it was not overblown from his perspective. In fact, it created a sense of safety, a feeling that I was present and interested.

Good listeners also do what the psychologist Carl Rogers called "checking his understanding"—sometimes called "reflective listening." While other writers think of this in terms of therapeutic effects and intentions, Rogers thought of it as just checking whether he was receiving the message the client was trying to send. This can be accomplished by statements beginning with stems like:

"Let me see if I understand . . ."
"The way you see it . . ."
"Let me see if I can summarize what you've been saying . . ."
"What I'm getting is . . ."
"You . . ."

The exact words are unimportant: The attitude is supremely important. It is also not so important whether or not you get it right. If the speaker responds, "No, that's not what I mean at all. What I mean is . . . ," that's good! Even getting it wrong has helped the other person be clear. And your willingness to be corrected shows how much you want to understand.

Reflect before Dispensing Advice

A skilled listener is slow to give advice. This cannot be a hard and fast rule. But in general, advice giving is a different interactional stance from the effort to understand. When we give advice, we communicate that our own ideas are more valuable than those of the person we are trying to listen to. Listening involves a trust in the inner wisdom or ultimate Buddha nature of the one speaking and his ability to find his way.

There is a further reason to be cautious about advice: It often has the opposite effect from what is intended. For example, if we are listening to someone who is sad, and we offer some well-meaning palliative, such as "Don't blow things out of proportion," there's a chance the person will feel that you just don't understand. Now she not only feels sad but also misunderstood and even more alienated and alone. She may try to convince you it really *is* that bad and come to feel even worse as she rehearses all her negative thoughts and feelings, perhaps even exaggerating them so you will see that she is entitled to feel upset.

Sometimes people need listening because they are confronting a major choice. If someone must choose between going in life direction A or life direction B, human nature is such that the person may pull all the more strongly for A as soon as we argue for B. This is not contrariness or pathology, it is thoroughly and completely human. When we feel torn or ambivalent about an issue and someone else pulls for one side, we naturally feel a pull to represent the other side. So what happens when we tell our friend she should leave her miserable, unhappy relationship? She of course begins to tell us all the wonderful reasons why she should stay in it.

If you understand this polar nature of conversation, you may be tempted to use it in a manipulative way. You might, for example, tell your friend to stay in her relationship as a clever way of getting her to actually leave it. Sometimes this may work. But it is very risky. For one thing, people seem to sense our real attitude despite what we say, and they respond to this rather than to our words. More important, this approach is not listening, but a manipulative form of advice giving.

All of this may sound intimidating at first, but with practice it can become second nature. Listening is a high art. No matter how good you are at it, you can always improve. Just do your best. Even professional listeners struggle with this, sometimes not being able to keep ourselves from throwing in unwanted and unrequested advice or the "brilliant" insights that do more to stroke our own egos than help the other person. But try to move your capacity to listen in the right direction. Let it be okay that you are not yet a fully realized Buddha. Remember to practice lovingkindness toward yourself.

∼ PRACTICE ∼

Listen Actively

The next time someone comes to you with a problem or concern, spend a little longer listening actively, focusing on just trying to understand. Use the stems given on page 199, such as "The way you see it . . ." and so on to help get you started. Avoid switching the topic to something else, or comparing it to your own experience. Try to wait, if you can, until the person asks for advice before giving it. (Notice how seldom people actually do this.) If you absolutely cannot restrain yourself from advising, bring mindfulness to this process, and at least ask if it is okay to offer a suggestion.

The point is not to eliminate all advice. Advice can help sometimes. But most of us need to rebalance in the direction of listening more. And then when we do advise, it will be more likely to be on target, and more likely to be received as well.

∼∼∼

Cultivate Loving Speech

As important as listening is, skillful speech is equally important. Right speech is important enough that the Buddha assigned it its own place in the eightfold path. In *The Heart of the Buddha's Teaching*, Thich Nhat Hanh expresses this teaching this way:

Aware of the suffering caused by unmindful speech and the inability to listen to others, I am committed to cultivating loving speech and deep listening in order to bring joy and happiness to others and relieve others of their suffering. Knowing that words can create happiness or suffering, I am determined to speak truthfully, with words that inspire self-confidence, joy, and hope. I will not spread news that I do not know to be certain and will not criticize or condemn things of which I am not sure. I will refrain from uttering words that can cause division or discord, or that can cause the family or the community to break. I am determined to make all efforts to reconcile and resolve all conflicts, however small.

Notice that in the Buddhist understanding, listening is already part of right speech. Speaking and listening are sides of the same coin.

Above all, right speech is loving speech. Its aim is to relieve suffering and create happiness. And if it is also to be rooted in truth, it is still more important that it be loving. There may of course be times when we have to speak words that will, in the short run, cause some pain, when we must be cruel to be kind. But this is a dangerous area. For one thing, when we get self-righteous about speaking the truth, we may often be rationalizing an intention to hurt, using our "truth" as a sledgehammer—an instrument of our anger. And for another, the "truth" we speak is our own, partial and relative. With mindfulness, you can discriminate between when you are telling a painful but needed truth, and when anger is at work.

Develop Skillful Speech

Psychology also has a valuable contribution to make regarding skillful speech. The following suggestions are ones I use regularly in my clinical practice. Some are obvious, some are subtle. Some I gleaned from research and other professional literature, some are part of therapeutic lore, and one or two are my own contribution.

1. *If you think you should discuss something with someone, you probably should.* While it is possible to do too much processing, for many of us, the temptation is more to avoid things that may be difficult to bring up. If you feel this issue may be effectively resolved with some discussion, then consider initiating one. Some very important questions remain, however, such as *how* and *when*. It is important to bring up difficult subjects skillfully, calmly, and at an appropriate time. It is generally not advisable to bring up a difficult discussion when someone is heading out the door to work or first thing when he or she arrives back home, tired at the end of a long day. But remember that no matter how hon-

orable your intentions are, your words will not always be received, particularly if the other person is simply not ready to hear the information you are sharing.

2. *Talk about how you feel.* First, talk about how *you* feel. Avoid mind reading your partner's unexpressed feelings or making assumptions about them. Second, talk about how you *feel*. Discuss your feelings rather than your judgments or your psychological analysis of the other person. "I felt hurt and angry when you shut the door so hard" is much better than "I felt you were being rude when you slammed the door in my face." Notice that the latter is a disguised judgment. Even if you say the words "I feel" at the beginning of a sentence, you may not be talking about your feelings. "Rude" is a judgment and so is "slammed the door in my face." When you discuss how you feel, you invite the other person to try to understand. When you judge, you invite defensiveness and argument. In this case, an argument could well ensue about what is and is not rude, or whether the way the door was shut constituted slamming. And of course no one wants to feel psychoanalyzed by a friend or partner. "I feel you're being defensive" or "I think you have a problem with your mother" are questionable in a therapy context. They are sparks on gasoline in personal relationships.

This rule is usually invoked regarding negative feelings. And that makes some sense, since those feelings are the more difficult ones. However, it helps to give *at least* equal opportunity to positive feelings as well. "I felt loved when you made my favorite meal for me."

Of course, before you can talk clearly about how you feel, there is a prior step. You must be able to know and respect your own feelings. You must be mindful of them and care for them. In this way, mindfulness with your own thoughts and feelings is the basis for skillful interaction.

3. *Take responsibility for your feelings.* "I felt angry when you closed the door so hard" is better than "*You made me* feel angry . . ." The second implies that you are helpless to take care of your own feelings and that the other person bears total responsibility for them. This is a subtle distinction, perhaps, but a useful one.

4. *Avoid labeling and name calling.* Of course. But I have worked with too many angry couples to avoid stating the obvious. Watch out for subtle forms of this as well. Diagnosing someone's psychological

problem is more sophisticated than calling someone a jerk, but it is the same thing at heart. Calling someone defensive, even if it's true, seldom contributes to a climate of openness.

5. *Beware of* always *and* never. First of all, these words are generally incorrect. One disconfirmatory instance makes the lie of them. If you say, "You *never* take the garbage out," your statement is not only provocative, but also untrue if only *one time* the other person took the garbage out. *Always* and *never* put the other person in a box. In this sense, they function a little like name calling.

When you find these words on the tip of your tongue, look for the feeling behind it and try to express it directly (guideline 2). Try: "I'm feeling frustrated with how we share household responsibilities." (Also see guideline 6.)

6. *Ask for what you want* (rather than complaining about what you don't want). Sometimes idealistic people are surprised by the notion that we have to ask for behavior change from people we love. There's a feeling that we should love people just the way they are. You may love them, but asking for change is a practical necessity. The only question is whether we do this skillfully or not. Compare the following:

"You never bring me flowers. What's the matter? Don't you love me anymore?"

and

"Darling, it makes me so happy when you bring me flowers. It would feel wonderful to me if you did that a little more often."

It is not hard to see which is more skillful. In the second example, the person being addressed is invited to change in a way that allows him to do so without feeling like he is giving in or losing.

7. *Avoid gunny sacking.* Gunny sacking is a hunting term. It refers to pulling ammunition out of a sack on your shoulder. In dialogue, this means bringing up past issues whenever you talk about a current one. Gunny sacking is a way to ensure that nothing changes. Nothing can be resolved if every minor discussion snowballs into an argument about past mistakes.

8. *Use humor.* Humor can be helpful. At the same time, be aware that it is potentially a two-edged sword. Humor can also carry our aggressive and hostile feelings, perhaps giving us a way to deal with them with a light touch, but also running the risk of hurting another unintentionally. Be especially cautious with humor at another's expense. Nowadays some people make excessive use of ironical humor and sarcasm. In this atmosphere, no one wants to risk making a simple direct statement about what she thinks and feels. Such humor prevents intimacy and can hurt others more than we know. If your humor is to be at someone's expense, let it be your own.

9. *Admit your part in the problem.* If you believe you are 100 percent innocent and the other person 100 percent at fault, you are most likely wrong. Even if you think your part is relatively small, to concede that you played some part in the difficulty is helpful and conciliatory. If the other person feels entirely blamed and made at fault, he is unlikely to experience this as a safe environment in which to change. But don't fake it. If you are insincere, or if you are conceding a point that is so trivial that it really just emphasizes how much you blame the other person, this will be ineffective.

10. *Find something in what the other says that you agree with.* If someone is speaking very unskillfully and resorts to calling you a jerk, even in this case, you can agree: "You know, you've got a point. I've probably done several jerky things already today." This is especially useful in dealing with someone hostile. You have agreed in part. You have not taken on the totality of the label "jerk"—you've just admitted to an aspect of it. Who has not done some things that may be considered jerky? This can be followed up with:

11. *Request more information.* That is: "Tell me more about what you mean when you say I'm a jerk." This one-two combination of agreement and requesting more information deflates anger in a powerful way. Note that this is not a violation of the principle of self-love. In fact, it takes real self-love to concede the possibility of having done some *particular* things in an unskillful manner, while maintaining an overall attitude of self-worth and self-acceptance. However, these things may prove difficult to do emotionally unless you have adequately prepared the ground.

12. *Avoid premature problem solving*. You know who you are, all you well-intentioned fixers and problem solvers out there. You can hardly help yourself; you rattle off the answers and solutions to other people's problems at the drop of a hat. "Why don't you just . . ." "All you need to do is . . ." But perhaps you have noticed, albeit with frustration, that others do not always seem to embrace your generous, freely offered wisdom. If you get frustrated because your suggestions are greeted with "Yes, but," consider this a message. The other person may be trying to tell you: "Please, I want to feel *understood*. Your advice sounds easy and then I feel silly for even having these feelings. Just try to understand."

If you are unsure whether the other person wants problem solving or sympathetic listening, there is an effective strategy: ask. But be careful. You must ask in a way that shows openness toward either possibility, not with a tone that subtly suggests, "You don't really want constructive help, because you are not open to advice."

13. *The stranger rule*. We sometimes are more polite to a stranger on the street than to the people we are closest to. Try to be at least as courteous with the people you are close to as you would be with a stranger. Say please. Say thank you, you're welcome, excuse me.

14. *Practice mindfulness of vocal tone, facial expression, gesture, and body language*. Often people respond more to the *way* in which we say something than to *what* we actually say. Sometimes I have had couples turn on a tape recorder before discussing an issue. This can be very revealing. On tape, people hear how their tone of voice contradicted the message they thought they were giving. An exaggerated example is the singsongy, sarcastic way the comedian Steve Martin used to say, "Well, ex-cuuuuuse meeeeeee!" If you do that in a discussion, later you can argue, "But all I said was, 'Excuse me.' I was just being polite!"

15. *Practice mindfulness of the effect of what you say and how you say it*. When do your words create closeness—an atmosphere of acceptance? When do they seem to create distance or defensiveness? If your words are not having the effect you wish, perhaps there is a more skillful way. No list of guidelines could ever be fully adequate. But if you pay attention to the feedback you get from others, monitoring whether your words create more openness and closeness or distance and defensiveness, you can guide what you say in the direction of greater effectiveness and skill.

16. *Don't make these guidelines a source of argument.* When anger is around, even positive tools can get pulled into it. I have worked with couples who, being introduced to these principles, then use them as another weapon in their arsenals, each accusing the other of not following them correctly. Use these ideas to guide your own behavior. That way, they work in your favor and help your relationships.

Sometimes You Have to Hiss

It is a Zen principle that rules can never be fully adequate guides to our behavior. When we are fully alive and awake in the present moment, we know what to do and what not to do. And while the above rules are useful, there is a time when they must be abandoned. This is killing the Buddha when you meet him, so that Buddha comes to life in you instead of being an idol.

In Christopher Isherwood's *Ramakrishna and His Disciples* the gentle Hindu saint Ramakrishna tells a parable about a guru who reforms a poisonous snake. But there was a problem: The guru's teaching had worked all too well. Since everyone knew he would no longer fight back, the poor snake, who previously had terrorized the neighborhood, was now himself terrorized and abused. When the guru saw the snake again, he was barely alive, so badly had he been treated. Hearing the account of what he had suffered from others, the guru said, "For shame! . . . Are you such a fool that you don't know how to protect yourself? I told you not to bite. I didn't tell you not to hiss. Why couldn't you have scared them away by hissing?"

Ramakrishna summarized: "You have to hiss at wicked people. You have to scare them, or they'll harm you. But you must never shoot venom into them. You must never harm them."

In another example, one of Ramakrishna's disciples returned from the marketplace only to discover he'd been cheated by a pious-talking shopkeeper. Ramakrishna told him: "The shopkeeper was there to do business, not to practice religion. Why did you believe him and get cheated? Just because you're a devotee, that's no reason to be a fool."

The reason to practice right speech is not ultimately about following rules or moralisms or even about being a good person. Speech is "right" when it leads in the direction of peace and happiness, when it liberates us and others from suffering.

And sometimes, right speech means you have to hiss.

Encourage Loving Action

Action, it is said, speaks louder than words. And certainly it is the case that loving, kind words carry little weight if not supported by loving, kind action.

When we make the heart larger through metta meditation, we find that loving action flows easily. Often it is not when we set about self-consciously doing some good deed that we are helpful, but when we just are who we are. A tree helps the world by being a tree and following its own nature. It does not have to tell itself, "I must do something to help the world! I must create oxygen, I must bear fruit!" Just being itself, it helps and blesses the world.

We, too, are generally most helpful when we just take good care of ourselves, practicing calmness and understanding. This is even true with professional helpers like therapists. When a therapist tries too hard, self-consciously attempting to be helpful, her efforts often backfire. When a therapist seeks, more modestly, simply to understand, taking care of herself so she does not get lost in sadness, this is often the most helpful thing of all. We help the people we are closest to most by cultivating happiness and peace in ourselves. Others feel better just being around such a peaceful, happy person.

But this is not to deny the importance of intentional action. It is a good practice to wake up in the morning and ask yourself, "What can I do this day to bring some happiness to the people I love?" and then seek to put a few such things into practice each day.

In behavioral therapy for couples, healthy human relationships are seen as a positive cycle of doing things for each other. The more George does loving things for Mary, the more she in turn is inspired to do loving things for him. And the more she does for him, the more George does back, and so on. This positive cycle of interaction contrasts sharply with what happens in troubled relationships. In troubled relationships, people trade hurtful behaviors in a negative, escalating cycle. Because George hurt Mary, Mary hurts George, who hurts her back, and so on. Unless something intervenes to change it, this negative cycle continues, often intensifying with each exchange.

Fortunately, positive cycles of interaction tend to continue their momentum as well. The goal of the couples' therapist is to take advantage of this fact and reestablish a positive cycle. Even if this is done in a mechanical way at first, it can continue and deepen once it has gained enough momentum.

It is difficult to restart the positive cycle. When you are stuck in a negative interaction cycle with someone, it is hard to cut across the grain of your hurt and anger by doing kind things for the other person. The fear of being taken advantage of comes into play. This fear is seldom warranted, as the documented effectiveness of this type of therapy shows. Most people will respond to repeated, consistent kindness. But in an emotional sense, it can be quite difficult to start doing nice things when you are angry and hurt. Practicing metta meditation can help a lot with this emotional barrier.

Identify What Loved Ones Truly Want

Sometimes people devote a lot of time and energy to doing helpful, loving things, but the effort is wasted because they are not the right things, or at least not the best ones. George might knock himself out fixing Mary's car, trying through many hours of difficult, dirty work to do something nice for her. But it may be that Mary would just as soon take the car to a mechanic. It may be that George would receive more appreciation for giving Mary fifteen minutes of deep listening about her work day than for many hours of hard labor on her car. Similarly, Mary might spend hours preparing a dinner for George that would put Martha Stewart to shame. But if George is basically a meat-and-potatoes guy, Mary's efforts are largely wasted. George might appreciate it far more if Mary watched a little football with him and honestly tried to understand the game and his passion for it.

If Mary and George do the wrong things for each other, not only are they wasting effort, but they risk feeling even more discouraged. "See, he never appreciates the things I do." "See, it doesn't matter how much I do for her." Out of discouragement, each then becomes less likely to make further efforts. *But if they look deeply and with insight, they will see that it is not so much the case that what they did was not appreciated, as that they were not doing the right things.* In fixing the car and preparing the meal, they were really doing what they themselves wanted, not what the other person wanted.

In these simple examples lies an important truth. Often when we say we are doing things for the other person, we have not seriously tried to understand what the other person really wants, but we do things we like to do, or things we want to be appreciated for. So how do we know for sure what the other person likes? The answer, which is again surprisingly simple, is to *ask*. In my work with couples, I have them rate how much they like a particular thing on a numeric scale. This artificial-seeming device clarifies a lot. Because if asked how much she likes having lasagna made for her supper and how much she likes having the shopping done, the answer may be, in both instances, "a lot." But if she rates it from 1 to 10 (with 10 being the most wonderful), the lasagna may be a 6 and the shopping a 9. This provides considerably more information than "a lot."

Talk to those you share life with about what they like so your energy can be focused appropriately. Otherwise, you may burn yourself out on kindnesses that are simply the wrong things, and then feel unappreciated.

Express Appreciation

Another important kindness is expressing appreciation in a meaningful way. Most people, if asked, would say that they make a point to express appreciation to others. Yet most of us would also agree that the world we live in is short on appreciation. How can both be true? If you were to actually monitor how many times in a week you express meaningful appreciation to someone—appreciation that goes beyond what might be considered bare politeness—you would be surprised at how infrequently you do this. Yet honest, warm, sincere appreciation is one of the things that contributes profoundly to our sense of connectedness, for both the giver and the receiver, and is essential in maintaining positive cycles of interaction.

Some people object to the behavioral description of human interactions as too mercenary, too much of a trade or a business and not enough of the heart. Yet it is undeniable that positive cycles of interaction do have an aspect of exchange or trade, and this is necessarily so. But in healthy, positive cycles there is no literal tit for tat, no close keeping of accounts. The Buddhist view of no self sheds light here. Once you see that we are not as separate as we generally believe, the boundary between giving and receiving blurs. I give, at the same time knowing that, since I am interconnected with others, I have not lost anything by this. For making the people around me happy contributes to my happiness. Also, by taking care of my own happiness and well-being, I give to those around me. So the apparently selfless act of giving contains a selfish element, and the apparently selfish act of self-care contains a generous element. The point is not just that it is better to give than to receive, but that both are part of the same overarching process. In reality, there is not one thing called giving and another called receiving, but a cycle called giving-receiving.

No self helps us see these connections. It challenges the moralistic view separating selfishness and generosity, and opens up a world that is all one, or as the Buddhists would prefer to say, not two. In this world, there is no giver and no receiver, nothing given and nothing received. We are interconnected by countless acts of lovingkindness.

Learn to Let Go

In a journal entry dated October 23, 1836, Ralph Waldo Emerson said this about the experience of bereavement: "My own faith teaches me that when one of these losses befalls me it is because the hour is struck in my own constitution, a crisis has there taken place which makes it best for my whole being, makes it necessary for my whole being that this influence be withdrawn."

Death is not the only reason this can happen. Sometimes also for reasons other than death a relationship reaches the point where, for the well-being of one or both parties, it is necessary to let it go. When you are caught in a destructive cycle and you have done everything, tried everything, it may be time to call a halt to your connection to that person.

In couples therapy, I've seen people desperately try to find the love they need from their partner. Sometimes, the more frustrated they become in meeting this need, the harder and more desperately they try to force it out of their partner. At this point it is much better to step back a little, and simply try to see clearly: Who is this person I am trying so hard to please, to get love from? What is his true nature? Does she have the capacity to love me in the way I want to be loved? If you are honest, you may recognize that you are trying to get blood from a stone. This person may not have what you need.

Sometimes when a friend becomes separated by distance, you are wise not to pursue a relationship too hard. Sometimes a parent is so disordered and abusive that the adult child must stay away if he is to have a chance to live any sort of decent life. Sometimes a son or daughter or sibling may be so psychologically disordered that a relationship with that person will only be destructive. These are sad truths. And while we think it good much of the time to try to avoid further disconnection and maintain the relationship, we know that sometimes this just cannot be. We would be remiss if, by not discussing this, we added to your guilt about it.

Even if you have reached the sad conclusion that a continued connection is impossible, you can still practice metta toward that person. Send her love and compassion. Release your resentment, anger, and sadness. And entrust her to the benevolence of the universe.

Open to a Different Reality

Metta meditation, together with the practice of skillful listening, speaking, and doing, when pursued with a gentle, patient persistence, creates a new world. This new world is like a mirror image in which you must move the opposite way from what you expect. The things we do in this world are strangely backward. The more we grasp, the less we have. The more we give away, the happier we feel. Nor is this a matter of doing anything noble, self-sacrificing, or in any moralistic way praiseworthy. It is simply that you come to see that certain actions have certain results. Some actions create suffering. Some create happiness. Contrary to so-called common sense, reality is not divided up in such a way that my happiness and yours are at odds, with an increase in one representing a decrease in the other. In fact, since we are not two, there is no split in happiness, no collection of competing happinesses. I give to you knowing that it will increase your happiness, which will increase mine, which will again increase yours, and so on. I receive your giving knowing that it will help make me happy, which will help you to be happy, and so on. Every act of giving spreads like ripples in a pond and rebounds to us.

It is a little difficult to get one's bearings in this topsy-turvy, upside-down, mirror-image world. We need patience with ourselves as we slip back into old ways and try to separate out our happiness from that of others. But that is okay. It is part of the play of maya—of illusion—that human growth comes in this awkward, two-steps-forward, one-step-back manner. As long as we do our best to remain mindful, we see the consequences when we slip, and adjust accordingly.

Kindness is "not two." Just as it makes no sense to be kind to ourselves and separate this from kindness to others, so it makes no sense to practice kindness toward others, but be exceedingly unkind toward ourselves when our newfound insight falters.

Practice for Week Nine

1. Continue meditation (twenty-five minutes twice daily), a day of mindfulness, reading, walking meditation, and work with dreams.
2. Spend one or both of your daily meditation periods on metta meditation (pp. 188, 191).
3. In all of your interactions this week, focus on listening a little more deeply to others. Make a space for them. Use the exercises in this chapter to help:
   • "Observe Filters" (p. 198)
   • "Listen Actively" (p. 201)
4. Focus all week on right speech. Avoid spreading rumors, participating in gossip, or saying anything about anyone that you would be unwilling to say to her face. Concentrate on speaking only that which is useful, helpful, encouraging, and true. Meditate on the guidelines in this chapter and seek to put them into practice. Add your own insights to the practice as you learn from your experiences and reflection.
5. Focus on kind action, without seeking credit or recognition. This may be for the most part little things, simple and undramatic. Let the other car get in front of you. Be the one to empty the dishwasher. Straighten up. Show others your smiling face.
6. Focus this week on awareness of how others help you. Express this awareness. Tell the other person you appreciate it. Especially notice simple things: the sales clerk who is friendly. The kind word. The people who drive reasonably and courteously (instead of focusing on the relative few who drive aggressively, as we are wont to do).

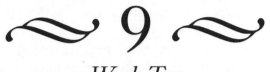

9

Week Ten

MEDITATE ON PAPER

Your own treasure house already contains every thing you need.
Why don't you use it freely, instead of chasing after something
outside yourself?

—Ma-tsu (A.D. 709–788)

Create a Vessel

Jewish mystical tradition teaches that while the divine light is everywhere, it is necessary to forge a container to hold it. Psychologically, this is a way of saying that the divine, the center within, must be consciously held. A personal journal provides such a container. Journaling is a powerfully healing practice, a way to take stock of your life, to gain perspective, to weave together seemingly disconnected and disparate strands. Whereas public autobiographies must maintain a public face and seek to make a certain impression or protect against misunderstandings, a personal journal is a private autobiography, where one can say honestly and boldly whatever one is thinking and feeling in the moment.

In your journal, you can listen to your life and tap out its secret rhythms. It is a place for total honesty about your life experiencing, including things you might normally condemn about yourself. While great journal writers of the past such as Emerson or Thoreau maintained a lofty, dignified persona in their journals, you can be free from that in private journaling. If you cannot be candid with yourself in your own journal, where can you be? Your journal is a place of freedom from the public self. It is a place to acquaint yourself with all that you are, including your less presentable aspects.

In our fragmented world and even more fragmented experiencing, many of us feel a need for some container, some way of holding the fragments together. A journal can do this. Research has demonstrated that journaling has effects similar to, though not as large as, the effects of psychotherapy.

The process of journaling parallels psychotherapy. Like therapy, journaling requires a process orientation. That is, placing more attention on *how* things unfold than on the result. To benefit from keeping a journal, it is better not to expect immediate relief and profound insight each time you write. In fact, trying to force this out of each session is a mistake. Let it be enough to listen to your life, to explore raw, unvarnished thoughts and feelings. In itself, this is a unique experience. In itself, this is already healing. And as you do this over a period of time, you find a greater ease with yourself and with your life, a more accepting and open attitude toward yourself and others, and an increase in your capacity to unabashedly feel what you really feel and to feel it deeply and clearly. In your journal, you do not need to force your experience to fit into the categories of some prescripted and unexamined life story. Journaling is an experience of self-acceptance, of freedom from your public face.

Regular journaling cultivates a positive spiral of increasing awareness. At first, you record events and feelings of the day, trying to recall them clearly, with understanding and self-acceptance, exploring their connection, perhaps, with ongoing life issues and themes. At this point, your journaling does not affect the rest of your day—your day affects your journaling. What you experience during the day becomes the material you later record. As you continue, however, the effect begins to work in the other direction as well; your journaling begins to affect your day. During the day you become more sharply aware of your thoughts and feelings, knowing that you will write about them later. When you reach this point, a positive feedback cycle has begun.

Manage Difficulties

If journaling can accomplish so much, why doesn't everyone do it? Of course, for some people, the thought of picking up pen and paper and looking within is as appealing as scraping sandpaper over your tongue. For many, writing has simply become too aversive. The memories of critical teachers and others are simply too strong.

But even for people who are otherwise comfortable with writing, there are roadblocks to keeping a journal. Three such difficulties are: (1) the slow pace of journaling; (2) the difficulty of finding the time for it; and (3) the temptation to let journaling become primarily a repository for negative thoughts and feelings.

Enjoy the Slower Pace

Today when information speeds at incredible rates from computer to computer on the World Wide Web, even talking seems slow. Trying to connect with others can feel like trying to get Alice's March Hare to stretch out his legs and have a leisurely chat. "I'm late! I'm late!" he protests, and there is no time to stop and talk. No wonder taking up a pen and recording your private thoughts, feelings, and images can seem quaint and cumbersome, like a horse and buggy in a space shuttle age.

Yet it is this very slowness that makes journaling valuable. Like most of the approaches for increasing awareness in this book, it, too, is most essentially a way of slowing down, of allowing our monkey minds to calm and settle, of breathing more deeply, of sensing more clearly. The slower speed that makes journaling seem quaint is the very thing that gives it value.

If the slowness of writing is aversive, you can use your computer's program that translates the spoken word into type. But you might like to experiment with the old-fashioned method first. In some ways, there's no substitute for pen and paper.

Create the Time

The second problem, finding time, is an aspect of the problem of speed. For people who feel a constant pressure to do things quickly, journaling will seem like an extravagance of time. Some methods of journaling contribute to this problem by having burdensome time requirements. The psychologist Ira Progoff, for example, created a wonderful approach called "Intensive Journaling." He initiated people into this process at special retreats and through the books he wrote about these retreats. It's a good method, especially for a period of life transition, and if you are very interested in journaling as a technology for personal growth, you might enjoy Dr. Progoff's books or even try a workshop. However, the process he describes is time intensive.

If you keep your journaling process simple, it need not require large amounts of time. There can also be great flexibility—times when you write a lot and times when you write a little or skip altogether, according to your needs and the demands of your schedule. You don't need to record every passing thought and experience. Just by attending to major themes, you can gain a great deal of insight.

Avoid any hard, compulsive, or forced quality about your journaling. Let it be the emotional equivalent of stepping into a warm, bubbly Jacuzzi at the end of a hard day. One is unlikely to stick with any personal growth project that becomes heavy with pressure, guilt, or obligation.

But what if you feel like you don't have the energy, even if you can find time? Even if your journaling is kept simple, at the end of the workday one can easily feel this way. And the thought of doing it in the morning before work, or cramming it in between work activities during the day, can seem unappealing or impossible. And there are times when it is, of course. Yet for many of us, though we say we are busy, we spend a lot of time on passive pursuits such as television. It is as though we have two modes: completely on and completely off. In the on mode, the mode we usually think of as our life, we are busy rushing and doing. This is the aspect of our lives we are thinking of when we say we are busy. When we come home, it is easy to take the path of least resistance. Now we are off duty. We want to do things that place minimal demands on us. Watching a *Seinfeld* rerun seems a lot easier than writing in a journal, meditating, reading, or playing music.

Examine Your Busyness

We have already discussed how our busyness connects with the myths of struggle and self-importance; if you feel that you don't have time to journal, you may wish to examine that perception. Often this just means that a particular task is less important to you than other things that you want to do.

Still, finding time can be a little difficult. Part of the problem is that our daytime, workday life is so out of balance, so rushed and hectic, that we need to rebalance into the opposite. We move from being totally on all day to being totally off and out of service. If this is the problem, we may need ways to alter our rhythm during the workday hours if we are to spend our evenings differently. For if we get stuck in this pattern, life becomes all work except for those scarce and precious weekends and holidays.

If you say you are too busy, you might examine time spent watching television. Some people conquer television by getting rid of it altogether. As many alcoholics know, with some behaviors it is easier to abstain than to attempt moderation. If you are stuck in this pattern but don't want to throw out the television, there are less radical steps. Make a deal with yourself to write in your journal or read for half an hour before you turn it on. Intentionally spend an evening without television now and then, or even do a television fast for a week or so. When you reduce the time spent in passive modes of entertainment, you'll be amazed at how much time you really have. And you've solved the problem of finding the time for journaling or other pursuits. Wouldn't it be interesting to find out what you would do with your time if you stopped passive entertainment?

But when you find yourself surfing channels at light speed because none of what's on appeals to you and it's all commercials anyway, perhaps you can mindfully, with love and acceptance toward yourself, acknowledge that for now this is the choice you are making and explore what it feels like to be making this choice.

Keep It Constructive

Finally, nothing can make journaling more unpleasant than if it becomes solely a record of negative, angry, or depressing thoughts and feelings. If all you do in your journal is recycle and rehearse such feelings, it can be harmful. Sometimes this happens because popular culture has infected us with the feeling that being honest means being negative. So feelings of anger or sadness are accepted at face value, while feelings of happiness or love are suspect. This is a carryover from diluted Freudian thinking, where inner exploration means figuring out what we *really* feel and what our *real* motivations are (and what others *really* feel, which is even more fun)—all with the underlying assumption that real feelings are negative and positive feelings are not real.

Of course, most journalers will have dark, gloomy entries from time to time. This may even continue for whole periods, especially if there has been a major loss or life change. But if it continues too long, if journaling itself seems to get you depressed, this is worth paying attention to. Perhaps you need to focus your mindfulness on positive aspects a little more. Focus for a time on simple pleasures: that cup of coffee in the morning, the sound of your friend's voice on the phone, the comforting warmth of your bed on a winter night. Just drawing breath is pleasurable when experienced in the right way. You don't have to deny the negative feelings or try to manufacture anything that isn't real. Just consciously open to whatever is there that is healing and positive, *in addition to* any difficult feelings and thoughts.

Our consciousness is like a garden, with weeds, flowers, and vegetables—a whole mixture. Sometimes it is as though we are watering and fertilizing the weeds instead of the flowers. Try watering the flowers for a while. Devote a week to noticing the good things that are there and recording them in your journal.

Keep It Private

Privacy is essential in journaling. If you write in your journal knowing that others may view what you have written, this may hinder the candid flow. Your journal is a place for the raw feeling, the unprocessed sadness or joy. If you are being very honest and noting that you feel joy in someone else's misfortune and at the same time guilt for feeling that way, you need to be with those feelings without judgment and without worrying that someone may be hurt by reading about them later. Given the way feelings flow and change, you may reach other, more socially acceptable and compassionate feelings later, which you don't record. Someone who happens upon your journal entry, however, won't know that, and may be hurt needlessly. But in any case, you just should not have to worry about this.

How can you protect your privacy? Leonardo da Vinci taught himself to write in mirror image so that no one looking over his shoulder would be able to decipher what he was writing. But most of us will not need to go to such lengths. Usually it is enough to: (1) *Explain to those you live with why you consider privacy important.* If you have not communicated your expectations about this, you are as much to blame as they are if they snoop. (2) *Always put your journal away.* You should not have to bury it in the backyard, but if you leave it open on the kitchen table, you are actually encouraging prying eyes.

In addition, some people like to get a locking diary, or, if journaling on the computer, to encrypt the file.

Find the Right Time and Place

Though you can journal anytime, morning and evening are ideal. One practical reason for this is that journaling can easily be interrupted or pushed out of your schedule altogether if you plan to do it during the day. Choosing morning or evening as journaling time helps prevent this.

Morning and evening journaling each have a different quality. In the morning, we approach the process with the clarity of a night's sleep. Dream material may be more of a focus in the morning, since the traces of our dreams are more accessible. Morning writing reviews our life from a higher level, less in touch with the details, but seeing the larger themes more clearly. Morning writing can also set us up for a positive day if we use it to voice intentions about how we want to live.

Evening writing, on the other hand, contains richer detail about the day. Sometimes these details contain the real fruit of journaling. Writing at the end of the day helps us let go of the day's events, ensuring a sleep less troubled by undigested worry and anxiety. It also facilitates productive dreaming, bringing important themes from the day into focus for exploration in our sleep. You may find one time works best for you, or you may want to get the rewards of both morning and evening by varying when you write or even doing both.

Make a Quiet Space

As much as possible, let your journaling be surrounded by *quietness*. Find a peaceful, comfortable place for writing and choose a time when you will not be interrupted. Put the answering machine on, activate your voice mail, or just unplug the phone. Let the people you live with know what you are doing and enlist their cooperation. You may want to use a favorite pen or choose a special notebook. These are ways of *respecting* the process. When we respect the process, it is more likely to reward us. Sit down, write the date on the paper, close your eyes, and gently breathe in and out. Let your mind review recent life events, perhaps focusing on what has happened since your last entry. Let images, feelings, and thoughts come spontaneously, without forcing anything. Be with all of this without judgment; in fact, hold sympathy for yourself and acceptance of your life.

The Felt Sense

The psychologist Eugene Gendlin coined the term *felt sense* to describe the bodily sensation connected with a particular life issue or problem. The felt sense contains much useful wisdom about a life issue unavailable to the verbal, linear, and rational mind. To get to the felt sense, think of one of the problems or issues in your present life—relationships, money, career, or whatever—something of importance to you. Keep your awareness of the problem sharp and clear, letting all of your feelings come up. Then focus on the area of your body between your neck and waist. Notice where the sensations related to these feelings are located. Is it primarily in the shoulders? The chest? The stomach? Notice the exact nature of the sensation you experience. To focus on the sensation, ask yourself questions about it. Are the feelings hot or cold? What color would they be if they had a color? What is this sensation like? Prickly, tight—whatever it is, note it carefully. Keep the feelings, thoughts, and sensations vivid. When you begin to write, write *out of* this felt sense, letting the felt sense itself speak. When the answers are just more cognitive chatter of the sort you normally engage in already, the felt sense stays more or less the same. But when you have allowed something new to happen, when you have let the felt sense itself speak, the physical sensation shifts and changes. Record the answers that come out of this felt sense. There may be many small steps or shifts involved in changing a life problem, so do not be in too much of a hurry. By paying attention to the felt sense, you reach deeper layers of knowing.

Writing from the felt sense of a problem prevents us from getting stuck in those tightly rational, but ultimately self-defeating loops many of us know too well.

Journaling to Remember

While insufficient in itself for the in-depth healing a journal can bring, journaling to remember is a good place to start. Sometimes you may want to skip this level, but there are times when this level is important. Beverly used this level extensively during some of her travels. She wanted to simply be aware and remember her experiences. It can also be a useful level to get started when you don't know where to begin. As you record life events, notice what thoughts and emotions are attached to them. Then begin to gently explore these. In fact, if you have difficulty identifying feelings in a particular area of concern, often it helps to begin by noting the concrete, external facts first. By being in touch with these, the feelings flow more easily into awareness.

Build a Memory Bridge

Life experiences are connected to prior life experiences with a similar emotional tone. When we suffer grief or loss, these experiences are understood in the light of previous losses, and amplified by them. When something wonderful happens, these experiences are also enhanced or muffled by what has gone on before. You can learn about how your life story filters current experience through the lens of the past by building a memory bridge between significant present events and past events that evoke a strong response. To do this, first notice an event that either is significant in itself or one that evoked a stronger response than you would have expected. Be with these feelings and focus on the felt sense. Then let memories emerge that are connected to the present experience. Note the passive quality in the word *let*. Rather than trying to figure things out, you want to let connections emerge. The connection between memories may not always be apparent logically, but they are connected emotionally. Then begin with this earlier memory and holding it clearly in awareness, wait for another memory to emerge, continuing this process until it comes to a natural halt. Then finally, take a look at the whole chain of memories. What does it tell you about the roots of your current issue or difficulty?

Use Stream-of-Consciousness Journaling

Of course, strictly speaking, recording your stream of consciousness is not possible, since you can think many times more quickly than you can write. But the idea is to *let* thoughts and emotions stream on to the paper without trying to control the outcome. It is a process of serendipity, of discovery. Let whatever comes come, even if it seems silly, disconnected, nonsensical, irrational, or disgusting. The intention is to accept rather than judge these inner processes. But since in reality you can't always force yourself to be accepting—which is a self-contradiction anyway—simply note any judgments that come up as another thing to observe, be with, and befriend. A simplified example might go something like this:

> Feeling a little off today, and I don't know why . . . Hearing that clock again. I never notice how loud it is until I sit to write. Seemed to have just gotten out of bed this way . . . There were those disturbing dream images, being chased by some kind of animal, a dog or something, intense fear . . . Such a strange feeling, really. Boy, I didn't know all that was in there. Feelings of judgment. I have trouble liking the parts of me where this came from. What am I doing this for, anyway? I should be getting to work. I have so much to do, there isn't time . . . Such feelings of pressure . . . My boss's face comes to mind, looking angry. Like the time I came to work an hour late last month . . .

Your entries will be more personal than this sample, but it demonstrates the principle of being with whatever comes up, gently exploring it without trying to change it or do anything but *hear yourself*, listening in on your internal process. Once the writing seems to run out of energy, it is helpful to go over the entry, even to read it out loud to yourself if you are alone, and listen lovingly to the flow of your inner life. When we begin to journal regularly, the first things to surface are often things we are uncomfortable with, since that is what most needs to be healed, acknowledged, and accepted. But sometimes we can also reach strange and beautiful realms that we never would have suspected lie within us. We reach them best, however, by having no particular expectations to reach anything, by a willingness to accept whatever comes up.

Inner Guide Journaling

Emerson wrote, "We are wiser than we know." There is in each of us an amazing wisdom. The problem is not that this wise voice does not exist. The problem is that it is difficult to hear it over the cacophony of other voices, especially the voices of worry, fear, and gloom.

It can help to use imagery to access the wise voice. There are many ways to do this. You might imagine a holy figure such as Jesus, Mary, Krishna, the Buddha, Avalokiteshvara, or any representation of the wise woman or wise man within. Perhaps you will see the emaciated form of a Hindu yogi, wearing a simple dhoti (loincloth). Perhaps you will see a native shaman, or a wise old rabbi with flowing beard and prayer shawl. Be creative. Use whatever images help you to tap your inner wisdom. It isn't necessary to believe that you are really talking to the Buddha (though you indeed may be more than you realize). The image you use is a way of focusing your attention and finding your own wisdom. Imagine yourself approaching this person with imagery that suggests going deeper into the self to a bright center of your being. Here is an example you can start with to tap into your own existing beliefs and images. If you like, try recording it into a tape recorder and listening to it with your eyes closed.

> I see a series of 10 steps going down before me. It is cool and dark, and gets more so with each step. I feel my legs moving, taking each step, feel each foot as it touches the stone . . . 10 . . . 9 . . . 8 . . . deeper into coolness, into peaceful, comforting depth, 7 . . . 6 . . . 5 . . . I see that the old stone steps beneath my feet are worn smooth with centuries of use. Many seekers have come this way . . . 4 . . . 3 . . . I see before me now a heavy wooden door with a metal handle. The door is arched at the top, and seems ancient and solid . . . 2 . . . 1 . . . The door is right in front of me now. I reach for the handle, feel the cool, strong metal in my hand. I

sense the heavy weight of the door, though its hinges operate smoothly, easily. As the door opens I walk into the sunlit courtyard before me. There is a colonnade around the perimeter, and at the far end, a glowing figure in white, with a long beard, thin, seated in full lotus posture, surrounded by flowers, eyes half-closed, smiling. Though he does not move I feel him beckon me to approach. Instinctively, I remove my shoes. I am on holy ground. I approach the wise one. While I bask in the warm sunlight of this courtyard and of the wise one's presence, the grass beneath my feet is cool, damp, and refreshing. I feel each step, then sit on a mat before the wise one. His eyes open fully, though they retain their inward quality. They are full of love and peace. The love is both impersonal and personal at the same time, both a universal love and a love for me alone. Silently, he bids me to ask my question, remaining silent for a moment after I speak, mindfully drinking in what I have asked, then he says . . . [then write down what comes to you].

It is important that the figure you imagine is a loving one. If you encounter other feelings from this person, feelings of judgment, anger, or even playfulness, experiment with some different imagery. Ask for someone else to appear. You probably are not in contact with that aspect of yourself that can help you—in Jungian terms, the wise old man or the wise old woman.

After a while, you may not need the imagery to contact your wise inner self. If your attention becomes unfocused or you are experiencing especially stressful times, you can always go back to it.

Listen to Your Wise Inner Self

What might you hear from your guide? This depends on your need and the situation for which you are seeking guidance. And your guide may be a very different character from someone else's. Some guides have quirky personalities. Some are talkative, others say little. But we can share a few generalities from our own experience, and a few caveats as well.

Perhaps you have had this kind of experience: A friend of yours comes to you with a problem. Say it's a relationship problem. After lay-ing out her griefs, she asks you what you think. Should she break it off? Sensing the trap of giving an opinion, you say something truly banal, like, "I think you've got to follow your own heart." Your friend gets angry at you. How could you tell her such a thing? How could you dispense such cheap, trite advice? Obviously, you just do not understand her pain and the complexity of her situation.

A few days later, your friend calls. She has seen her therapist, and she is feeling better now. You ask what the therapist told her, and she tells you that the therapist said she needed to follow her own heart. You try to remind her that this is the very thing you had said, and which she found dramatically unhelpful a few days before. Your friend stoutly denies that you ever said such a thing.

What is going on here? One thing is that therapists study timing. They develop a sense of when advice is likely to be received and when it will be difficult for the client to hear it. They don't always get it right, either. But then they know how to process these "empathic failures" with a client. But there is another reason why this could happen. It has to do with *preparedness to hear*. We may be more receptive to hearing some truths from our therapist than from our friends, because we have invested a certain role and a certain kind of expectation in the therapeutic relationship.

Inner guide journaling prepares us to receive these truths. The advice you hear from your guide may sound cliché or trite if you told a friend about it. It may indeed be of the caliber of "Follow your heart." The skeptic, or the skeptical aspect of each of us, may have some doubts about this process when your guide seems to come out with such truisms. But the difference is that the contemplative process of journaling has prepared you to receive a truth that you could not have heard before. The soil of your psyche has been plowed, fertilized, and cleared of rocks and debris. Now the seed is received into the soft ground. But without this preparation, the seed cannot take root.

Furthermore, consider what makes something cliché. Things are often cliché, not because they are not true, but because they are profoundly true though overused. Take the slogan "One day at a time." Said at the right time, to "prepared soil," this can be both wise and helpful. But if said in an unthinking, reflexive way, as a kind of Band-Aid for another's pain or indeed as a way of distancing from the other's pain, it can be incredibly unhelpful or even destructive.

Our experience suggests that guides can talk in ways that might sound trite at times, but that we usually do not experience them as trite. In fact, these truths often captured something we needed to hear or needed to remind ourselves of.

You might be looking for very specific advice from your guide. For example, if your problem is money, you may hope your guide will say, "Take everything you own and hock it and invest in XYZ stock." Or if your problem is loneliness, you might hope for an answer like, "Go to the Walgreens down on the corner and smile at the first person you meet there." We have never had this happen. And in fact, while we do not exclude the possibility that there could be truth in such oracular pronouncements, we suggest skepticism about them, particularly if the advice is risky. Use common sense.

More likely what you will get from your guide is an apt summation of the circumstances you find yourself in and the issues involved. This can be very accurate and bring you to a new level of understanding of your present circumstances and how they relate to ongoing life themes and issues. Or at times a guide may refocus your attention. All of this can be very helpful, even if it does not yield an immediate solution.

Watch for bodily shifts as you write or reread the message from your guide. Shifts in our understanding are often connected with long sighs or changes in the felt sense of the problem. These give a clue that something important has changed in your understanding.

Patiently Untie the Knots

A major life issue is like a large, tight knot. A difficult knot must be tugged at here, pulled on there, gradually loosened, bit by bit, until it unravels. Then at some point, the solution emerges. Issues reaching back into childhood or involving years to reach their present state of complexity are seldom resolved in a quick way. Instant answers are suspect.

You may recall the legend of Alexander the Great and the Gordian knot—a knot that no one had been able to untie. Alexander simply drew his sword and cut it right through. Problem solved. Some problems are like this. If we are not caught in a certain cognitive set—in this case, that knots are something to untie rather than cut—simple solutions will sometimes emerge. Yet for the most part, this is not the way we grow and change and solve complex human life dilemmas. The sword may cut the knot, but it may be at the expense of severing too much of our humanity.

Beverly once had the privilege of clinical supervision by the noted family therapist Braulio Montalvo. In one supervisory session, Montalvo crumpled a piece of paper loosely and threw it on the floor. Everyone watched as the paper unfolded itself, slowly, bit by bit. The point was clear: Progress in therapy, or any significant process of human growth, is often a slow and gentle unfolding. It cannot be rushed.

Dialogue with Significant People

Sometimes when writing in your journal, you may think of a particular person, whether from your present life or from your past. Or you might find yourself at times just daydreaming about someone, giving him a piece of your mind or talking something over with him. This indicates unfinished business with this person. Your journal presents a special opportunity to bring this business to completion.

One way to do this is to engage this person in an inner dialogue in your journal. As usual, begin in quietness. Breathe in and out. Invoke the feelings and images associated with that individual. Touch the felt sense of these issues. Try to come as much as possible from a centered place, where you perceive your feelings, whatever they are—hurt, anger, fear, whatever you feel—but where these feelings are gently, lovingly held and contained. Then write what you have to say to this person.

The next step is a little harder to do but also more rewarding. This involves putting yourself in the situation of the other person, and hearing what he has to say in response. Don't worry whether you correctly infer what he would actually say. Ultimately, this exercise is more about you than about the other person. It is about the part of yourself that this other person represents. And in this sense, there is no way you can get it wrong. Just let the other person speak, telling you his side of things. If you have some trouble putting yourself into the mindset of the other person, get up from where you were writing as yourself and sit somewhere else to write as the other. The physical act of moving helps you separate from your own perhaps all-too-familiar perspective and enter a different one.

After you take in the other person's point of view, carefully, lovingly notice your reactions. Does it trigger more anger in you? Do you find yourself defending something? Whatever it is, be with those feelings, and then begin to respond in your journal to what the other has said, perhaps changing your seat again as a way to activate a shift in perspective. You then simply proceed in this fashion until the process seems to come to a natural halt. As a final step, return to quietness again, breathing gently in and out, and with love and acceptance, read the dialogue over to yourself again. Try to see each side not so much as right or wrong, but as different perspectives, each partial, incomplete, and distorted by the person's own needs and issues. Doing this may trigger more feelings that you want to dialogue about, which you can then pursue if you wish. Or you may feel that you have gained a greater degree of resolution in your relationship with this individual than you had before. This is an indication that it is time to stop the dialogue process, at least for now.

Resolution is always relative and to some extent incomplete. There is always more that could be said. For this reason, you never have to feel that you must go on and on until you reach perfect peace about an issue. A process orientation is called for, a willingness to live with some incompleteness. When other life issues become more pressing and these occupy your attention, you have done enough with this one for the time being. Respect the flow of your own psychological energy. When your attention shifts to something else, it is time to move on to that issue and leave this one for now. You can always return to it later if you wish.

The Other Person Is You

In such a dialogue, you are ultimately dealing with *yourself* more than with the other person. If you are in conflict with another person, in this kind of dialogue you are dealing with the *internal aspect* of that conflict. Another way to say this is that you are dealing with a conflict in yourself, between different aspects of yourself, or with what that person *represents* to you more than the actual human being. For example, you may discover through this kind of process that at least part of your problem with another person is connected with ongoing life issues or themes that are part of a negative schema. In this way, your fight with Kathy is not just with her, but it is also about your sense of never getting what you need from others. This does not mean that Kathy is right and you are wrong because all the issues are yours. Kathy brings her own issues to the situation as well. And anyway, the whole point of this kind of process is to move us beyond blame. Blame divides us from others and from ourselves by fostering unending cycles of defensiveness, attack, and counterattack. Part of the inner meaning of your fight with Kathy is about resolving this issue of feeling that you can't get what you need from others. Your fight with Kathy is an opportunity for you to find a greater degree of resolution of this ongoing problem.

How will this process then affect your relationship with the other person? If it is someone from the past, it may just mean that you have reached a greater harmony regarding that person and whatever he or she represents to you. Alternatively, you may find that you wish to be in touch with that person again in some way. If so, the outer action and the inner action support each other. Your attempt to reach out to the other is also an acceptance of that part of yourself with which you are in conflict, and your acceptance of that part of yourself also may enable a new kind of relationship.

If the person you are writing about is in your present life in an ongoing way, your journal work may help to deepen or heal that relationship. However, this is not always the case, and at other times, resolution may not be possible. Yet again, you might find that interactions with this other person no longer affect you so deeply, though the outer relationship is more or less the same.

There are many possible outcomes. But by honoring this material with your attention and mindfulness, you vastly increase the odds of finding a more satisfying way to deal with this person, and even more important, with the issues this person represents in your life.

∽ PRACTICE ∽

Write Your Life Chapters

There are very many ways to use a journal. Some people choose journaling as their main tool for mindful living, for avoiding what Plato called the unexamined life. Such individuals journal religiously. Others will journal more or less frequently, depending on need. When life is chugging along without major difficulties, they seldom think of journaling. And when life throws them a curve, they intensify their journaling efforts.

Life chapters is an approach we have adapted from Ira Progoff. It is a journaling exercise that can be useful at any time, but perhaps especially during times of difficulty or stress. To engage in this process, come to quietness. Listen to your life. See it in its sweep, from its earliest beginnings to the point where you are today. Find the felt sense of your life as a whole. Then, just as if you were about to write your autobiography, let the times of your life organize themselves into life chapters, perhaps eight or twelve of them. Do not think about it too much or agonize over it. Simply let the chapters emerge. Then write out the chapter headings, with a one- or two-sentence summary of the content of that chapter of your life.

When you have completed this task, review your life chapters quietly. Take in the movement of your life. If it is difficult for you to feel accepting about some things in your life, look at it the way you would look at the life story of someone you love and admire. Tune in to your felt sense of your life as a whole, and notice whether it shifts as you write.

You cannot predict the results of this process. You may gain something from it altogether unexpected. But in general, this exercise puts you in touch with the movement and direction of your life. Ask yourself these important questions: If the trends you have just summarized continue, where is your life leading you? If you do not like what you see, what is your life calling forth from you? What change is needed? It is more important to hold the question in awareness and dwell with it than to get answers.

If you do this exercise some weeks or months apart, you may come up with quite different chapters. That is because the place you start from is so different that it spontaneously evokes a different narrative organization. Repeating the life chapters exercise at different times puts you in touch with the flow of your life story so you can see it multidimensionally. It also can help you change it if you choose to. It can give you a sense that, since things have changed before, they need not be stuck in the present configuration, either. You can feel the changes and perceive more clearly that the way things are need not be the way things remain.

Hold to the Center

It is said that if a Masai warrior is incarcerated, he will die. Lacking a concept of the future, he assumes that the way life is now is the way life will always be. To an extent, we are all a little this way. Psychological research has shown that our memories are compartmentalized according to our emotional states. When we are happy, it is easy to recall happy times and events in our lives, and difficult to recall sad times. When we are sad, the reverse is true. This is how the brain is organized. For this reason, we can easily get locked into compartments of sadness or other negative emotions, finding it difficult to recall things that give us joy or hope.

One of the things the life chapters exercise can do is give you a direct experience of what the Buddhists call impermanence. If your life is a point on the rim of a bicycle wheel, then as the bicycle moves forward in space, the point on the rim also travels up and down. Similarly, our lives go up and down. But whatever we face today, it is no more permanent than what we faced yesterday. The point of the medieval figure of the wheel of fortune (still seen in tarot decks) is that if you live on the surface of life, on the outer rim, you are either going down or going up. Only if you live at the center do you have any stability. The life chapters exercise helps you see these ups and downs in perspective, and puts you in contact with the center of the wheel, the still point, what we have been calling the center within. And when you view several instances of the life chapters exercise, your perspective broadens out from the present to take in your whole life as a single gestalt. You gain freedom from the tyranny of the present, one-sided view of things, and see it *sub specie aeternitatis*—from the perspective of eternity.

Find Your Creativity

A journal can be useful as a repository for creative thinking. As noted above, by befriending our difficult thoughts and feelings, we begin to find more creative ways of dealing with life dilemmas. But more than that, we can also record artistic inspiration. If you write, here is where you can record an idea for that wonderful novel. Or perhaps you have an idea that does not fit anywhere you can think of right away, but you note this fragment, trusting that it may fit somewhere. Perhaps you have an idea for a song lyric, the solution to a physics problem, a sketch of a new painting, or a solution to a business dilemma.

Each of us has our own creative genius. To find it, we have to begin to trust our inner process—to begin to trust ourselves as essentially creative and reliable guides, as Buddhas in the making. Einstein trusted his instincts and developed his theories of special and general relativity, overturning established notions about the nature of the universe. The only certain path of failure is to ignore your own flashes of illumination. Emerson wrote: "A man should learn to detect and watch that gleam of light which flashes across his mind from within, more than the lustre of the firmament of bards and sages." Journaling is a way to pay attention.

In Essence

Journal writing is a technology for seeing new options. It is one way to be with our feelings—even our most troubling ones—and calm them sufficiently to find new ways of dealing with them. It is a way, as a wise client said about psychotherapy, of being "side by side" with these feelings without being overwhelmed by them or controlled by them.

Journaling is an effective way to get in touch with your inner depths, and thereby find creative solutions to problems, whether these be problems in living, esthetic problems, scientific, or spiritual ones. It is a tool of mindfulness. Whereas Buddhist meditation is predicated on the concept of *anatta* or "no self," journaling can be especially helpful to some because it is compatible with our western culture and its valuing of the individual person.

It is worth giving journaling a chance by doing it regularly enough for a long enough period that it becomes a habit. If it is helpful, if it is on your path, you will come to value this as an important tool for living. You will even miss your journal when you have been away from it too long.

Practice for Week Ten

1. Increase your meditation time to thirty minutes twice daily.
2. Continue with the day of mindfulness practice, reading, walking meditation, and work with dreams.
3. Start a journal. Try to spend some time each day this week writing in it. Experiment with each of the approaches in this chapter:
    *   "The Felt Sense" (p. 222)
    *   "Journaling to Remember" (p. 223)
    *   "Build a Memory Bridge" (p. 223)
    *   "Use Stream-of-Consciousness Journaling" (p. 224)
    *   "Inner Guide Journaling" (p. 225)
    *   "Dialogue with Significant People" (p. 229)
    *   "Write Your Life Chapters" (p. 231)
    *   "Find Your Creativity" (p. 233)

PART IV

~o~

Arriving Home

Thich Nhat Hanh says life is a walk. That is to say, life is a matter of taking each step, of facing each thing that comes along with mindfulness. If there is work to do, we work mindfully. If it is time to play, we play mindfully. If sadness comes up in our consciousness, we take care of the sadness with our mindfulness. If joy comes up, we strengthen it with mindfulness.

Arriving home is the same as continuing the walk—continuing the journey so that with each step we already arrive in the realm of nirvana. Each step is a fulfillment already, and we are no longer looking forward to some other kind of fulfillment, nor stuck in the past.

Now that you have made a beginning, you face the issue of how you want to continue your journey. How will you do that so you do not lose the momentum you have been building over the last weeks? While there may be some basics such as meditation that you need to practice all the time, your practice will grow and evolve in accord with your changing need and circumstance.

Only you can answer the question of how you shall continue. But in the following chapter, we offer some principles for guiding your decision.

❧ 10 ❧

Week Eleven and Beyond

WHAT KIND OF BUDDHA ARE YOU?

❧o❧

Beware of confining yourself to a particular belief and denying
all else, for much good would elude you—indeed the knowledge
of reality would elude you. Be in yourself a matter for all forms
of belief, for God is too vast and tremendous to be restricted to
one belief rather than another.
> —Ibn al-'Arabi, Sufi master (1165–1240)

According to Buddhist teaching, there are 84,000 dharma
doors—84,000 ways to find peace, to liberate oneself from suffering, to enter nirvana. If anything, that may be an underesti-
mate. How does one then go about deciding which modes of practice
are best? How will you best practice the dharma? What kind of Buddha
will you be?

A Western Buddha-Dharma

When Buddhist teaching left the metaphysical atmosphere of the Indian subcontinent, it was already startlingly pragmatic. The Buddha

was not interested in speculation; for the forty-nine years of his teaching career, he insisted repeatedly that he taught only suffering and the end of suffering. While the pristine essence remained constant, as the teaching entered China, it underwent transformation. It became Chinese. Again, as it reached Japan, the dharma became Japanese. It became Korean in Korea. In each place, the dharma has had to meet the people of that language and culture.

At this critical point, the dharma is encountering the culture of the Western world. The rough outline of a new form of the dharma is emerging. Here are some of the characteristics we see:

1. *A Western Buddha-dharma will not be primarily for priests, monks, and nuns.* Most practitioners will be "lay practitioners." This term itself probably needs revision, since it already sounds somewhat pejorative. The democratic spirit runs too deep for monasticism and ordination to be considered more important than so-called lay practice. While monks and nuns will also play a role, the Buddha-dharma in the West may be above all for those who remain in the world, who marry or have committed relationships, have families, drive on crowded freeways, and struggle to earn a living; who transport children to soccer games, and seek a healthy and enriching sexuality.

2. *Most practitioners of the Buddha-dharma will not become "Buddhists."* We have already mentioned there is no word in the East for Buddhism. Buddhism is a term invented in the West to try to fit it into our own categories as a "religion" among other religions. The closest Eastern term is Buddha-dharma—the teaching of the Buddha. In keeping with this insight, most people will seek to incorporate Buddhist practice and teaching into their own lives in their own ways. Atheists and agnostics will tap these teachings in ways consistent with their point of view. Most Christians will remain Christians, and most Jews will remain Jews, if they are already connected with their tradition in a helpful way. The dharma will help them connect with their own traditions more deeply, rather than causing them to reject them. Many practitioners will claim no formal religious affiliation at all. And a few will identify themselves as Buddhists.

Buddhist teaching is not another ideology. It is not about becoming Buddhist rather than some other tradition. The dharma teaches us that such divisions are based on concepts, and concepts have no ultimate reality. If we are to connect with the spiritual in a way that can bring healing in this post–September 11 world, we must give up our tendency to harbor the secret or not-so-secret belief that our way is the only true way. For this thought contains a seed of violence that inevitably will at some point break out and infect the world, as it has again and again.

3. *Western Buddha-dharma will be psychological as well as spiritual.* The Tibetan master Chögyam Trungpa said, "Buddhism will come to the West as a psychology." This should not be surprising. Buddhism is deeply psychological, and our culture is a psychological one. Everyone uses terms like *complex, ego, libido, defense mechanism, conditioning,* and *reinforcement.* Many of the same people who are most interested in the peace and liberation of Buddha-dharma will be the ones already most acquainted with psychology. We believe this connection is vital if Buddha-dharma is to remain healthy in the West. *Finding the Center Within* is a contribution toward connecting dharma and psychology in practical ways.

4. *Western Buddha-dharma will remain individualistic.* Individualism runs too deep in the West for us to abandon it. The question here will not be so much about how to become a Buddha but about how to become the sort of Buddha that you, as an individual, are meant to be. There are quiet Buddhas and outrageous Buddhas. There are Buddhas who dance and sing and Buddhas who sit in unruffled silence. There are Buddhas who move like mountains and Buddhas who move like a swift mountain stream. What kind of Buddha are you?

There are paradoxes here. How do we combine no self with individualism? When viewed as concepts or logical categories, they seem like blatant contradictions. However, they are not irreconcilable. The teaching of no self can loosen our anxious, clammy grip on our individuality, recognizing that, on the ultimate level, this is all emptiness. This can free us from the *cult* of individuality—ultimately just another conformity. And when we are freed to understand no self, we can become most deeply that which we truly are.

On a practical level, a problem here is how to tap the support of community (sangha) while retaining the freedom of individual practice. So far, most people are attempting to practice on their own and only a few are joining in community practice on a regular basis. New models are needed to help us tap the strengths of community, while allowing space for individuality.

Wholeness Rather Than Holiness

When a person becomes religious, or adopts some form of self-improvement regimen, something happens. Suddenly that person develops a split in herself—a split between where she is and where she would like to be, between how she is now and her new ideals. Whether it is the newly converted Christian, who now wants to convert her friends, or the coworker who just got back from an assertiveness workshop and now deals roughly with everyone's feelings but his own, we say such people have gotten religion. It is not a compliment.

Buddhism shares this problem. In Zen circles, they talk about people who reek with the "stench of Zen." These are the people who are self-consciously religious and spiritual, afraid of their humanity. But the essence of enlightenment is an open heart. To be enlightened is to be fully human.

The Buddha compared his teachings to a raft. The purpose of the raft is to take you to the other shore. In itself, the raft has no value. Its purpose is to bring you to the other side, from the shore of suffering to the shore of liberation. It makes no sense to make the raft an object of veneration. It makes no sense to carry it around on your head. It makes sense only to use the raft to get across.

Spiritual paths are like homeopathic remedies. They cure by giving a small amount of a substance with the same effect as the symptoms. Rather than fighting against the symptom, the homeopath works with the symptom, strengthening it slightly, thereby (in theory) stimulating the body's natural tendency to correct an imbalance. Religion, the very word meaning to bind together what was separate, likewise temporarily exacerbates the split. For a time, the person is more divided within himself and with the world than ever before. Thus we have the irony, witnessed again and again throughout history, of spiritual traditions dividing people from each other rather than uniting them in understanding and love.

Ultimately this is why you must kill the Buddha you meet on the road. Buddhas and Buddha-teachings are concepts you employ to defeat concepts, so you can achieve that which was already there to begin with—your clear, undistorted, true nature, your face before your parents were born, the suchness of things just as they are, without commentary or analysis. It is the means for coming into the kingdom of God, for living in the eternal now. In the end, therefore, you have to abandon the raft and destroy the beloved concepts if you are to reach the goal. For ultimately any ideal, no matter how holy or helpful, is just another concept.

Sometimes people who start down the spiritual path try too hard to be good. Trying so hard cuts them off from the true goal, which is not so much about being good—or at least not primarily so—but more about being true, being complete, being whole. "Be ye *perfect*," taught Christ. And the Greek word means "brought to completion" or "whole," having nothing to do with perfectionism or never making a mistake. For trying so hard to be good, we destroy our naturalness. And rather than undergoing a true transformation, we only repress whatever does not fit the ideal.

The words *wholeness* and *holiness* are closely related. In origin, they had the same meaning. They are both related to the German word *heil*, meaning "healthy," "whole," or "salvation," and the English word *hale*. To be whole is to be holy and to be holy is to be whole. In their modern form and usage, however, we prefer the word *whole* over *holy*. For making holiness the goal often makes you even more divided and alienated from yourself. Trying to be holy, you repress anger, since anger does not fit your image of holiness. Ultimately this does not work. Anger leaks out unconsciously in ways more destructive than if you had just let it alone and let it be in the first place. The same fate awaits any human emotion or inclination that does not fit the ideal of holiness. Whether it be sexuality, aggression, envy, sadness, or whatever does not seem to fit, by repressing it to live up to an ideal, the impulse will only be expressed anyway, but now it comes out twisted and deformed, with a destructive power exponentially multiplied.

So forget holiness. Aim to be whole. Try to be a decent human being. Aiming at wholeness keeps you on track, because true holiness is a transformation of all that we are and not repression. The way is neither repression nor a shallow "letting it all hang out" approach. By aiming at wholeness, we continue to work with all that we are instead of trying to force or contort ourselves into being what we are not and can never be, for it has no reality in the first place. It is the television evangelist who gets caught in the seedy motel with a prostitute, precisely because he tries to project an image of purity. In contrast, true spiritual giants never quite fit our pretty fantasies. Zen masters hit students on the head with their sticks; Christ curses the fig tree for not having fruit even though it was not the season for fruit; and Ramakrishna teaches us to hiss at those who would harm us in self-protection. The psychologist Carl Rogers—whom many feel had a saintly quality and whom many associate with the phrase "touchy-feely"—also believed in being genuine and authentic, and for this reason, would tell people when he felt uncomfortable or angry. It is even reported that on at least one occasion he walked out of a classroom in anger when he was a professor. These odd, unanticipated qualities attest to the authenticity of such individuals when seen against the larger context of all that they are and teach.

The Prime Directive

Anyone with a passing familiarity with *Star Trek* in any of its multiple incarnations will recognize the term *prime directive*. In these shows, the prime directive was a rule to not interfere with the development of other cultures in the galaxy, but to let each develop in its own way and at its own pace.

How shall you, as an individual, practice? Shall you join the Zen center down the street? Will you do a lot of sitting meditation or more walking meditation? Will you emphasize metta meditation, journaling, or work with dreams? How will this emphasis change over time?

As you seek to become the Buddha you are meant to be (and already are), there is a prime directive, a central hermeneutic to follow in making these choices: *You must seek to practice in such a way that you feel lighter, happier, more peaceful, and more loving.* This above all. Any form of practice that has an effect other than this is suspect. We suggest that you keep this principle in mind as you decide, for example, what combination of practices you will employ and how much of each—sitting meditation, walking meditation, dream work, metta meditation, and whatever else you find helpful to you in moving in the direction of peace and wholeness. If what you are doing feels heavy and obligatory—if it makes you feel anxious or sad, find another way. Find a way to make it enjoyable and light. The highest form of worship is simply to be happy.

You need not be black and white about this. For example, if your meditation causes you to feel heavy, you do not have to conclude altogether that meditation is not for you. Instead, ask yourself: How can I practice meditation so that I can enjoy it, feeling happy and light and peaceful? Perhaps you will want to set aside your focus on the breath for right now and work with a mantra for a while. Perhaps you will want to shorten the meditation periods, or do more walking meditation and less sitting meditation. The question is not practice or no practice, but *how* to practice joyfully.

The distinctively American voice of Ralph Waldo Emerson resounds: "Nothing is at last sacred but the integrity of your own mind." For Emerson, this is part of his trumpet call to be your true self. For us, perhaps a little less stridently, it means to place nothing above our peace, calmness, and sanity. The world may say this is selfish, but the moment we listen to this criticism and sacrifice our calm, in that instant we become not only more distressed ourselves but also less help to the world.

THE EXPERIENCE (TOM)

As I'm meditating this morning, my cell phone rings. This triggers a round of thinking: "Why does this always happen when I meditate?" And, "Someone really needs you. Better stop what you are doing, it could be serious!" I breathe in and out. I remind myself, it is not true (or is at least exaggerated) to say that my phone *always* rings during meditation. That is the easier of the two challenges. The second one is more difficult: Shall I continue to care for my mind and meditate, or respond to the call? Breathing in and out, I decide to meditate. Not only is this honoring the prime directive, but I know I will be more helpful when I do return the call.◇

As you find your way to become the Buddha you already are, take care to maintain your peace, joy, happiness, and well-being. Let this principle show you what to practice, how to practice, and what to avoid. It is the key to understanding the dharma and what it means in your own individual life. When you wake up in the morning, form the intention to protect this peace above all, all day long. For there is no such thing as Buddha: There is only you being the Buddha that you are. And the moment you return to peace and joy, you are that already.

It is at the same time the greatest gift you can give yourself and the greatest gift you can give the world.

The Ten-Week Program: A Recap

∾o∾

Practice for Week One

1. Do the practices contained in the chapter:
   - "Where Are You?" (p. 8)
   - "Acknowledge Your Many Roles" (p. 10)
   - "Reconnect with Your Roots" (p. 15)
   - "Be Aware of Self-Punishing Thoughts" (p. 17)
   - "Become the Beloved" (p. 20)
2. Try this special daily practice: "Take Up Your Robe, Sandals, and Begging Bowl" (p. 22).

Practice for Week Two

1. Perform the practices for this week:
   - "Count the Breath" (p. 27)
   - "Find Your Self" (p. 38)
   - "Tea Meditation" (p. 41)
2. Try this special daily practice: "Moments of Mindfulness" (p. 42).

Practice for Weeks Three and Four

Because establishing a regular practice of meditation is so important, we suggest you spend two weeks just doing that. This is in fact only a minimum period of time, but at least you can make a beginning.

1. During week three, practice sitting meditation for at least ten minutes once a day. Then during week four, add a second sitting of the same length—for example, sitting once in the morning and once in the evening. Remember to keep it enjoyable and not struggle.
2. Every day, reread a little of chapter 3 to help you keep the right attitude and spirit. In this way, you can keep us with you as you take your first steps in formal meditation practice. By the end of week four, you may have read the chapter two or three times.

3. There is always a way to enter and encourage the meditative state. Experiment during this period with the different methods in this chapter during your meditation periods:
   - Mantra meditation (p. 58)
   - Breath meditation (pp. 59, 60)
   - Remember you are not trying to force peaceful feelings but to work with what is ("Peace Is the River," p. 49)
   - "Practice Mere Recognition" (p. 61)
   - "Encourage Yourself" with coping thoughts (p. 65)
   - "Use Gathas" (p. 66)
   - "Dwell with a Word or a Phrase" (p. 67)
   - Begin with breath, then body awareness, then awareness of thoughts and feelings (p. 67)
   - "Practice the Four Immeasurable Minds" (p. 69)
   - "Go from Sound to Silence" (p. 71)
   - "Go from Motion to Stillness" (p. 71)
   - Practice inner light meditation (p. 71)
   - "Take a Break" (p. 72)
   - "Take Refuge" (p. 73)
   - "Walk the Path of Devotion" (p. 74)

   You don't need to try all of these. Just experiment with those that have the most intuitive appeal.
4. In addition, try a little walking meditation (p. 72). Use it as a way to take a break from your work during the day whenever you need to.
5. Continue the moments of mindfulness practice you began in week two (p. 42).
6. Begin collecting books for your inspirational bookshelf. (p. 74).

Practice for Week Five

1. Increase your meditation now to fifteen minutes twice a day.
2. Continue to practice a few minutes of inspirational reading each day—in the morning if possible.
3. Add a second moment of mindfulness (p. 42).
4. Practice walking meditation at least once or twice this week.
5. Try the exercises and suggestions in this chapter:
   - Visualize slowing down (p. 85)
   - Practice radical medicine (p. 85)

- Practice *wu-wei* (pp. 85)
- "Begin and End the Day Intentionally" (p. 87)
- "Find Bells of Mindfulness" (p. 88)
- "Ask: Where Am I? What Am I Doing?" (p. 90)
- "Allocate Attention to Centering" (p. 90)
- "Cultivate a Balanced Lifestyle" (p. 92)
- "Examine Your Environment" (p. 92)
- "Let Your Peace Return to You" (p. 93)
- "Stay in Charge of the Task" (p. 94)
6. Practice a day of mindfulness (or at least a part of a day) (p. 96).

Practice for Week Six

1. Increase your meditation time to twenty minutes twice a day.
2. Continue daily reading.
3. Practice walking meditation when you can.
4. Continue with two moments of mindfulness (p. 42).
5. Practice the exercises in this chapter:
   - "Practice the Five Remembrances" (p. 105)
   - "Change *Must* to *Prefer*" (p. 167)
   - "Practice Mindful Consumption" (p. 113)
   - "Challenge Your Busyness" (p. 116)
   - "Choose a Living World" (p. 121)

Practice for Week Seven

1. Continue to practice meditation (twenty minutes twice daily), mindful moments, daily reading, and walking meditation (chapter 3).
2. Begin to record and work with your dreams, using the suggestions and ideas in this chapter. If you do not always have the time in the morning to work with a dream, at least jot some quick notes to jog your memory. Then record it more fully later in the day.
3. Continue to practice a day of mindfulness (chapter 5).
4. There's a lot of information in this chapter. If it is largely new, you may want to read it several times as you work with your dreams this week.

Practice for Week Eight

1. Continue with the practices of a day of mindfulness, moments of mindfulness, reading, walking meditation, and dream work.
2. Increase your meditation time to twenty-five minutes twice daily, if you feel ready to do so.
3. Practice the exercises in this chapter:
   - "Challenge Depressive Thinking" (p. 161)
   - "Identify Your Maladaptive Schemas" (p. 167)
   - "Twenty-five Healing Things" (p. 171)
   - "Work with Anger Thoughts" (p. 178)
   - "Work with Worries" (p. 179)
4. In general, this week give special attention to your emotional life. Read this chapter at least twice. When negative emotions surface, recognize them. Don't try to push them away, but don't wallow or get lost in them either. Breathe in and out, making a calm, open space to experience them fully and clearly. Look into the roots of the problem. Do something to nurture yourself from your list of twenty-five healing things.

Practice for Week Nine

1. Continue meditation (twenty-five minutes twice daily), a day of mindfulness, reading, walking meditation, and work with dreams.
2. Spend one or both of your daily meditation periods on metta meditation (pp. 188, 191).
3. In all of your interactions this week, focus on listening a little more deeply to others. Make a space for them. Use the exercises in this chapter to help:
   - "Observe Filters" (p. 198)
   - "Listen Actively" (p. 201)
4. Focus all week on right speech. Avoid spreading rumors, participating in gossip, or saying anything about anyone that you would be unwilling to say to her face. Concentrate on speaking only that which is useful, helpful, encouraging, and true. Meditate on the guidelines in this chapter and seek to put them into practice. Add your own insights to the practice as you learn from your experiences and reflection.

5. Focus on kind action, without seeking credit or recognition. This may be for the most part little things, simple and undramatic. Let the other car get in front of you. Be the one to empty the dishwasher. Straighten up. Show others your smiling face.
6. Focus this week on awareness of how others help you. Express this awareness. Tell the other person you appreciate it. Especially notice simple things: the sales clerk who is friendly. The kind word. The people who drive reasonably and courteously (instead of focusing on the relative few who drive aggressively, as we are wont to do).

Practice for Week Ten

1. Increase your meditation time to thirty minutes twice daily.
2. Continue with the day of mindfulness practice, reading, walking meditation, and work with dreams.
3. Start a journal. Try to spend some time each day this week writing in it. Experiment with each of the approaches in this chapter:
    *   "The Felt Sense" (p. 222)
    *   "Journaling to Remember" (p. 223)
    *   "Build a Memory Bridge" (p. 223)
    *   "Use Stream-of-Consciousness Journaling" (p. 224)
    *   "Inner Guide Journaling" (p. 225)
    *   "Dialogue with Significant People" (p. 229)
    *   "Write Your Life Chapters" (p. 231)
    *   "Find Your Creativity" (p. 233)

Sources and Readings

~o~

For additional information and resources, visit our Web site at MindfulPsychology.com.

Benson, Herbert. *The Relaxation Response*. New York: Avon, 1975.
———. *Beyond the Relaxation Response*. New York: Berkeley, 1985.
Bien, Thomas, and Beverly Bien. *Mindful Recovery: A Spiritual Path to Healing from Addiction*. New York: John Wiley & Sons, 2002.
Bowen, Murray. *Family Therapy and Clinical Practice*. New York: Jason Aronson, 1978.
Burns, David D. *Feeling Good: The New Mood Therapy*. New York: Avon Books, 1980.
Campbell, Joseph, with Bill Moyers. *The Power of Myth*. New York: Doubleday, 1988.
Chopra, Deepak. *The Way of the Wizard: Twenty Spiritual Lessons for Creating the Life You Want*. New York: Harmony Books, 1995.
———. *How to Know God: The Soul's Journey into the Mystery of Mysteries*. New York: Three Rivers Press, 2000.
———. *Awakening to the Sacred: Creating a Spiritual Life from Scratch*. New York: Broadway, 1999.
———. *Awakening to the Buddhist Heart: Integrating Love, Meaning, and Connection into Every Part of Your Life*. New York: Broadway, 2000.
Chuang Tzu. *Chuang Tzu: Basic Writings*. Translated by Burton Watson. New York: Columbia University Press, 1964.
Cooper, David A. *A Heart of Stillness: A Complete Guide to Learning the Art of Meditation*. Woodstock, Vt.: SkyLight Paths, 1999.
Csikszentmihalyi, Mihaly. *Flow: The Psychology of Optimal Experience*. New York: HarperPerennial, 1991.
Dalai Lama. *Opening the Eye of New Awareness*. Boston: Wisdom Publications, 1999.
Das, Lama Surya. *Awakening the Buddha Within: Eight Steps to Enlightenment*. New York: Broadway, 1997.
Dickinson, Emily. *The Complete Poems of Emily Dickinson*. Edited by Thomas H. Johnson. Boston: Little, Brown, & Co., 1960.

Dossey, Larry. *Healing Words: The Power of Prayer and the Practice of Medicine*. New York: HarperCollins, 1993.

Eckhart, Meister. *Meister Eckhart: The Essential Sermons, Commentaries, Treatises, and Defense*. Translated by Edmund Colledge. New York: Paulist Press, 1981.

Elliott, Charles H., and Maureen Kirby Lassen. *Why Can't I Get What I Want?: How to Stop Making the Same Old Mistakes and Start Living a Life You Can Love*. Palo Alto, Calif.: Davies-Black Publishing, 1998.

Emerson, Ralph Waldo. *Selected Writings of Ralph Waldo Emerson*. Edited by William Gilman. New York: New American Library, 1965.

Freud, Sigmund. *The Interpretation of Dreams*. New York: Avon, 1965.

Fromm, Erich. *Man for Himself: An Inquiry Into the Psychology of Ethics*. Greenwich, Conn.: Fawcett, 1947.

———. *The Forgotten Language: An Introduction to the Understanding of Dreams, Fairy Tales, and Myths*. New York: Grove Press, 1951.

———. *The Art of Loving*. New York: Perennial Classics, 1956.

Gendlin, Eugene T. *Focusing*. 2nd ed. New York: Bantam, 1981.

Goldstein, Joseph. *Insight Meditation: The Practice of Freedom*. Boston: Shambhala Publications, Inc., 1993.

Goleman, Daniel. *The Meditative Mind: The Varieties of Meditative Experience*. New York: Tarcher/Putnam, 1988.

Isherwood, Christopher. *Ramakrishna and His Disciples*. New York: Simon & Schuster, 1965.

Johnson, Robert A. *Inner Work: Using Dreams and Active Imagination for Personal Growth*. New York: HarperCollins, 1986.

Julian of Norwich. *Showings*. Translated by Edmund Colledge and James Walsh. New York: Paulist Press, 1978.

Jung, Carl G. *The Symbolic Life*. Princeton, N.J.: Bollingen Press, 1954.

———. *The Archetypes and the Collective Unconscious*. Princeton, N.J.: Bollingen Press, 1959.

———. *Man and His Symbols*. New York: Doubleday, 1964.

———. *Memories, Dreams, Reflections*. Recorded and edited by Aniela Jaffe. New York: Vintage, 1965.

———. *Dreams*. Princeton, N.J.: Bollingen, 1974.

Kelly, Thomas R. *A Testament of Devotion*. New York: Harper & Row, 1941.

Khan, Pir Vilayat Inayat. *Awakening: A Sufi Experience*. New York: Tarcher/Putnam, 1999.

Krishnamurti, J. *Commentaries on Living, First Series*. Wheaton, Ill.: The Theosophical Publishing House, 1984.

Langer, Ellen J. *Mindfulness*. Reading, Mass.: Addison-Wesley, 1989.

Laubach, Frank C. *Letters by a Modern Mystic*. New York: Student Volunteer Movement, 1937.

Lawrence, Brother. *The Practice of the Presence of God*. Edited by Donald Demaray. New York: Alba House, 1997.

Levine, Stephen. *Turning Toward the Mystery: A Seeker's Journey*. New York: HarperSanFrancisco, 2002.

Lewinsohn, P. M., and C. S. Amenson. "Some Relations between Pleasant and Unpleasant Mood-Related Events and Depression." *Journal of Abnormal Psychology* 87 (1978): 644–54.

McGuire, William, and R. F. C. Hull, eds. *C. G. Jung Speaking: Interviews and Encounters*. Princeton, N.J.: Bollingen Press, 1977.

McKay, Matthew, Peter D. Rogers, and Judith McKay. *When Anger Hurts: Quieting the Storm Within*. Oakland, Calif.: New Harbinger, 1989.

Merton, Thomas. *Mystics and Zen Masters*. New York: Delta, 1967.

Milgram, Stanley. "Behavioral Study of Obedience." *Journal of Abnormal Psychology* 67: 1963.

Mitchell, Stephen, trans. *Tao Te Ching*. New York: HarperPerennial, 1991.

Nhat Hanh, Thich. *Breathe! You Are Alive: Sutra on the Full Awareness of Breathing*. Berkeley, Calif.: Parallax Press, 1986.

———. *Being Peace*. Berkeley, Calif.: Parallax Press, 1987.

———. *Transformation and Healing: The Sutra on the Four Establishments of Mindfulness*. Berkeley, Calif.: Parallax Press, 1990.

———. *The Heart of the Buddha's Teaching*. Berkeley, Calif.: Parallax Press, 1998.

———. *Anger: Wisdom for Cooling the Flames*. New York: Riverhead, 2001.

Prabhavananda, Swami, and Christopher Isherwood. *How to Know God: The Yoga Aphorisms of Patanjali*. New York: New American Library, 1969.

Progoff, Ira. *At a Journal Workshop*. New York: Dialogue House Library, 1975.

Rogers, Carl. *On Becoming a Person: A Therapist's View of Psychology.* Boston: Houghton-Mifflin, 1961.

———. *The Carl Rogers Reader.* Edited by Howard Kirschenbaum and Valerie Land Henderson. Boston: Houghton Mifflin, 1989.

Rosenberg, Larry. *Breath by Breath: The Liberating Practice of Insight Meditation.* Boston: Shambhala, 1998.

Salzberg, Sharon. *Lovingkindness: The Revolutionary Art of Happiness.* Boston: Shambhala, 1995.

Suzuki, Shunryu. *Zen Mind, Beginner's Mind.* New York: John Weatherhill, Inc., 1982.

Tillich, Paul. *The Eternal Now.* New York: Charles Scribner's Sons, 1963.

Watts, Alan. *The Way of Zen.* New York: Vintage, 1957.

———. *Psychotherapy East and West.* New York: Random House, 1975.

Welwood, John. *Toward a Psychology of Awakening: Buddhism, Psychotherapy, and the Path of Personal and Spiritual Transformation.* Boston: Shambhala, 2000.

———. "The Psychology of Awakening." *Tricycle: The Buddhist Review* 9, no. 3 (spring 2000): 43–48.

Wilson, Edward O. *Consilience: The Unity of Knowledge.* New York: Alfred A. Knopf, 1998.

Young, Jeffrey E., and Janet Klosko. *Reinventing Your Life.* New York: Dutton, 1993.

Index

∼o∽